EXPRESSIONS OF PHENOMENOLOGICAL RESEARCH
CONSCIOUSNESS AND LIFEWORLD STUDIES

The Fielding Monograph Series is published by Fielding Graduate University, 2020 De la Vina Street, Santa Barbara, CA 93105.
Phone: (805) 898-2924. Fax: (805) 690-4310.
On the web: www.fielding.edu

Expressions of Phenomenological Research
Consciousness and Lifeworld Studies

Edited by
David Rehorick, PhD
Professor Emeritus
University of New Brunswick & Fielding Graduate University

Valerie Malhotra Bentz, PhD
Professor, Fielding Graduate University

With a foreword by
Michael Barber, PhD
Professor, Saint Louis University

TABLE OF CONTENTS

4

FOREWORD

In *The Phenomenology of the Social World*, Alfred Schutz, discussing objective, already-constituted meanings, comments on the possibility of getting behind these meanings to uncover subjective meaning, that is, the intentional operations of consciousness which originally conferred such meanings. When Schutz does so, he discovers the wondrous streaming of consciousness, a new world that is at every moment one of becoming and passing away. As a consequence, Schutz affirmed that the problem of meaning is always a problem of inner time. In this discussion, Schutz exemplified the spirit of phenomenology that starts with what is established, static, fixed, and taken for granted, subjects it to the most vigorous criticism, and finds behind it a whole new undreamt-of world to which one's naïve presuppositions have blinded one. This unsuspected domain is the *other* of the unexamined world that one begins with, and phenomenology regularly reveals such regions of investigation as lovely, rich, enlightening, unsettling, and edifying. This book of essays, *Expressions of Phenomenological Research: Consciousness and Lifeworld Studies*, edited by David Rehorick and Valerie Malhotra Bentz and produced by eight of their former graduate students, illustrates precisely the spirit of phenomenology that guided Schutz as he disclosed the uncharted terrain of subjective meaning.

Like Schutz, the authors of this book take seriously inner time insofar as they look back, some of them from as much as ten years later, upon their formation in phenomenology at the Fielding Graduate University. They recollect their first encounters with phenomenology and

6

what attracted them to it, and at the same time they demonstrate how that past has taken on unexpected, diverse, and abundant new meanings, as if the past itself is never complete and ever awaits new interpretations that help reconceive it. Perhaps, because of this phenomenological un-derstanding of time, all the authors also allude to even their present un-derstanding of that past as itself unfinished, as not yet having reached a culmination, as if they were, like Edmund Husserl, perpetual beginners. Some of them refuse to segregate the experience at Fielding as a "break" in time, as a conversion away from their previous lives, and instead identify prior character dispositions that readied them for phenomeno-logical life. Furthermore, the authors' narratives elucidate how time and history are fluid, creative, and indeterminate, thereby blocking attempts to predict with any certainty the future the past will yield. Who, for instance, would have imagined that graduate training in phenomenolo-gy might produce, not the customary university philosophy professor, but these authors who are coaches for executives, human development professionals, sustainability entrepreneurs, directors of medical organi-zations, leadership specialists, company executives, professional violin-ists, and community-based social innovators? Indeed, phenomenology is now as central in their lives and as creatively exercised in what they do as it would be for any university philosophy professor.

The lack of rigidity, which the surprising unfolding of time and phe-nomenological thinking promote, further appears clearly in the authors' willingness not to restrict themselves to one version of phenomenolo-gy but to draw on insights wherever they are available, whether from Gadamer, Heidegger, Husserl, Schutz, Wolff, Wagner, Psathas, Van Manen, or Kenneth Burke. In fact, they even make use of phenomenol-ogy to greater or lesser degrees, as if phenomenology itself precludes any absolutizing of itself. Moreover, the authors in their research, sin-gle-mindedly devoted to uncovering the things themselves as they pres-ent themselves, resort without hesitation to whatever technologies will help, such as videos or photography. Hence, one author produces videos of chamber musicians' interactions so that those musicians' music coaches can see and reflect upon the bodily cues, postures, and physical placements that such musicians are unconscious of and yet reliant upon as they make music together. In addition, this volume's essayists' readiness to learn from any source becomes evident in the thoroughly interdisciplinary approaches they deploy. Hence, one finds them balancing a biomedical model of health care with a concern for the subjective meaning of clients, drawing on the achievements of both the natural and social sciences, and integrating phenomenology with managerial and clinical paradigms. Furthermore, these authors refuse to compartmentalize diverse disciplinary paths so as to be better able to resolve practical problems that require comprehensive solutions, such as those called for by nonprofit organizational development. Just as phenomenology tends to progress beyond its present confines, so these authors are unwilling to abide within the comfortable bounds of phenomenological/ philosophical theory itself. Instead, they seek to bring its resources to bear on a variety of practical concerns in such a way that it is impossible to think of them in any other way than as the "Scholar-Practitioners" that they call themselves. One wonders if this openness to insights from whatever quarter that may arise or to the application of phenomenology to domains that might seem distant or irrelevant to it might be traced back to the leregogical method of their mentors, Bentz and Rehorick. This method dissolves any rigidly defined roles distinguishing teachers from students since the vast expertise students bring with them into the Fielding program deserves respect and since instruction should be welcomed from whatever source it emerges.

The progressive movement of phenomenology to take account of what might lie beyond its purview also is manifest in the way that the authors pay attention to the physical, locational, and emotional substrata of experience on which thinking depends and of which it is often unmindful. For instance, one finds the graduates of Fielding speaking frequently of "pathic knowing" and "cognitive love" to acknowledge that emotional, physical, and geographical dimensions are inextricably interwoven with thinking. These authors are attuned to the bodily gestures, facial expressions, and physical proximity that can foster the interactions of chamber musicians and to the architectural features (e.g., spacious halls as possible meeting sites rather than as mere thruways to other locations), gardens, or art displays that can humanize community-based organizations. Finally, they reflect on the effects that place can have on consciousness that may only become visible when we change places, occupy different places at different times, observe the different effects that the same place can have on different cohabitants, engage in activities (e.g., biking, running, or beer-brewing) that are inseparably associated with certain environments, or find the places we inhabit functioning diversely for us, as, for instance, the context, center, or source of our conscious experiences. Fielding's own curricular emphasis on somatics has no doubt played a role in shaping their graduates to heed, like good phenomenologists, those aspects of experience so easily overlooked or taken for granted since they are as so close to us, such as our affects, our bodies, or the environments that function as horizons fringing our thematic foci.

Repeatedly the authors, like many of their distinguished predecessors at Fielding and in the history of phenomenology, find in intersubjectivity perhaps the quintessential site for phenomenological astonishment. Following Gadamer, one author admits how her (and our) prejudices and fore-projections can distort the understanding of others of which we need to be aware if we are to understand another at all. Yet this same author also aspires to the freedom from prejudice in the tradition of the phenomenological *epoché* and the Gadamerian fusion of horizons. Those taking hermeneutic approaches recognize how an interpretive framework can shape the questions directed to another, as one author reflecting on the manuscripts of Nelson Mandela explains, and yet this author documents how Mandela became her pedagogue. A theme running throughout the book is the hope, based on phenomenological striving beyond itself, of reaching the surprising, rich, and different world of the other. Frequently, the authors emphasize how the traditional, unreflective typifications through which we approach others can impede entrance into their world and appreciation of them, whether one speaks of biomechanical categories that need to give way to patient-constructed narratives; the classifications of marginalized people as "homeless," "addicted," or "mentally ill" that should be traded for the typification of them as "citizens"; or labels of others according to their jobs instead of drawing near to them more after the fashion of a Buberian Thou. One author makes use of Kurt Wolff's schema of "surrender and catch," equating "surrender" with Heideggerian "letting go," with recognizing the vulnerability of the other, with accompanying the other into the other's experience of disorientation, and with refraining from offering others advice. This author explores how Wolffian "surrender" is of central significance for his vocation, not as a sociologist, but as a coach for company executives. These authors conceive the subjective meaning of the other as lying beyond the barriers that our customary ways relating and thinking impose between us and the other and that phenomenology continually invites us to transgress and transcend.

Finally, it is no coincidence that this receptivity to novelty, challenge, illumination, and diverse viewpoints is to be found in authors who have integrated the phenomenological style of reflection into their own way of living. It is also no wonder then that all these authors concur with the way that Fielding and their mentors characterize phenomenology, namely as transforming anyone whoever deeply engages with it. The Gadamerian methodology, for instance, requires that in the interpretation of others one's own fore-projects will need to be revised constantly. Likewise, the surrender and catch methodology, which calls upon one to let go of oneself, to empathize with others' vulnerability, and to embrace the personal disorientation of oneself that might result from such empathizing, entails that the phenomenologists themselves must incessantly undergo substantive change. The authors suggest that

10

the practice of anxiety-releasing meditation and continual practice at listening to others flow from and strengthen the phenomenological mode of life. Because of this life-long immersion in a phenomenological way of existing, these authors characterize themselves as more dialogic and empathetic than ever, as better able to be leaders or friends or lovers, and as capable of carrying out their life projects as organizational professionals or executives better than they ever would have been able, had phenomenology not become an intimate part of who they are and who they will continue to be.

Michael Barber
Professor, Department of Philosophy
Saint Louis University

INTRODUCTION

The collection title, *Expressions of Phenomenological Research*, arose from our long-standing collaboration to research, write, teach, and share our knowledge and enthusiasm for the domains of phenomenology, hermeneutics, and interpretive studies. It is a story about the intersection of two scholarly lives, each committed to advancing understanding and application of phenomenological inquiry to doctoral dissertation research for mid-career professionals and practitioners who chose to study at the Fielding Graduate University. The collection sub-title, *Consciousness and Lifeworld Studies*, signifies the primary thematic orientation of doctoral dissertations. The conceptions of "consciousness" and "lifeworld" are central to the Western tradition of phenomenological scholarship, which aims to deepen our understanding of socio-cultural life. Below, we share a brief origin narrative that displays how we each "came to phenomenology", and then into collaboration at Fielding.

The story begins with Valerie's decision to join the Fielding faculty. While teaching in a traditional sociology doctoral program in Texas, I found that students in the helping professions were particularly attracted to phenomenology and hermeneutics because of the direct connection to actual work situations. Because of my connection with Professor Richard Owsley, I became acquainted with the work of Martin Heidegger. He also introduced me to the Society for Phenomenology and Human Sciences (SPHS), and the Society for Phenomenology and Existential Philosophy. There I met Helmut Wagner, author of Alfred Schutz's intellectual biography. In the summer of 1978, Wagner taught a graduate course in my department, and his curriculum became the basis of his book, *Phenomenology of Consciousness and Sociology of the Lifeworld* (1983).

While on sabbatical in 1991 at the University of California, Santa Barbara, Rich Appelbaum introduced me to The Fielding Institute where Jeremy Shapiro and Don Bushnell were program directors in the Human and Organization Development Program. I was attracted to the idea of joining Fielding because of its openness to alternative ways of knowing, exemplified by their "cultures of inquiry" approach. The HOD faculty represented a wide range of social sciences disciplines. They worked together to assist professional student learners in connecting research to practice. I was reminded of Edmund Husserl's (known as "the father of phenomenology") call "back to the things themselves," as well as his concern that scholars were being shunted into academic "silos." Husserl's call to address the paramount issues of the day resonated with my felt sense of Fielding, a place where phenomenology and hermeneutics were front and central.

The challenges adult professional learners grappled with in applying their research to practice led to my writing of *Mindful Inquiry in Social Research* (1998) with Jeremy Shapiro. Here the researcher is in the center of the process guided by four cornerstones of phenomenology, hermeneutics, critical theory and Buddhism. We also introduced the concept of "mindfulness" as a component of the research process, a notion that has since gained wide currency today as anything from meditative to marketing practice.

In 1971, David Rehorick stumbled into the phenomenological domain in the midst of preparations to conduct formal demographic and statistical dissertation research. My dramatic methodological and topical shift to a theoretically oriented phenomenological dissertation set in motion a lifelong interest in what phenomenology and interpretive studies could bring to our understanding of the lifeworld. My first academic appointment called for teaching an array of program-required courses. It was several years before I was granted permission to offer an

MA and PhD graduate course called "Interpretive Studies", focusing on phenomenological inquiry.

Opportunities to expand my knowledge and research interests were accelerated during my first sabbatical leave in 1980-81 at Boston University, where regular contact and dialogue with scholars such as George Psathas, Kurt H. Wolff, E. Kohak, and Jeff Coulter broadened my grasp of phenomenology. It also expanded my understanding of new burgeoning domains such as phenomenological sociology, ethnomethodology, and conversational analysis. This year launched my involvement in the journal *Human Studies*, as author, then member of the Editorial Board, and eventually Review Editor.

I became a regular presenter at SPHS, bringing me into wider contact with kindred thinkers, and the chance to experience the wisdom of Helmut Wagner during several formative long walks. It was at these annual meetings that I met Valerie Bentz, and was inspired by her creative presentations.

As interest in studying phenomenology increased at Fielding, Valerie called for additional faculty support through informal university networks and SPHS meetings. In October 1995, I agreed to join Fielding as Consulting Research Faculty, with a mandate to support doctoral dissertation development, especially in qualitative methodologies and phenomenology.

Taken as a whole, this edited collection stories *Expressions of Phenomenological Research* retrospectively. Our account is taken from the final course syllabus that we used to co-teach in 2015. Our discussion of how phenomenological research unfolded is drawn from a survey of relevant doctoral dissertations completed between 1996 and 2016. Our retrospective account signals a shift to an expanded framework within which phenomenology and hermeneutics remain vital, baseline components of the changing curriculum at Fielding.

The relevance of our stories only makes sense when placed in a broader context, one where we asked several alums to give voice to their experiences at Fielding and beyond. The chapters in this collection by Jim Marlatt, Lee Knobel, Jo-Anne Clarke, Carol Laberge, Lori Schneider, Ayumi Nishii, Dorianne Cotter-Lockard, and Michael and Ann Wilson are testimony to what happens when one enters the phenomenological and hermeneutic domains. While their chapters share the results of their dissertation research, the discussions reveal equally as much about their journey into, through, and beyond phenomenological scholarship. As a way to help our authors kick-start their reflections, we generated "Drafting Prompts", which were never intended to direct the content or form of their expression. The prompts included:

(1) Generate a chapter that discusses how phenomenology and/or hermeneutics contributed to what you discovered in your dissertation research.

(2) Perhaps address how phenomenological scholars influenced the ways you came to see what your central research question was.

(3) Comment on your learning process in coming to understand and apply the methodology of phenomenology and its central concepts. Consider the learning environment created by Bentz and Rehorick through their seminars and workshops. This is about your learning pathway.

(4) Comment on the continuing relevance of phenomenological thinking for your life and professional practice.

(5) The chapter is more than a summary of your dissertation research, methodology, and findings. It is a reflective discussion of the broader experience with the domains of phenomenology and hermeneutics (communique to authors, November 6, 2016).

The result is eight bold and engaging chapters, each of which echoes features of what is described as our teaching and learning approach in Chapter 1.

The impetus for this edited collection arose in the spring of 2016 when we asked ourselves: So, what has more than two decades of scholarly collaboration meant to us, and for the students who embraced phenomenology and hermeneutics as a mode of research and way of understanding? Our commentary on learning, doing, and being, coupled with meaningful reflections by eight past student participants, is an expression of what transpired.

We are most thankful to all students at Fielding, and beyond, who joined with us on a special learning journey, one that was transformative for everyone. Our collaborative explorations were rich, insightful, sometimes even magical.

We acknowledge formative sources for our own inspiration: Helmut Wagner, George Psathas, Kurt H. Wolff, Richard Owsley, and Richard Jung. The Society for Phenomenology and the Human Sciences (SPHS) has been a long-term source of support for the development of phenomenology, its applications, and as a forum to introduce our students to a broader cadre of prominent phenomenological scholars.

At Fielding, we recognize the vision of Dr. Katrina Rogers, President, for creating pathways to preserve Fielding's intellectual heritage. We acknowledge Dr. Jean-Pierre Isbouts, Series Editor for Fielding University Press (FUP) for sensing the potential of our project, and bringing it forward as a research monograph.

Ms. Casandra Lindell, Associate/Copy Editor, compiled the draft chapters into a full manuscript, and offered many editorial suggestions that have enhanced the clarity of the text. Ms. Abby Rae, Fielding Librarian, guided the reference search for relevant, completed HOD dissertations with ties to phenomenology and hermeneutics (Appendix B).

We are most appreciative for the Foreword generated by Dr. Michael Barber, offering his overview of the relevance and place of our book within the wider domain of phenomenology.

In thinking of our work as more than just a legacy, we are thankful for the on-going contributions of Fielding faculty, alumni, and current students who have participated in the creation of Somatics, Phenomenology, and Communicative Leadership (SPCL), a new curriculum concentration. Our legacy becomes a new horizon for scholarship at the

Fielding Graduate University.

We hope that readers of this collection will be captivated by the stories of our authors, and how they became engaged with phenomenological inquiry.

David Rehorick, Senior Editor   Valerie Malhotra Bentz, Editor
Vancouver, British Columbia   Santa Barbara, California

CHAPTER 1
The Emergence of Transformative Phenomenology: Two Decades of Teaching and Learning at Fielding

David Rehorick, PhD

Professor Emeritus, Fielding Graduate University &
University of New Brunswick, Canada

Valerie Malhotra Bentz, PhD

Professor, School of Leadership Studies
Fielding Graduate University

Abstract

This chapter displays the pathways, developed by David Rehorick and Valerie Bentz over two decades, to share and teach phenomenological inquiry to doctoral dissertation students. It is a retrospective account of what they discovered worked best, and how learning about phenomenology can enhance one's research and transform one's life. An empirical examination of seventy-six completed dissertations revealed contributions that can be described as phenomenologically inspired, oriented, or based. Their Fielding experience is contextualized relative to broader issues and trends within the phenomenological movement. This chapter is like an umbrella, under which one can make sense of the subsequent offerings by eight alumni who studied with Valerie and David.

Keywords: phenomenology, hermeneutics, consciousness, lifeworld, transformation, scholar-practitioner, adult learning, leregogy, sociology, psychology, qualitative research

Introduction

What constitutes phenomenological inquiry? What is the place and relevance of phenomenology in the social and human sciences? What makes sense to students who come to the phenomenological domain for the first time? What might be the utility of phenomenology and hermeneutics to professional practitioners who are introduced to different epistemologies and research approaches? These are some of the big, bold questions we posed in the context of more than two decades of co-creating and co-teaching doctoral research seminars and workshops within the School of Human and Organizational Development (HOD) at the Fielding Graduate University.

In this chapter, we address: (1) what arose as the central tenants of our course content, (2) what became our teaching style, (3) what seventy-six completed doctoral dissertations can tell us about phenomenological research in HOD, and (4) where we locate our contributions within the broader domain of phenomenological inquiry. We have always been surprised by how few in-coming students are aware of Western contributions to the study of "consciousness" emanating from the phenomenology of Edmund Husserl. The outward turn for knowledge, driven by objectivist concepts, dominates the scholarly landscape. By framing the social world a "lifeworld," our flesh is intertwined with life forms and meaning structures.

While there have been expressions of phenomenology within the Schools of Psychology and Educational Leadership at Fielding, the most systematic and sustained development occurred within HOD. Between 1996 and 2016, we identified a pool of seventy-six completed doctoral dissertations that display engagement, to varying degrees, with phenomenology and/or hermeneutics in research design and methodology (see Appendix B). This dissertation pool provides an empirical base for illuminating how phenomenological inquiry developed and unfolded within the Fielding graduate program. While we have relevant experience at other universities and as invited external readers, our focus in this project is specifically on what emerged at Fielding.

Discovering What Works: Reflective Insights
from a Course Syllabus

As graduate students in the 1970s, Bentz and Rehorick were schooled to begin reading original philosophical texts (preferably in the original, but often in translation) for central figures such as Edmund Husserl, Martin Heidegger, Jean-Paul Sartre, Maurice Merleau-Ponty, and Paul Ricoeur, among others. Eschewing the notion that phenomenology is a methodology, there has always been push back against attempts to articulate something akin to a step-by-step approach to phenomenological inquiry. During the 1970s and 1980s, increased interest in phenomenology among social and human scientists created an atmosphere calling for a reduction of phenomenological terms and approach to make the material more accessible. As reference to phenomenology increased in non-philosophical published journal articles, James Heap and Phillip Roth (1973) drew attention to the uncritical, metaphorical transfer of phenomenological concepts into other social science domains. Such publications distorted the meaning of phenomenological concepts and fuelled misunderstanding, even suspicion, of what phenomenology is. Moreover, some scholars sought to uncover and display the "methods" within the methodology of phenomenology. For instance, Richard Hycner (1985) published what became controversial guidelines for the phenomenological analysis of interview data. While struggling to present phenomenological thinking in its own terms, Hycner remained caught by an apologetics to thinkers who judged the efficacy of phenomenology with reference to their established research platforms. These examples are part of a much larger story which cannot be told here. But it sets the atmosphere within which we sought to find ways to teach "what is phenomenology" and to demonstrate "how to do it."

We will refer to our 2015 course syllabus (see Appendix A) as we comment on how our teaching of phenomenology and hermeneutics emerged. This syllabus represents the cumulative wisdom of what appealed to our students, and how we shaped the curriculum over time to make phenomenology meaningful to them. The course is organized around three central texts—our book *Transformative Phenomenology: Changing Ourselves, Lifeworlds, and Professional Practice* (2008), Max van Manen's *Researching lived experience: Human science for an action sensitive pedagogy* (1997), and Helmut Wagner's *Phenomenology of consciousness and sociology of the life-world: An introductory study* (1983a). Other readings from original philosophical writings, published journal articles, and secondary books and chapters were introduced into the course in a "just-in-time" manner. Earlier course iterations were structured differently; however, we discovered that by focusing on three selected texts, our students grasped more and felt more confident in their first excursions into phenomenological thinking.

Our book, *Transformative Phenomenology*, was a response to the recurrent call of our students to show them "how to do phenomenology." It introduces foundational concepts of phenomenology along with essential methodological practices and strategies. Nine (of thirteen) chapters written by Fielding alumni provides convincing evidence that "you too" can harness the insights of phenomenology to enhance your research agenda.

In our introductory chapter, we delineated ways in which the phenomenological lens clears and clarifies one's vision (Rehorick & Bentz, 2008, pp. 3-31). A person's view of the lifeworld, understandings, and situations of others are clouded by his preconceptions, scientific and popular constructs, and media images and distortions. Over time, these may blind us one to what is apparent to the unclouded phenomenological eye, much as cataracts impair one's vision. As a point of departure, we oriented new learners to the work of four primary scholars: Husserl, Schutz, Merleau-Ponty, and Heidegger. We taught bracketing, imaginative variations, and horizontalization as beginning strategies for students to assess descriptive accounts of their experiences. We fully acknowledged that our work exists in and though writing and interpreting texts of words and images. Above all, we emphasized the work of Alfred Schutz (1967, 1970) as providing a platform from which our graduate students could explore lifeworld topics relevant to their personal lives and professional activities.

We focused also on Hans-Georg Gadamer as our chief hermeneutic strategist, since we found that most of our students gravitated to his writings. We also introduced them to the hermeneutics of Heidegger, Johann Droysen, and Paul Ricoeur (Gadamer, 1975; Palmer, 1969). In explicating Gadamer's hermeneutics, we conjured up the image and metaphor of a wild horse to illustrate his three hermeneutic levels. In the first level, one interprets the text on the basis of the context of the lifeworlds upon which it rests and within which it exists. This is akin to seeing and describing the wild horse from a distance. The second level depicts the multiple voices, which connect with and challenge each other within the text. Here, one approaches the wild horse and observes it running, walking, and engaging with other horses. Gadamer's third level exposes the ways in which the interpreter herself changes because of engaging with the text. This is where she jumps on the wild horse and tries to ride (Rehorick & Bentz, 2008, pp. 20-23). This can be risky, and she might be taken away from her destination, or even thrown and injured. But this is the nature of entering into phenomenological inquiry where a person must embrace ambiguity and uncertainty as part of the process of coming to see "as though for the first time."

To introduce the theoretical and conceptual thinking of Schutz, and to locate it within its historical context, students work with the second central text, Wagner's (1983a) *Phenomenology of consciousness and sociology of the life-world: An introductory study*. This book, not well-known in the circles of phenomenological scholarship, is a solid, clear, and holistic expression of Schutz's work. Wagner articulates how Schutz bridged Max Weber's vision for interpretive studies with selected features of the methodology of phenomenology in Husserl's thought. As such, Wagner's text is a pathway to understanding the rise of the domain of social phenomenology. At this intersection, many of our graduate students saw the potential and relevance of applying Schutzian thinking to the questions, issues, and problems arising from their professional practice (also see Wagner, 1973; Wagner, 1983b).

The third central text is van Manen's *Researching lived experience: Human science for an action sensitive pedagogy* (1997). This book has proven to be the most accessible and appealing source for phenomenological newcomers. Van Manen strikes just the right chord between the charge to read foundational phenomenological tomes, and calls for methodological directives on how to do phenomenological analysis. Indeed, all of van Manen's writings provide solid guidance without falling back on the methodological reductionism that has permeated the social, human, and educational sciences for the latter half of the twentieth century. Van Manen's more recent synthesis of his past writings (2014) pulls together the strands of his life's work in a single volume. While van Manen provides an excellent introduction to phenomenological and hermeneutic philosophy, he does not address the rich tradition of social phenomenology emanating from the work of Schutz.

The decision to select three central textbooks as introduction to phenomenological inquiry arose organically over time as we experimented with various reading mixes. Earlier syllabi introduced secondary published articles, book chapters, and an array of original writings (in translation) from central phenomenological philosophers. Over time, however, these sources shifted to the periphery and became supplementary items in a supporting reference list. As our course unfolded, we referred to and substantively laced features of past readings into the discussions. But we found that over several iterations of the course, students who began with the more limited three-textbooks better understood what phenomenology is and how it might serve their dissertation research agendas. As busy working professionals undertaking doctoral studies, our students reported that our approach gave them confidence without causing them to feel overwhelmed.

Our experience teaching pre-dissertation workshops and courses informed by phenomenology, hermeneutics, interpretive studies, and phenomenological sociology, along with mentorship through doctoral research, leads us to make two claims. First, we sustain Husserl's vision for phenomenology as invoking "complete personal transformation, comparable in the beginning to religious conversion" and to the "greatest existential conversion" of humankind (Husserl 1954/1970, p. 137; quoted in Rehorick & Bentz, 2008, p. 26). Second, our work with mid-career practitioners who return to doctoral studies later in life has led us to see that "phenomenological inquiry is an essentially practical activity, and the model of the scholar-practitioner is an inherently educational mission for the twenty-first century" (Rehorick & Bentz, 2008, p. 26).

Characterizing Our Teaching Style:
Leregogy as an Umbrella Conception for Adult Learning

As much as our course syllabus, choice of reading texts, and practice of phenomenological writing were shaped by our scholarly lifeworlds, our teaching style was shaped by what our students brought to the face-to-face and online classroom encounters. As established professionals and practitioners, Fielding students have a vast knowledge base, often in topical areas where they, not always the faculty, can claim content expertise. What students lacked (often a source of learning anxiety) was knowledge of the research process. In particular, many students had not been exposed to the wide array of qualitative methodological approaches, and most had never heard of phenomenology and hermeneutics. They were challenged to comprehend the supporting epistemological frameworks, which contrasted sharply with what they had been taught previously as constituting "correct research". As much as we endeavoured to introduce them to phenomenology, our students in

24

turn were teaching us how to teach them because many struggled with the uncertainty and ambiguity elicited by "coming to phenomenology for the first time."

It is relevant to briefly comment on the nature of the Fielding learning model, since this provides the context within which learning takes place. In chronicling the rise of the Fielding Institute from its inception in 1974 through 1985, Keith Melville informs us that the learning model revolves around two core principles: (1) that doctoral programs "should be judged by the real-world impact of what students learn," and (2) the model should reflect Malcolm Knowles' principles of andragogy (Melville, 2016, p. 27). In distinguishing pedagogy from andragogy, Knowles ushered in new horizons for higher education. As adjunct faculty at Fielding late in his career, he influenced the direction of the learning model (Melville, 2016, pp. 114-116). For our purposes, we draw on remarks by Steven Schapiro (2003) who offers an informative account of the relations between adult learning theory as applied to the Fielding Graduate University program in Human Organization and Development. He displays the development of the program from beginning principles of andragogy and mentoring, following the lead of Knowles, to a more collaborative and critical model of adult (midlife) education (see Dirkx & Mezirow, 2006; Herman & Mandell, 2004; Taylor, 2007). While locating the Fielding program within the broader conceptions of adult learning, Schapiro adopts a critical perspective to show the limitations of andragogy and self-directed learning (2003, p. 151). In reviewing how Fielding faculty and students have migrated toward more interactive and collegial modes of learning, Schapiro draws upon elements from critical and collaborative pedagogy to display how the Fielding program has evolved (Garrison, 1997; Knowles, 1973). His discussion explicates how Fielding has depicted its learning model over time. Moving beyond andragogy as a central organizing concept, we propose that our approach to teaching and learning phenomenology is best characterized by a new conception "leregogy," which originated within David Rehorick's research and writing.

The conceptions of pedagogy and andragogy have a rich and extensive socio-historical and intellectual trail. In contrast, the conception of leregogy emerges outside these traditions, within a project where I (David) collaborated with Gail Taylor to enhance our understanding of the phenomenological and hermeneutical domains. We published an article entitled "Thoughtful incoherence: First encounters with the phenomenological-hermeneutical domain" (Rehorick & Taylor, 1995). We asked, "How do separate individuals with varying experience come into collaborative being?" The neologism "leregogy" was coined to capture what was experienced as partners on a learning mission.

> *Leregogy* is a term coined to try and bridge the indomitable severing of roles between teacher and learner. It implies a transactional and shifting set of "roles" wherein both people are, at various times and sometimes synchronously, both teachers and learners. It also gets by the accepted term for adult learning (andragogy) which has its linguistic roots in maleness; and the authoritarian role-sets implied by the term pedagogy. (p. 411)

As a conception, leregogy invites us to create a new, fresh way to conceptualize adult learning to include an engaged adult learner role and a relational component of the adult learner as being co-present. In a leregogical relationship, participants are open and mindful to learning from and within the relationship. "Leregogy" is more suited to describe the nature of learning interactions, and how it is possible to tolerate periods of personal incoherence while moving toward a mutual goal of enhancing understanding. "Leregogy" has roots connected to the English verb "to learn." *Lere* is derived from an obsolete English verb, with roots in Old German, meaning "to teach," "to guide, lead," and "to learn, study" (retrieved from http://en.wiktionary.org/wiki/lere). As leregogues, we are called to practice more tolerance for incoherence as an essential part of learning (Rehorick & Taylor, 1995, p. 406).

In struggling to make sense of phenomenological texts, Gail and I speak of accepting exegesis as an important step in grasping new ideas in unfamiliar domains of inquiry (Rehorick & Taylor, 1995, pp. 395-396). Repeating what is said in one's own words in an important first step in understanding challenging material. The tendency of educators to press too quickly for students to adopt a critical stance fails to permit uncertainty and incoherence to be an explicit and valid part of the learning process. In documenting our co-learning journey, we distinguished insider from outsider views of the process:

> While an outsider to our process might interpret our activities as merely confused or unformed, our own experience of inchoation was marked by a certain persistent faith that periods of painful disorientation, as well as the eruptions of energy that piecemeal clarity gave rise to, would lead us ineluctably towards something both interesting and new. The incoherence, in other words, was always *thoughtful.* (p. 397)

Our co-created journey into phenomenology revealed the relevance of embracing periods of doubt and chaos during the learning process, of accepting silence as a learning component, and of placing less emphasis upon appearance when trotting ideas out into the public arena. In a leregogical relationship, participants are open and mindful to learning from and within the relationship. Much as leregogy emerged within a context of experiential transformative learning, teaching phenomenology at Fielding was a leregogical activity, one that allowed others to experience the transformative nature of phenomenology for their research and their lives.

Phenomenology in Dissertation Research:
Three Expressive Threads

To shift from understanding to applying phenomenological thinking, all students in our (David & Valerie's) graduate seminars and workshops were required to engage in the practice of phenomenological writing. This is about generating rich, in-depth, first-person descriptions of any phenomenon of interest. While many students selected topics related to their dissertation research, some choose themes grounded in their experiential lifeworlds.

Most students expressed how difficult they found writing from the perspective of the "I" since the normative, socio-historical research agenda has taught us that only third-person, so-called scientific writing is legitimate and acceptable. The turn to first-person experiential expression is foundational to phenomenological inquiry. To help kickstart their writing, we directed students to van Manen (1997, chapter 5; see also Bentz, 1995), who offers guides as to what phenomenological writing can encompass. In addition, we continued to generate and refine notes that provided ways for students to get started (Bentz & Rehorick, 2013). After the publication of *Transformative Phenomenology*, chapters by Fielding alums illustrated how descriptive phenomenological texts and interview data became an integral part of the research process (see Novokowsky, 2008; Haddad, 2008).

It was through this learning strategy that newcomers to phenomenology began to see its utility first and foremost for clarifying and deepening what was offered as a preliminary central research question to their dissertation studies. As course facilitators, we had learned from past experience that what one thinks, at first cut, to be one's central research question is often misleading. Only through a deep dive can one see what tacit, taken-for-granted assumptions might be shaping and distorting the quality and crispness of one's foundational question. If a person does nothing further with phenomenology than harness it to help clarify his research question, his study could be characterized as "phenomenologically-inspired." The deeper connection to phenomenological thinking may not be evident explicitly in the final dissertation product; however, formative engagement with phenomenology as a way of knowing serves to ground the broader research agenda in a way that enhances clarity of expression and purpose. We call "phenomenologically-inspired" the first expressive thread in the relevance of phenomenology to dissertation research.

More explicit and direct ties between dissertation research and phenomenological thinking can be characterized by two further expressive threads—as "phenomenologically-oriented" and as "phenomenologically-based." This is where the degree of engagement with writing and re-writing becomes central to the research quest. In phenomenological social and human science, "writing does not merely enter the research process as a final step or stage.... Human science research *is* a form of writing. Creating a phenomenological text is the object of the research process" (van Manen, 1997, p.111).

To empirically demonstrate the distinctions between "phenomenologically-inspired," "phenomenologically-oriented," and "phenomenologically-based" Fielding HOD dissertations, I (David) did a library search for dissertations completed between 1996 and 2016 where the work had some reference to phenomenology and/or hermeneutics (see Appendix B). All dissertations were completed at Fielding Graduate University (formerly The Fielding Institute March 1974 to June 2001, and Fielding Graduate Institute July 2001 to December 2004). I identified and assigned one of three classification designations to seventy-six dissertations: PB = phenomenologically-based, with a count of 30; PO = phenomenologically-oriented, with a count of 24; and PI = phenomenologically-inspired, with a count of 22. This classification arose from an examination of both abstracts and tables of contents for each dissertation. We then conducted a "final expert's check" since one or both of us had direct knowledge of most dissertations since we had served as either committee member or chairperson. The characteristics of each of the three expressive dissertation threads are specified below, and the specification for each dissertation can be found in Appendix B.

Characterizing a Phenomenologically-Based Dissertation (PB)

Dissertations in this category typically display some mix of the following characteristics:

(1) Both substantive and methodological ties to phenomenology and hermeneutics exist.

(2) Insight into the "whatness" of a phenomenon or experience, often accompanied by a sense of wonderment at unexpected aspects of the experience, is provided.

(3) Ideas and concepts from central thinkers such as Husserl, Merleau-Ponty, Heidegger, and Schutz are laced into the fabric of the research literature review.

(4) Both the methodological framework and the specific methods or strategies used in data collection are phenomenologically grounded. Sometimes the research extends and adds to existing phenomenological methods or strategies.

(5) The research demonstrates a change in our understanding of the lifeworld, as well as the being of the researcher.

Characterizing a Phenomenologically-Oriented Dissertation (PO)

Dissertations in this category typically display some mix of the following characteristics, and may echo some characteristics listed under PB:

(1) References and citations to phenomenology and hermeneutics are often present in the introductory and methodology/methods chapters.

(2) There is usually acknowledgement of how phenomenological thinking helped clarify the central research question, and how the quality and clarity of data collection methods (most often interview schedules) were enhanced by it.

(3) The work may blend methodological approaches—for instance, something from phenomenology with something from other qualitative approaches such as narrative inquiry or autoethnography.

Characterizing a Phenomenologically-Inspired Dissertation (PI)

Dissertations in this category display characteristics such as:

(1) Formal acknowledgement of how earlier study of phenomenology helped shape formulation of the research question.

(2) Limited direct reference to phenomenological scholarship and thinking, yet an informed reader would "sense" the impact of phenomenological scholarship on the formative stage of the research. Thus, the impact is implicit.

(3) Sometimes there is an expression that, in a next round of research, more focus would be given to doing a phenomenological study, building from what was accomplished in the current study.

This retrospective examination of what surfaced in the phenomenological dissertation pool reflects both the direction of influence that we had on students who engaged to varying degrees with the phenomenological research literature, and our way of bringing it forward. In the next and final section, we seek to locate what emerged at Fielding among other phenomenological scholarship.

Contextualizing Transformative Phenomenology: Phenomenological, Sociological, and Psychological Influences

Having addressed the development of phenomenology at Fielding, the question arises as to where to locate our contribution within the broader domain of phenomenological inquiry. Phenomenology is the study of consciousness and objects of consciousness. Phenomenology requires the researcher to begin and end from within her own embodied consciousness. In the West, Husserl is considered the founder ("father") of the phenomenological movement (Husserl, 1954/1970; Natanson, 1973). After Husserl, the movement might be depicted as "spokes radiating away from a central hub." While phenomenology began as a philosophical enterprise, scholars in domains such as psychology, sociology, and psychoanalysis (to mention only a few) sought ways to harness features of Husserlian thinking to enhance their own investigations (Wagner & Srubar, 1984).

As the impact of Husserl's phenomenology moved beyond the confines of European philosophy, two geographically oriented attitudes arose: (1) Most European scholars maintained separation between phenomenological philosophy and other domains; and (2) North American scholars sought a synthesis between phenomenology and their individual disciplines (Embree, 1988; Nasu, 2012). The academic fields of psychology and sociology are typically not conceptualized from "within consciousness," thus the introduction of phenomenology was resisted by scholars who view themselves as "scientific" and using an "objective" lens to view individuals and social life. In their view, studying the human and social world is about explanation, or cause-effect prediction. In contrast, researchers who embrace phenomenological thinking seek understanding, or meaning and interpretation. There was accelerated attraction to the phenomenological attitude in mid-1960s America. Many younger scholars were feeling disillusioned with positivistic and behaviorist ways of thinking. It is interesting to note that both Valerie (in the U.S.) and David (in Canada) were graduate students in sociology departments during the late 1960s and early 1970s.

What emerges from our collaboration at Fielding is a blended style of phenomenological inquiry. A more Husserlian focus, including hermeneutics, is represented in the writings of van Manen (1997, 2014), Amedeo Giorgi (2009), and Clark Moustakas (1996). These writers explicate what constitutes a phenomenological methodology, and how phenomenology can be done. A second component arises from the extension of Husserl's writing about the "lifeworld" as the source of experience. Alfred Schutz sought to bridge selected features of Husserl's methodology with the interpretive sociology emanating from Weber

(Burger, 1976; Schutz, 1967). Schutz's writings border on the socio-logical side of phenomenology, displayed through central thinkers such as Wagner (1983a, 1983b) and George Psathas (1973, 1989). Having spoken about Wagner's contributions earlier in this chapter, we now comment briefly on Psathas' contributions.

A formative and influential publication appeared in 1973, Psathas' edited collection entitled *Phenomenological Sociology: Issues and Applications.* This collection introduced uninitiated readers to phenom-enology. It also demonstrated the relevance and application of phe-nomenology to a wide range of traditional social science topics such as communication, interaction, organizations, groups, and society. Psathas displayed how Schutz provided direct entry into the new paradigm called "phenomenological sociology" (Eberle, 2012, pp. 139-140). In contrast to typical sociological research, which begins from a concep-tual level, the new paradigm does not study social reality through pre-conceived theoretical concepts. What is captured phenomenologically must find expression through language, thus text becomes an object for hermeneutic interpretation (Eberle, 2012, p. 148). Psathas understood the link between phenomenology and hermeneutics in the study of so-ciological phenomena, mirroring what van Manen (2014) displayed in his studies of pedgagogy and educational issues.

Our particular blending of perspectives also reflects the nature of Fielding as a multi-disciplinary institution. Since HOD students are practitioners, they tend to focus on both the psychological and the so-cial realms, and they are exposed to both phenomenology of individual experience and of the lifeworld. Students first become used to working from within their own consciousness through the practices espoused by Husserl. These include writing rich descriptions of an experience including the bodily and emotional components. They learn to set aside assumptions about the experience through bracketing, imaginative variations, and working from with the epoche (setting aside everyday meanings). Through writing and rewriting, in a leregogical, collaborative setting, they gain clarity about a nature of a phenomenon. At the same time, they learn to control the workings of their cognitive faculties, bringing about more flexibility and creativity in their work.

On the "sociological" side, students learn to describe the typifications and relevances operating in the lifeworlds they are researching. According to Schutz, there should be no conflict between the findings of phenomenologists and other social scientists using objectivist methods. Rather they should corroborate each other even though they start from different premises. Phenomenological inquiry seeks to display the dialectical interplay of objective and subjective meaning contexts. In reality, however, there has been push and shove between objectivist and phenomenologically based social scientists.

The publication of our book, *Transformative Phenomenology: Changing Ourselves, Lifeworlds, and Professional Practice* (2008) documents the essential ingredients of what worked at Fielding. Taken together, our course syllabus (Appendix A) and "Transformative Phenomenology: A Scholarly Scaffold for Practitioners" (Rehorick & Bentz, 2008, Chapter 1) provide a concrete account of where we ended up. Our leregogical educational approach created a collaborative environment whereby our students helped us delineate what made sense to them, and what was better left behind. The selection of phenomenological thinkers, research approaches, and strategies was influenced by the nature of real lifeworld issues and problems our practitioner-scholars chose to research. On reflection, two formative research strands emerged: (1) thinking that stemmed from a blend of hermeneutics and phenomenology, and (2) thinking that drew substantively and methodologically from the thought of Schutz.

Expressions of Phenomenological Research: Consciousness and Lifeworld Studies offers empirical evidence to display the ways in which teaching and learning phenomenology was expressed both as a research endeavour and as a transformative experience for the researcher. The identification of "three expressive threads" among the dissertation pool surveyed, adds a new character dimension to the efficacy of phenomenology and hermeneutics. We maintain that exposure to phenomenological thinking can contribute in three significant ways: research that is phenomenologically-inspired [**PI**], research that is phenomenologically-oriented [**PO**], and research that is phenomenologically-based [**PB**]. Thus, there are three ways that "transformative" expression and experience appear. Akin to a three-layered cake, each of the three research threads has something valuable to offer. PB research encompasses all three cake layers, thus one is fully immersed substantively, methodologically, and personally. PO research is two-layered, whereby the quality of the research question and the methods and strategies used to gather data are enhanced by having explored the phenomenological domain. There is only a single-layer to the PI research cake, but in turn exposure to phenomenological thinking enhances the base and clarity of the research question posed, whatever the ultimate methodological approach. In effect, the transformative nature of the research is a matter of degree, each in turn profoundly contributing to the thoughtfulness of one's study.

In the following chapters, eight authors show us how coming to understand phenomenology and hermeneutics, then applying it in their dissertation research, became meaningful for both the immediacy of the research project and beyond. They reveal how phenomenology was transformative personally and professionally, thus becoming an embodied way of knowing and being.

End Notes

These are some of the big, bold questions we posed in the context of more than two decades of co-creating and co-teaching doctoral research seminars and workshops within the School of Human and Organizational Development (HOD) at the Fielding Graduate University. In 2016, the structure and organization of programs within the Fielding Graduate University were modified significantly. Prior schools of HOD (Human Organization and Development) and ELC (Educational Leadership Change) were re-organized into the School of

Leadership Studies (SLS). However, we will continue to refer to HOD in this book since the dissertations were begun and completed under the HOD umbrella.

While there have been expressions of phenomenology within the Schools of Psychology and EducationalLeadership at Fielding, the most systematic and sustained development occurred within HOD.
One of Fielding's three founders, Renata Tesch, wrote about and taught phenomenology, and she saw it as "transformative" (see Tesch 1980; 1990).

These examples are part of a much larger story which cannot be told here.
More recently, Jonathan Smith, Paul Flowers, and Michael Larkin (2009) claimed to have generated a recipe for phenomenological analysis. However, their writing displays the problematic of uncritical, metaphorical transference of phenomenological concepts (see Heap & Roth, 1973). In this closing chapter, Smith reflects on calling their approach "interpretative phenomenological analysis (IPA), and states that a better conception would have been "experimental qualitative psychology" (EQP) (pp. 203-206).

In explicating Gadamer's hermeneutics, we conjured up the image and metaphor of a wild horse toillustrate his three hermeneutic levels.
Our metaphor sprang from an exquisite painting of a wild horse by Wan Chang-Hamachi. This image is imprinted on the front cover of our edited collection, *Transformative Phenomenology*.

As much as we endeavoured to introduce them to phenomenology, our students in turn were teaching ushow to teach them because many struggled with the uncertainty and ambiguity elicited by "coming tophenomenology for the first time."
Illustrative accounts of what it means to experience "coming to phenomenology for the first time" can be found in Rehorick & Taylor (1995) and Rehorick & Bentz (2008, pp. 8-11).

As adjunct faculty at Fielding late in his career, he influenced the direction of the learning model(Melville, 2016, pp. 114-116).
Former Fielding President, Judith Kuipers (2011), also offers an informative commentary about the learning model.

The neologism "leregogy" was coined to capture what was experienced as partners on a learningmission.

Two independent database searches (March & August 2009) found no entries for "leregogy" prior to the coining of the term by Rehorick and Taylor in 1995. The searches indicate that the term had been picked up only very selectively in no more than two or three publications which referenced Rehorick and Taylor as the originators. These searches were done in conjunction with the preparation of a conference paper by Rehorick & Jeddeloh (2010). In a parallel vein, the concept of "heutagogy" began to surface around the same period that "leregogy" was coined. At inception, *heutagogy* was oriented to the nursing profession. More recent literature on heutagogy emphasizes the centrality of the learner, relegating the teacher to that of facilitator (Hase & Kenyon, 2013). By contrast, leregogy, from original conception, takes it a step further. The roles of student-teacher and mentor-mentee fall away, as at varying times all are teaching and learning together, without formal learning boundaries.

Much as leregogy emerged within a context of experiential transformative learning, teachingphenomenology at Fielding was a leregogical activity, one that allowed others to experience the transformative nature of phenomenology for their research and their lives.

Further applications of the conception of "leregogy" can be found in Rehorick, Jeddeloh & Lau-Kwong (2014), and in Rehorick & Rehorick (2016).

To shift from understanding to applying phenomenological thinking, all students in our (David &Valerie's) graduate seminars and workshops were required to engage in the practice ofphenomenological writing.

The practice of phenomenological writing is referred to by other conceptions such as "phenomenological protocols," "phenomenological research writing," "phenomenological protocol commentary," and "phenomenological protocol statement." In our teaching experience, we found that the term "protocol" elicited uncertainty and even anxiety; therefore, we eventually settled on "phenomenological writing" as our introductory conception.

Having addressed the development of phenomenology at Fielding, the question arises as to where to locate our contribution within the broad-

er domain of phenomenological inquiry.

Herbert Spiegelberg (1982) generated one of the best and well-known historical introductions to the phenomenological movement. His focus is on the philosophical development, arising with the work of Edmund Husserl. The distinction between European and American orientations emerged when phenomenology was introduced to the social and human sciences. Recently, Nasu (2012) has published a consolidated and detailed account of the development of the movement within the United States.

In the West, Husserl is considered the founder ("father") of the phenomenological movement (Husserl, 1954/1970; Natanson, 1973).

A sustained study of the nature of consciousness has been a part of the tradition of scholarship in India for more than 2000 years (Chattopadhyay, Embree, & Mohanty, 1992; Bentz, 2016).

Having spoken about Wagner's contributions earlier in this chapter, we now comment briefly on Psathas'contributions.

In *Festschrift for George Psathas*, I (David) remarked that one scholarly generation after George, I followed a similar scholarly trajectory, moving from formal demography and statistics to the unfamiliar waters of phenomenological sociology (Rehorick, 2012, pp. 29-30). In this respect, I reflect Eberle's suggestion that varying perspectives arose from followers of a particular scholar.

The publication of our book, Transformative Phenomenology: Changing Ourselves, Lifeworlds, andProfessional Practice (2008) documents the essential ingredients of what worked at Fielding.

Since the publication of the book in 2008, we are saddened by the passing of Sandra K. Simpson, Bernie Novokowsky, and Gloria L. Cordova. Their contributions remain a permanent statement to who they were and what phenomenology meant to them.

*We maintain that exposure to phenomenological thinking can contribute in three significant ways:research that is phenomenologically-inspired [**PI**], research that is phenomenologically-oriented [**PO**],and research that is phenomenologically-based [**PB**].*

There are two possible results of applying the phenomenological method to sociology: a sociology that would be intrinsically phenomenological in its categories and claims, or a sociology that is based upon a metatheoretical position that is phenomenologically grounded. In the first instance, we might say that the end product of applying a phenomenological approach to sociological analysis is a "phenomenological sociology," whereas in the latter case the result is a "phenomenologically *based* sociology." Our contention is that only the latter alternative is truly possible (Rehorick, 1974). More than four decades after making these claims in my doctoral dissertation, I find it fulfilling to have generated an extended vision that views PB, PO, and PI as legitimate ways that phenomenology can transform and augment the quality of research.

References

Bentz, V. M. (1995). Husserl, Schutz, Paul, and me: Reflections on writing phenomenology. *Human Studies*, *18*, 41-62.

_____. (2002). From playing child to aging mentor: The role of *Human Studies* in my development as a scholar. *Human Studies*, *25*, 441-8.

_____. (2016). Knowing as being: Somatic phenomenology as contemplative practice. In V. M. Bentz and V. M. B. Giorgino (Ed.) *Contemplative social research: Caring for self, being and lifeworld* (pp. 50-79). Santa Barbara, CA: Fielding University Press.

Bentz, V. & Rehorick, D. (2008). "Transformative Phenomenology: A Scholarly Scaffold for Practitioners." In D. Rehorick and V. Bentz (Ed.), *Transformative Phenomenology: Changing Ourselves, Lifeworlds, and Professional Practice* (pp. 3-31). Lanham, Maryland: Lexington Books.

Bentz, V. M. & Shapiro, J. (1998). *Mindful inquiry in social research.* Thousand Oaks: SAGE.

Bentz, V. & Rehorick, D. (2013). *On phenomenological writing: Collected notes* (2009–2010). Unpublished seminar documents, Fielding Graduate University, Santa Barbara, CA.

Burger, T. (1976). *Max Weber's theory of concept formation: History, laws, and ideal type.* Durham, NC: Duke University Press.

Chattopanhyaya, D., Embree, L., & Mohanty, J. (Ed.). (1992). *Phenomenology and Indian philosophy.* Albany, NY: State University of New York Press.

Dirkx, J. M., & Mezirow, J. (2006). Musings and reflections on the meaning, context, and process of transformative learning: A dialogue between John M. Dirkx and Jack Mezirow. *Journal of Trans-*

formative Education, *4*(2), 123-39.

Eberle, T. (2012). Phenomenology and sociology: Divergent interpretations of a complex relationship. In H. Nasu and F. C. Waksler (Ed.), *Interaction and everyday life: Phenomenological and ethnomethodological essays in honor of George Psathas* (pp. 135-52). Lanham, Maryland: Lexington Books.

Embree, L. (Ed.). (1988). *Worldly phenomenology: The continuing influence of Alfred Schutz on North American Human Science*. Washington, DC: The Center for Advanced Research in Phenomenology and University Press of America.

Gadamer, H.-G. (1975). *Truth and method*. New York, NY: Seabury.

Garrison, D. R. (1997). Self-directed learning: Toward a self-directed model. *Adult Education Quarterly 48*(1), 18-33.

Giorgi, A. (2009). *The descriptive phenomenological method in psychology: A modified Husserlian approach*. Pittsburgh, PA: Duquesne University Press.

Haddad, D. (2008). Intentionality in action: Teaching artists phenomenology. In D. A. Rehorick & V. M. Bentz (Ed.), *Transformative phenomenology: Changing ourselves, lifeworlds, and professional practice*, (pp. 193-206). Lanham, MD: Lexington Books.

Hase, S., & Kenyon, C. (Ed.). (2013). *Self-determined learning: Heutagogy in action*. London, England: Bloosmbury Academic.

Heap, J. L. & Roth, P.A. (1973). On phenomenological sociology. *American Sociological Review, 38*(3), 354-67.

Herman, L., & Mandell, A. (2004). *From teaching to mentoring: Principle and practice, dialogue, and life in adult education*. New York, NY: Routledge Falmer.

Husserl, E. (1954/1970). *The crisis of European sciences and transcendental phenomenology: An introduction to phenomenological philosophy*. (David Carr, Trans.). Evanston, IL: Northwestern University Press.

Hycner, R. H. (1985). Some guidelines for the phenomenological analysis of interview data. *Human Studies, 8*(3), 279-303.

Knowles, M. (1973). *The adult learner: A neglected species*. Houston, TX: Gulf Publishing.

Kuipers, J. L. (2011). PhD and EdD degrees for mid-career professionals: Fielding Graduate University, *New Directions for Adult and Continuing Education*, 129, 63-73. Hoboken, NJ: Jossey-Bass.

Lewin, P. M. (2010). Problems and mysteries: Book Review of Rehorick and Bentz (Eds.) Transformative Phenomenology. *Human Stud-*

ies, 33, 333-8.

Melville, K. (2016). *A passion for adult learning: How the Fielding model is transforming doctoral education*. Santa Barbara, CA: Fielding University Press.

Merleau-Ponty, M. (1962). *Phenomenology of perception.* C. Smith (Trans). London: Routledge & Kegan Paul.

Moustakas, C. (1996). *Phenomenological research methods.* Thousand Oaks, CA: SAGE.

Nasu, H. (2012). Phenomenological sociology in the United States: The developmental process of an intellectual movement. In H. Nasu and F. C. Waksler (Eds.) *Interaction and everyday life: Phenomenological and ethnomethodological essays in honor of George Psathas* (pp. 1-21). Lanham, MD: Lexington Books.

Natanson, M. (1973). *Edmund Husserl: Philosopher of infinite tasks.* Evanston, IL: Northwestern University Press.

Novokowsky, B. (2008). Personal power: Realizing self in doing and being. In D. A. Rehorick & V. M. Bentz (Eds.), *Transformative phenomenology: Changing ourselves, lifeworlds, and professional practice* (pp. 129-140). Lanham, MD: Lexington Books.

Palmer, R. E. (1969). *Hermeneutics: Interpretation theory in Schleiermacher, Dilthey, Heidegger, and Gadamer.* Evanston, IL: Northwestern University Press.

Psathas, G. (Ed.). (1973). *Phenomenological sociology: Issues and applications.* New York, NY: John Wiley & Sons.

_____. (1989). *Phenomenology and sociology: Theory and research.* Washington, D.C.: Center for Advanced Research in Phenomenology & University Press of America.

_____. (2008). Forward. In D. A. Rehorick & V. M. Bentz (Ed.). *Transformative phenomenology: Changing ourselves, lifeworlds, and professional practice* (pp. xi-xiii). Lanham, MD: Lexington Books.

Rehorick, D. A. (1974). *The hermeneutics of social action: A study in the convergence of phenomenology and sociological theory.* Unpublished PhD Dissertation. Edmonton, Alberta, Canada: The University of Alberta.

Rehorick, D. A. (1980). Schutz and Parsons: Debate or Dialogue? *Human Studies, (3)*4, 347-55. Reprinted in Kurt H. Wolff (Ed.), *Alfred Schutz: Appraisals and Developments.* The Hague, Netherlands: Martinus Nijhoff, 1984.

Rehorick, D. A. (1984). Review, H. R. Wagner's Phenomenology of consciousness and sociology of the life-world. *Human Studies*, 7(2), 255-7.

Rehorick, D. A. & Buxton, W. (1988). Recasting the Schutz-Parsons Dialogue: The Hidden Participation of Eric Voegelin. In L. Embree (Ed.), *Worldly Phenomenology: The continuing influence of Alfred Schutz on North American human science*, (pp. 151-69), Washington: The Center for Advanced Research in Phenomenology and University Press of America.

Rehorick, D. A. & Taylor, G. (1995). Thoughtful incoherence: First encounters with the phenomenological hermeneutical domain. *Human Studies*, 18(4), 389–414.

Rehorick, D. A. (2002). I/Human Studies. *Human Studies*, 25(4), 435-9.

Rehorick, D. A. & Bentz, V. M. (Ed.). (2008). *Transformative phenomenology: Changing ourselves, lifeworlds, and professional practice.* Lanham, MD: Lexington Books.

Rehorick, D. A. (2012). Revisiting Psathas: A personal and hermeneutic reappraisal. In H. Nasu and F. C. Waksler (Eds.), *Interaction and everyday life: Phenomenological and ethnomethodological essays in honor of George Psathas* (pp. 29-37). Lanham, MD: Lexington Books.

Rehorick, D. A. & Bentz, V. M. (2012). *Re-envisioning Schutz: Retrospective reflections & prospective hopes.* Paper presented at the Annual Meetings of the Society for Phenomenology and the Human Sciences (SPHS), Rochester, NY, November 2012.

Rehorick, D. A. (2014). Discovering leregogy: Transformative phenomenology as conduit. In A. Nicolaides and D. Holt (Ed.), *Spaces of transformation and transformation of space* (pp. 81-3). Proceedings of the XI International Transformative Learning Conferences, Teachers College, Columbia University, New York, NY.

Rehorick, D. A. & Jeddeloh, S. (2010). *Discovering leregogy: A phenomenological account of improvised collaborative transformation.* Paper presented at the 29th International Human Science Research Conference, Seattle University, Seattle, WA, August 2010.

Rehorick, D. A., Jeddeloh, S., and Lau-Kwong, K. (2014). At the boundary of transformative learning: Empirical, phenomenological, and conceptual insights. In A. Nicolaides and D. Holt (Ed.), *Spaces of transformation and transformation of space* (pp. 81-93). Proceedings of the XI International Transformative Learning Conference, Teachers College, Columbia University, New York, NY.

Rehorick, D. A., & Rehorick, S. (2016). The leregogy of curriculum design: Teaching and learning as relational endeavours. In A. Tajino, T. Stewart, & D. Dalsky (Ed.), *Team teaching and team learning in the language classroom: Collaboration for innovation in ELT* (pp. 143-163). London, England: Routledge.

Ricoeur, P. (1991) *From text to action: Essays in hermeneutics, II.* K. Blamey and J. Thompson (Trans). Evanston, IL: Northwestern University Press.

Schapiro, S. A. (2003). From andragogy to collaborative critical pedagogy: Learning for academic, personal, and social empowerment in a distance-learning PhD program. *Journal of Transformative Education, 1*(2), 150-166.

Schutz, A. (1967). The phenomenology of the social world. G. Walsh & F. Lehnert, (Trans.). Evanston, IL: Northwestern University Press.

Schutz, A. (1970). *On phenomenology and social relations: Selected writings.* H. Wagner (Ed.). Chicago: University of Chicago Press.

Smith, J. A., Flowers, P., & Larkin, M. (2009). *Interpretative phenomenological analysis: Theory, method, and research.* Thousand Oaks, CA: SAGE.

Spiegelberg, H. (1982). *The phenomenological movement: A historical introduction* (3rd ed.). The Hague, Netherlands: Martinus Nijhoff.

Taylor, E. W. (2007). An update of transformative learning theory: A critical review of the empirical research (1999–2005). *International Journal of Lifelong Education, 26*(2), 173-191.

Tesch, R. (1980). Phenomenology and transformative research: What they are and how to do them. In Handlon, J. & Stomff, D. (Eds.). *Fielding Occasional Papers.* Santa Barbara, CA: The Fielding Institute.

_____. (1990). *Qualitative research: Analysis types and software tools.* New York: The Falmer Press.

van Manen, M. (1997). *Researching lived experience: Human science for an action sensitive pedagogy* (2nd ed.). London, Ontario, Canada: The Althouse Press.

_____. (2014). *Phenomenology of practice: Meaning-giving methods in phenomenological research and writing.* Walnut Creek, CA: Left Coast Press Inc.

Wagner, H. (1973). The scope of phenomenological sociology: Considerations and suggestions. In G. Psathas (Ed.), *Phenomenological sociology: Issues and applications* (pp. 61-87). New York, NY: John Wiley & Sons.

_____. (1983a). *Phenomenology of consciousness and sociology of the life-world.* Edmonton, Alberta, Canada: The University of Alberta Press.

_____. (1983b). *Alfred Schutz: An intellectual biography.* Chicago, IL: University of Chicago Press.

Wagner, H., & Srubar, L. (1984). *A Bergsonian bridge to phenomenological psychology.* Washington, D.C.: University Press of America.

Wolff, K. H. (1978). Phenomenology and sociology. In T. Bottomore & R. Nisbet (Ed.), *A History of Sociological Analysis*, (pp. 499-556). New York, NY: Basic Books.

CHAPTER 2

The Transformative Potential of Conversations with Strangers

James Leonard Marlatt, PhD

Executive Coach and Organizational Development Consultant

Fielding Graduate University Alumnus

Abstract

In this chapter, I provide a commentary on my experience as a doctoral student encountering the field of phenomenology for the first time at Fielding Graduate University. My evolution as a scholar-practitioner is situated at a nexus where David Rehorick and Valerie Bentz' project of transformative phenomenology meets Kurt H. Wolff's project of surrender-and-catch. I present selected outcomes of my phenomenology-based doctoral study on the role of executive coaching relationships in facilitating transformative learning within organizational settings. These outcomes point to ineffable aspects of learning-in-relationship. An approach to scholarship offered by my Fielding mentors is depicted from a social phenomenology perspective as an encounter with archetypal strangers. I include a related experience of surrender-and-catch is recorded as a testimony to the transformative power of phenomenology.

Keywords: adult learning, "leregogy," the stranger, transformative phenomenology, surrender-and-catch, mindful inquiry, transformative learning, executive coaching

Prologue

Now in the next piece you'll see—naturally I saw it
first, but it took me some time too—that I am beginning all over again. I have forgotten everything—"everything" in quotation marks, of course (as in "everything" is pertinent and "everything else" vanishes—the
pertinence of "everything" of surrender). It's not that I
have not begun before—we are no longer on page one.
But, as you read, while I thought that the title "Sociology, Phenomenology, and Surrender-and-Catch" gave
me a program to follow, the venture turned out to be not
nearly as discursive as that idea of the title's role and
this of the nature of the essay anticipated.... In writing
I forgot about the title—more accurately, I held it in
abeyance, suspended it; I distrusted its imposed con-
ceptualization, even though it had been imposed by no
recognizable source other than myself....
–Kurt Wolff, *Surrender and Catch* (1976, p. 152)

Husband, father, son, brother, engineer, geophysicist, geologist,
explorer, manager, leader, coach, consultant, scholar-practitioner, and
caregiver—serendipity and transformation: *applied natural scientist*
meet budding *applied social phenomenologist.* Illuminating my lifeline,
my lifeworld, and my autobiography in a sentence through the lens of
a handful of typifications provides a map that takes me closer to understanding my territory. Marveling, in wonderment, at the same lifeline
that has evolved as more of a random walk toward the discovery of
the transformative power of phenomenology requires a more intentional
glance, beyond the taken-for-granted. This is a challenging ambition for
a middle-aged man with a life, and a lifeworld, programmed in the scientific method yet grappling with the phenomenological domain. What
follows is more than a solipsistic account of my particular doctoral journey. It is the account of a discovery of a different sort, catalyzed by hermeneutic encounters with guiding-strangers from the past, present, and
unanticipated future. Through these encounters, I grew to understand

phenomenology as more than a research methodology and method. Phenomenology has become my personal standpoint, and foundational philosophy, that informs my way of being. From this standpoint, I continue to encounter the variegated history and beauty of different philosophies, epistemologies, and theories, with openness and curiosity. Phenomenology beckons me to move beyond any sense of culmination, of having arrived, in the face of my current stock-of-knowledge, to continue to learn and transform.

A Scholarly Project: An Emerging Pathway
to Phenomenology
First Encounters with Phenomenology

I have a clear recollection of my first encounters with David Rehorick, my future committee chair, during an interview related to my application for doctoral studies at Fielding Graduate University. We had another encounter while walking on the beach at the new student orientation held in Santa Barbara. Through brief dialogic moments—encounters—I was struck by what I sensed as David's natural, innate curiosity and his sense of wonderment, openness, interest, humility, and acuity. This was something different from what I had taken for granted as the more conventional relationship between professor and student, where power differentials can distort things. I later came to understand these characteristics to be a manifestation of typifications that I made of David as a phenomenologist, and David as a teacher. He coined the neologism "leregogy" (Rehorick & Taylor, 1995)—where teacher is student, and student is teacher. I interpret the term to encompass a guiding and supportive stance between teacher and learner, de-void of power, accepting of faultiness, and naturally conscious of the impact of reward and criticism, a relationship where the teacher walks beside the learner as an equal. A "leregogic" practice—teacher-as-guide, where social distance and commentary mitigates dependence, spawns creativity and acknowledges that there are many possible pathways to the learner's destination. This is a relationship where the mentor (but not quite a mentor) learns from, and with, the mentee (but not quite a mentee) who is embarking on a unique self-directed learning journey of scholarship and self-discovery. In retrospect, those early meetings constituted my first encounters with a self-declared anomaly, an *applied social phenomenologist*, a scholar with many interests, a jazz musician, an *intellectual high plains drifter*, a *mentor-stranger*—I think that I was hooked on phenomenology before I knew what phenomenology was all about (Excerpt from personal diary).

When I began my doctoral studies at the Fielding Graduate University School of Human & Organizational Development (HOD), I had no idea of the transformative potential that conversations with strangers would come to have on me. In time, and following my embrace of David Rehorick and Valerie Bentz' project of transformative phenomenology, my doctoral study evolved into a phenomenological and hermeneutic exploration of the transformative role that personal relationships can play in executive coaching conversations (Marlatt, 2012; Rehorick & Bentz, 2008). The study was aligned with my deeper interest in exploring the experiential realms of humanistic coaching psychology and transformative learning, and understanding their relationship to human development (Boyd & Myers, 1988; Cranton, 2006; Dirkx, 2000; Dirkx, Mezirow, & Cranton, 2006; Mezirow, 2009; Rogers, 1985; Stober, 2006; Torbert, 2004). I was interested in understanding the catalysts and unacknowledged impacts of the coaching relationship. I was also interested in understanding how transformative learning might be accomplished through relationship, and how my study might inform the efficacy of coaching practice and the veracity of transformative learning theory.

As I progressed through the program, I began to recognize that my learning experiences were being grounded in conversations with *strangers*—recollections of my coach-past, my mentors, and through hermeneutic conversations with scholars from the past, present, and future. With the guidance of David and Valerie, I began to identify with Edmund Husserl's methodology. I experienced, and adopted, several phenomenological research methods for my study: the "openness" of hermeneutic epoché-reduction, and the "whatness" of the proper eidetic-reduction, complimented by hermeneutic dialogues with texts through approaches offered by Hans-Georg Gadamer (Husserl, 1931; Natanson, 1973; Palmer, 1969; Rehorick & Bentz, 2008; van Manen, 2016). I found meaning in Gadamer's depiction of such dialogues as encounters with a thing—even a familiar thing—as if viewed as a stranger, from a distance (Bentz & Shapiro, 1998).

Mid-stream in my research study, I turned toward the social phenomenology of the lifeworld to inform my research. This was through the unexpected discovery of the archetypal *stranger* in essays written by sociologist Georg Simmel and social-phenomenologist Alfred Schutz (Schutz, 1944, 1945; see also Wagner, 1983; Wolff, 1950). It was this significant entrance into the realm of the sociology of the lifeworld where I resonated with Schutz's practical focus on illuminating the natural attitude in the reality of everyday life (Barber, 2004). This was revelatory and led to subsequent encounters with Jürgen Habermas' concept of the colonization of the lifeworld (Eriksen & Weigard, 2003). My reading of Habermas revealed the potential for inquiry into the lifeworld to support social change. I reached an unanticipated zenith in more guiding, and foundational, encounters with the pre-phenomenological sociology of radical commitment invented by Kurt. H. Wolff (1976). His concept of *surrender-and-catch* became more central to my research, work, and life.

My decade-long exploration of the phenomenological domain can be described as a serendipitous developmental learning arc (Figure 1). The arc maps my pre-indoctrination in the scientific method, to phenomenological and hermeneutic research, toward social phenomenological inquiry, and onward to the pre-phenomenological—all realized through encounters with *strangers*. I have been both tangibly and ineffably transformed through an evolving journey, and a meaningful focus for my scholarship and practice—a vocation—continues to emerge as an outcome.

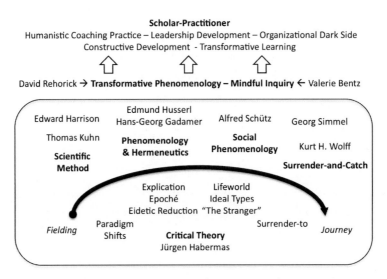

Figure 1: Conversations with strangers—a learning arc

Explication, Openness, and the Hermeneutic Epoché-Reduction

As both a researcher and research-participant (coach), I became embedded in my phenomenologically based study. My intent was to explore the subjective experience of three executive coaching relationships. Max van Manen (2016) offers a description of a process of the hermeneutic epoché-reduction followed by the eidetic reduction that I followed in my study. Through the hermeneutic epoché-reduction, I bracketed assumptions relevant to my inquiry by explicating theories and frameworks of coaching, transformative learning, and the sociology of small groups that I depicted through the lens of the sociological form of the stranger archetype. The explication of these perspectives brought their influence in misunderstanding the nature of the coaching experience to the forefront.

My open-state-of-mind emerged through the epoché, and insight into the meaning of lived experience and the lifeworld appeared through hermeneutic encounters with Simmel, Schutz, Habermas, and Wolff. I opened myself to the mystery of lived experience in different ways, including the adoption of a sense of wonder, openness, and concreteness—shifting away from theoretical abstractness—while engaged in my coaching encounters and research. I embraced and understood Carl Rogers's humanistic call for unconditional positive regard in helpful psychological encounters with others (Rogers, 1961). I recognized an alignment of his philosophy with Wolff's concept of "surrendering-to" my coachee's potential for transformation during my coaching conversations. I more fully understood the significance of active listening and the potential that is inherent in non-directedness, where I realized the futility of depriving the coachee of a transformative learning opportunity by providing advice.

An authority derived from evidence-based theories of psychology, cognition, personality, development, maturation, and other epistemic realms continued to devolve into secondary supporting mechanisms. Instead, I empathized with the captivating human condition and related behaviors experienced by my coachees that were beyond their immediate recognition and control. I attributed many of these behaviors to the colonization of their lifeworld by the social, political, and economic forces inherent in organizational settings. More productive humanistic and phenomenological coaching attitudes began to prevail as my conversations evolved to become more "leregogic" in nature. The essential phenomenological nature of humanistic coaching became apparent to me.

I explored the complexity of the executive coaching relationship through the exploration of the ideal types based on Alfred Schutz, Georg Simmel, and Margaret Wood's conceptions of the liminal *strang-*

er, *wanderer*, *immigrant*, *homecomer*, and *newcomer*. In this way, I was able to frame the dynamic and influential nature of social distance that exists between the coachee, coach, and other actors situated in the organizational context (Schutz, 1944, 1945; Wolff, 1950; Wood, 1969). The qualities of the *coach-as-stranger* became more apparent to me as an engagement that lacks the prejudice of presupposition. Simmel declared that the essence of a relationship based on strangeness "often receives the most surprising of openness—confidences which sometimes have the character of a confessional and which would be carefully withheld from a more closely related person" (Wolff, 1950, p. 404). Within this divulging relational space, the executive coach can adopt different identities (humanistic coach, mentor, expert, and evidence-based coach) and assist the coachee who is faced with disorienting dilemmas that surface in their lifeworld—dilemmas often rooted in typifications of the coachee by the host community. The humanistic coach adopts a phenomenological stance in the "we" relationship with the coachee, and helps mediate the coachee's expectations arising from encounters in the lifeworld with the "generalized other".

A Humanistic Coaching Methodology Emerges

A humanistic coaching methodology based on Wolff's pre-phenomenological concept of *surrender-and-catch* evolved from, and informed, my study. The methodology offers an ontological foundation from which to understand and follow an unorthodox phenomenological approach to coaching that embraces a free-flowing critical dialogue in support of transformative learning. This is different from a more conventional directive and goal-focused agenda (Figure 2). Wolff depicted *surrender-and-catch* as encompassing the unanticipated ephemeral and existential experience that rises out of *cognitive love* toward another: involving total involvement, suspension of received notions, recognizing the pertinence of everything, identification, and the risk of being hurt (Wolff, 1976, pp. 22-24). The experience of *surrender* can be understood as transformation, grace, flow, peak experience, being in the "coaching zone," and the coachee's "ah-ha" revelation (Csikszentmihalyi, 1991; Maslow, 1999; Stehr, 2007).

Surrender can be an unexpected, intense, existential experience leading to a revelatory, recognizable, transforming, cognitive *catch*. This might be recognized through reflection as an act of meaning making. When linked to theory, it can become an act of knowledge creation (Backhaus, 2003). In the act of *surrender-to*, we experience another person, or thing, in its essence, without preconceptions, through an attitude of extreme bracketing that takes us out of our common taken-for-granted way of understanding things around us (Backhaus & Psathas, 2007). As we *surrender-to*, we bracket with great intention and intensity but within the context of a critical stance because we understand our deep concern for the state of others in the lifeworld. From this stance, we can recognize the vulnerability of another person. From the act of *surrender-to* rises the potential for the ephemeral, affective, and existential experience of *surrender-and-catch*.

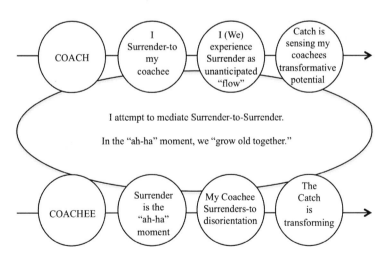

Figure 2: A methodology of surrender-and-catch *in the executive coaching relationship.*

The Eidetic Reduction Yields Some Ineffable Insights

So the eidetic reduction is not a simplification, fixation, or contraction of the world into a system of eidetic concepts—rather, it is the exact opposite: The eidetic reduction makes the world appear as it precedes every cognitive construction: In its full ambiguity, irreducibility, contingency, mystery, and ultimate indeterminacy. (van Manen, 2016, Chapter 8, Philosophical Methods, The Eidetic Reduction, para. 10)

I used transcripts of my coaching conversations and rich-descriptions (protocol statements) of my own personal experiences with transformative learning as a coachee as data to further my phenomenological and hermeneutic investigation. Husserlian eidetic reduction involved the reflective attitude in search of understanding the possible essential elements of meaning, or "whatness," of the lived experience. By leveraging the processes of imaginative variation and horizontalization, and by engaging my protocols and transcripts through Gadamers' three levels of hermeneutic understanding (Rehorick & Bentz, 2008), meaningful patterns began to emerge through my research. My phenomenologically-based study of the role of the executive coaching relationship in facilitating transformative learning within organizational settings revealed thematic patterns that are illustrated in Figure 3. Selected insights from my study are presented below.

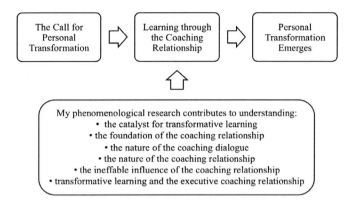

Figure 3: The influence of the executive coaching relationship in facilitating transformative learning.

The Catalyst for Transformative Learning

My study supports the premise that disorientation is necessary, but not sufficient, for transformative learning to occur. The executive coaching relationship can help the coachee cope with the impacts associated with enduring disorientation that is rooted in the actions of others in the work world. Jack Mezirow posits that the transformative perspective is born out of disorientation, understood through reflection, validated through discourse, and acted upon in the world (1981). Relationships play an important role at each of these stages, whether in catalyzing disorientation through interactions with other people in the work world, through ongoing debates with voices in the inner world in the face of disorientation, or through helpful dialogues with an executive coach.

The source of disorientation in the workplace can be rooted in the incidental, innocuous, unintentional, incompetent, or malicious acts of people in positions of authority. Unresolved psychological issues in the coachee's lifeworld, combined with disorienting encounters with people in positions of power in the world of work, can lead to ensuing anxiety and enduring disorientation. The reaction of coachees who are impacted by those acts may be guided by their habitual behavior of seeking approval, of servitude, capitulation, blind allegiance, or blind trust in a better tomorrow.

The coachee's emotional angst stemming from disorienting encounters with other people in the organization can remain unknown and inaccessible to the coach. However, the executive coach can help the coachee to elicit the rational from the emotional ground through dialogue, helping the coachee to come to terms with his disorientation. Disorientation can result in openness for the coachee to engage in executing coaching. If the executive coaching relationship forms at a time when the coachee is experiencing these impacts, he may very well reach out for the lifeline of hope for resolution of his dilemma. This hope, then, is a foundational element in establishing an effective executive coaching relationship.

The Foundation of the Coaching Relationship

My research affirmed that an evolving bond of trust is foundational to the executive coaching relationship. It can lead to a "shorthand" way of understanding each other. Eroding the trust bond between the coachee and executive coach can compound enduring disorientation, but might also push the coachee toward self-direction with less reliance on his coach. Trust is a sociological phenomenon and consists of an expectation that a person will realize a favorable outcome through the process of trust (Mollering, 2001). This expectation is based on an interpretation of experiences in our lifeworld that form the basis for believing that there are "good reasons" for the expectation. Georg Simmel described another element that relates to what happens between interpretation and the favorable outcome of a certain expectation. This in-between *thing* is an ineffable leap of faith involved in the process of trust where "there is no automatic logic connecting interpretation ('good reasons') to trustful favorable expectation" (p. 413). Mollering labeled this leap as *suspen-*

sion, "the bracketing of the unknowable which represents a defining aspect of the nature of trust" (p. 417).

The research identified an ineffable element in our executive coaching relationship that may be related to trust. I use the term *affinity* to depict an ineffable natural connection between a coachee and coach that can be apparent from the very start of the executive coaching relationship and which may be related to trust. Trust appears to be an important factor in assuaging the coachee's anxiety, but its relationship to the instant connection of *affinity* is less clear. The immediate natural connection between coach and coachee could be rooted in the process of developing trust. *Affinity* and *suspension* could be synonymous with, and an example of, what Kurt Wolff called *surrender*—in this instance, *surrender-to-trust.*

The Nature of the Coaching Dialogue

My research revealed that the coachee's authentic disclosure of the impacts of disorientation in their lifeworld can help to expedite the executive coaching process and contributes to transformative learning. Such authentic disclosures require that the coachee adopt a vulnerable stance in revealing part of his inner world to the coach. The prerequisite for authentic disclosure is a trusting relationship. My coachees arrived at similar states of anticipation in our executive coaching relationship. They anticipated that the executive coaching conversation would always lead to positive outcomes for the coachee. This state is an indicator of a productive executive coaching relationship. The conditioned expectation of positive executive coaching experiences is in itself trust-building and conducive to the coachee's ongoing authentic disclosure.

Authenticity is difficult to define but it is about being trustworthy and genuine in a relationship. Authenticity has been described from an educator's perspective as "being at the core of meaningful teaching and [that it] contributes to the spiral-like journey of individuation and transformative learning" (Cranton & Roy, 2003, p. 93). In addition, Cranton, in referring to Brookfield, described practical elements that contribute to authenticity in the teacher-student relationship. The elements include "making sure our behaviors are congruent with our words, admitting we do not have all the answers and can make mistakes, building trust with students through revealing personal aspects of ourselves and our experiences, and respecting students as people" (Brookfield, 1990 as quoted in Cranton & Roy, 2003, p. 93).

By comparison, the authentic humanistic coach exhibits consistent behavior (doing-what-you-say-you-will-do) and has unconditional positive regard (respect) for his coachee. However, authenticity is not necessarily related to admissions that the coach does not have all the answers or makes mistakes because the pure humanistic coaching model is founded on asking open-ended questions, which reduces the probability of this type of fallibility. It is only in the telling mode that the coach is vulnerable to perceptions of ignorance, failure to meet expectations (making mistakes), and inauthentic dialogue.

The Nature of the Coaching Relationship

The promotion and recognition of dialogic openings in the executive coaching conversation can lead to the appearance of discrete opportunities for transformative learning. Dialogic openings are ineffable learning opportunities that appear in those moments when an evocative coaching question or exchange catalyzes the coachee into a more reflective level of awareness. Dialogue or discourse is a fundamental element in Mezirow's epistemology of transformative learning, which is founded on Habermas's concept of communicative learning (Eriksen & Weigard, 2003; Mezirow, 2003). Mezirow depicts some of the elements that are associated with people who fully engage in critical-dialectical discourse. Having an open mind, developing empathy, bracketing premature conclusions, searching for common ground, and demonstrating emotional intelligence are among them.

Executive coaches can set the stage for serendipitous conversations that catalyze transformative learning. These are ineffable learning opportunities that appear through dialogic openings. A free-flowing "agenda-less" dialogue can be effective in facilitating deep learning and may be particularly relevant for coachees who are experiencing enduring disorientation. The coachee's agenda may not be the most effective agenda in supporting deep learning. In this mode both the coach and coachee do not have a presumptive attitude toward expected outcomes of the executive coaching dialogue. The coachee has faith in the coach's capacity to steer the dialogue in the right direction through his open-ended, or more direct, questions. The over-arching topic of the executive coaching conversation may or may not be the coachee's. The coach's agenda is focused on catalyzing reflection in the dialogic opening that may or may not appear in response to his question. The coach's patient capacity to persist through this uncertainty is rooted in his faith that a dialogic opening will appear. This may involve asking, repeating, or rephrasing questions, asking different open-ended questions, or on occasion asking more direct yes-no type of questions. It may even involve ending the specific executive coaching conversation without the coachee apparently experiencing any sort of revelation, in anticipation of a future conversation.

The free-flowing executive coaching dialogue is an evocative one and conforms to Mezirow's depiction. Mezirow's discourse elements are synonymous with the foundational elements of sound humanistic coaching practice as evidenced in the "transformative executive coaching gestalt" revealed throughout my study. These elements are also aligned with Wolff's concept of *surrender*. The free-flowing dialogue may have an analogy in Carl Rogers's non-directive teaching practice, which is an unstructured approach to learning that promotes student thinking through self-direction, and, in part, as a result of the teacher's positive and non-judgmental regard for all participants in the class (Rogers, 1961).

The Ineffable Influence of the Coaching Relationship

The themes identified by my research study attest to the ineffable influence of the executive coaching relationship on emerging transformation in the coachee's lifeworld. The themes map part of the learning process where affective and cognitive modalities in the coachee's lifeworld integrate to yield shifts in ways of being in the world. Indeed, executive coaching may lead to unknown, unacknowledged, and even dire consequences that can be emotionally or physically debilitating. Moving through emotional or physical catharsis is a part of transformative learning. Coming to terms with disorienting events in the workplace is a reflective process involving a pragmatic shift from an attitude of capitulation to the demands of others, toward the adoption of an attitude of self-control. Moving beyond the emotional angst associated with disorienting events in the workplace can coincide with the coachee's self-awareness that he has a growing capacity to deal with adversity in his lifeworld. This can lead to an adoption of a continuous learning perspective. The appearance of the dialogic opening in response to a coach's catalyzing question can represent an opportunity for transformative learning. Dialogic openings can lead to resurgent, or new, disorienting experiences that can catalyze the coachee toward further reflection. Ineffable shifts in the coachee's mindset can occur in the reflective space between executive coaching conversations. Reflection can take place over long periods of time, yet new ways of understanding can appear as more discrete fundamental "leaps" between old and new ways of seeing or being within those longer time frames. A "leap" might be realized as recognition of the essence of the coachee's disorienting dilemma. The "leap" might also lead to a pragmatic shift toward an attitude that involves taking more control of actions in the lifeworld.

Transformative Learning and the Executive Coaching Relationship

My study affirmed the veracity of the fundamental nature and importance of relationship in transformative learning theories. It supports Mezirow's (1981) alternative view that a catalyzing disorienting dilemma may be the result of a more evolutionary personal history in the learning process. The study also affirmed the efficacy of the practice of executive coaching from a humanistic perspective—as opposed to an evidence-based perspective—in assisting coachees who are facing enduring disorientation in their work world. The coach can take on a supportive role as the coachee copes with the psychological impacts that are associated with enduring disorientation that has a source in dysfunctional relationships with authoritarian individuals in the work place.

Implicating Transformation: Adopting a Phenomenological Standpoint

> The obligation of the philosopher to his contemporaries is to support their attempt to find the ground on which phenomena become, in the strictest sense, *evident*. Rather than being a mentor or guide in the classical sense of a companion who leads the novice, the phenomenologist strives to give the initiate autonomy from the outset, to place him in charge of himself. (Natanson, 1973, p. 10)

Maurice Natanson differentiates between a mentor or guide, and the phenomenologist charged with leading his initiate to the field. For me, coming to phenomenology has been a personal journey of discovery within the unique Fielding learning community. I have benefited greatly from an autonomy that initially relied on an introduction, and then an invitation to engage and wrestle with the intellectually demanding methodology of phenomenology—to engage with ideas rather than

61

a prescribed set of enabling research methods and rules. As a scholar-practitioner intent on the application of phenomenology in the life-world for the benefit of others, I find this priority for the beginner to be enabling. I feel some sort of synergy in knowing of Husserl's preference to present his ideas to non-philosophers coming to phenomenology because they brought "fewer prejudices and set positions" to the dialogue (Natanson, 1973, p.xx). Natanson also believed in a phenomenology that is accessible to non-philosophers (p.xii). For Husserl, the phenomenologist engages in a perpetual effort to understand things as if he were a *beginner*, intent on finding his own entry point into the philosophy again and again (Ntanson, 1973). Perhaps it is this refreshing innocence exhibited by the beginner that is a catalyst for my engagement in the phenomenological tradition.

David and Valerie appear to embrace Natanson's definition and model phenomenology as a way of being, while placing each student "in charge of himself." For Valerie, *Mindful Inquiry* is a foundation to research. She, along with Jeremy Shapiro (1998), developed *Mindful Inquiry* as a critical hermeneutic Buddhist phenomenology. Everyone can choose to integrate four knowledge traditions as a philosophical foundation for research, to engage in meaningful experience as a scholar and practitioner, and to make contribution in society. *Mindful inquiry* is a foundation, a philosophy, an orientation, a standpoint, for engaging in the world, and in the cultures of inquiry of all kinds. The mindful inquirer nurtures a capacity for mindful thought, alleviates suffering by critiquing origins of oppression, interprets things in the context of history and culture, and removes epistemological blinders by going back to the things themselves. For David and Valerie, *transformative phenomenology* is a central theme in bringing phenomenology to their "students" (Rehorick & Bentz, 2008). This is an approach to phenomenology that George Psathas in his forward to their book indicates can "show how we can experience renewal—through our readings, our study, our interviews, our organized protocols, our hermeneutic explorations, our understandings; in short, through all of the mysteries entailed in the transformative process…" (pp. xii-xiii). As an *applied social phenomenologist*, David believes in harnessing insights arising from a quest to examine the structures of everyday life through a phenomenological embrace of wonderment and, in my experience, transmits this way-of-being to novices while giving them "autonomy from the outset": "Others who have fully embraced the phenomenological domain can sense it, even if the words saying 'I'm doing it' are not always evident" (Rehorick & Bentz, 2008, p. 11).

Both David and Valerie acknowledge the trepidation that a novice may experience when encountering phenomenology for the first time (Rehorick & Bentz, 2008; Rehorick & Taylor, 1995). They offer guiding insights through their own writing to help others recognize that they are not alone in their sense of confusion when faced with the challenge of engaging with a demanding philosophy. Three of David's works continue to have great influence on me: his phenomenological study of an earthquake experience, in which I began to understand how human studies might inform natural science; his co-authored paper with Gail Taylor, which relays first encounters of a novice with the phenomenological tradition; and his authentic personal-growth-chronology of engagement with the Society for Phenomenology & the Human Sciences (SPHS). Valerie's works also continue to have influence. One is her reflections on phenomenological "writing from the heart"—from a place of origin, not reliant on conventional epistemologies. Another is her autobiographical account of embracing social phenomenology, which provides solace to an "initiate" encountering phenomenology for the first time. These offerings continue to encourage and model a way forward—to provide a vector and a driver—for embracing the opportunities that continue to surface before me (Bentz, 1995, 2002; Rehorick, 1986, 2002; Rehorick & Taylor, 1995).

I followed David's pattern in "I/Human Studies," recording my own selected chronology of coming to phenomenology. I depict this as the "factual" and the "actual"—the "what" and the "how"—of my journey toward engaging phenomenology: by choice, by accident, through exploration, and as a foundation, in part, for being in my world (see Table 1 below). This depiction is mapped, in an eidetic sense, by several experiences: recognizing the transformative significance of dialogic moments; turning to embed in a "sociological tradition" (Collins, 1994); realizing the impact of my "leregogic" guides through formative encounters; taking tentative steps toward authorship (Marlatt, 2011; Marlatt & Kyser, 2011); recognizing the value of autonomy in intellectual discovery; growing confidence; and meaning-making and personal transformation through phenomenological experience. Through the Fielding HOD doctoral journey I grew to understand the transformative potential of phenomenology as an echo from Husserl. By "bringing to reflective awareness the nature of the event experienced in our natural attitude, we are able to transform or remake ourselves in the true sense of *Bildung*" (van Manen, 1997, p. 7)—where *Bildung* is "a self-directed, creative, growth process leading to human development with the aid of education" (Siljander & Sutinen, 2012, p. 4). As an outcome, I continue to adopt phenomenology as a foundation for personal transformation as experienced through continuous learning.

Perhaps my defining hermeneutic encounters with the biographies and philosophies of Simmel, Schutz, Habermas, and Wolff were inevitable, given that my exploration occurred within the scholarly "container" held by David and Valerie—and expedited through their "leregogic" personas and guiding syllabus. These self-directed and creative encounters seemed to be serendipitous, emergent, mysterious, wonder-full, and meaning-full. Trusting my *mentor-strangers* to circumscribe, with a wide berth, my scholarly enculturation has been foundational to this outcome. During the course of my research, I grew to understand the transformative potential of phenomenology as stemming from the participative activity of research and practice. Wagner argues that whenever there are significant gaps in understanding between sociological researchers and people being studied, the sociologist needs to "live among the people, to learn about their lives through 'participant observation' or, better, 'observing participation'" (1983, p. 134). The goal is to understand the lives of the people before engaging in the collection of data. For Kurt Wolff, the sociologist cannot be a dispassionate, detached observer (Psathas, 2003). In this context, Wolff refers to the "before" period of living among the people as *surrender*, where the sociologist brackets both the intent of the research and knowledge from secondary sources in order to experience the people and the situation as they are. Only after this enculturation does the researcher stand apart from the experience, remove the brackets, and view the *catch* "hidden in his remembrances of the period of surrender," in part a result of the researcher's direct experience (Wagner, 1983, pp. 134-135). Understanding and embracing this participative vantage in my doctoral research and practice, and beyond, has been central to my phenomenological embrace.

The Factual	The Actual
2006 – Rehorick interviews Marlatt for entrance into the HOD program—a dialogic moment.	Rehorick's comments on Marlatt's description of an existential encounter with mathematical language. Marlatt recognizes Rehorick as a unique observer.
2007 – Rehorick and Marlatt walk on the beach and talk face-to-face at New Student Orientation for the first time —a dialogic moment.	Rehorick briefly expresses wonderment at Marlatt's way of seeing the world "through a geologist's eyes." Marlatt "sees" "David-the-Phenomenologist" for the first time.
2009 – Rehorick and Bentz remark on Marlatt's paper that focuses on situating in the history of the microinteractionist tradition after a Fielding intensive program on phenomenological inquiry.	Bentz and Rehorick model the phenomenological way during the intensive and beyond. Marlatt discovers that academic lineage and biography matter—a turning point.
2010 – Rehorick's "leregogic" orientation is neither, "directive' or "prescriptive" in "mentor-mentee" encounters.	Rehorick provides thoughtful, authentic, feedback. Marlatt is "cast adrift" to locate himself in a tradition and "catches" Simmel, Schutz, Habermas, and Kurt. H: Wolff along the way.
2010 – Rehorick solicits Patricia Cranton to be an External Examiner on Marlatt's Committee.	Marlatt is excited to raise the bar with an authority. Cranton challenges Marlatt to develop a meta-theory of transformative learning. Can I do it?
2011 – Bentz and Rehorick encourage Marlatt to present a paper as a doctoral candidate at an SPHS conference. Philip Lewin critiques Marlatt's paper.	Marlatt overcomes his trepidation and presents as a doctoral candidate for the first time. Lewin confirms Marlatt's take on the ineffable.

2011 - Marlatt's peer reviewed article is published in the Society of Economic Geologists Newsletter.	Marlatt injects HOD insights on adult development and knowledge broking into the natural sciences.
2011 – Rehorick responds to Marlatt's dissertation drafts.	Rehorick "gets" Marlatt's approach and Marlatt recognizes that he has something to "say."
2013 – Marlatt presents as a PhD for the first time at a phenomenology conference.	Marlatt is comfortable in contributing as a newly minted PhD among his peers.
2015 – Bentz organizes a working group for a new Fielding concentration.	Marlatt feels accepted as an alumnus adding value to a working group in the Fielding community.
2016 – Marlatt evacuates from a wildfire.	Marlatt experiences "surrender-and-catch," recalls Rehorick's "earthquake" paper, and emerges as a budding "applied social phenomenologist."
2016 – Rehorick and Bentz invite Marlatt to write a book chapter—a dialogic moment.	Marlatt is energized by the possibility, "surrenders-to" the opportunity, and returns to phenomenology "again and again."

Table 1: David, Valerie, and Me: A Selective Chronology

The Authentic Scholar-Practitioner: The Inevitable Ineffable

We believe that the person is always at the center of the process of inquiry—that you will always be at the center of your own research, which in turn will always be part of you. We believe this to be true not only in a psychological sense—for example, in the way that being insecure about your intellectual ability can create ambivalence about your work or that your personality style can shape your choice of a research method—but in a philosophical sense—for example, in seeing re-search not as a disembodied, programmed activity but rather as part of the way in which you engage in the world. (Bentz & Shapiro, 1998, pp. 4-5)

My path to the Fielding HOD doctoral program and beyond, and my discovery of phenomenology, has been a serendipitous and emergent affair that continues to stem from my thirst for knowledge. The strangers that I have encountered, and continue to encounter, are my guides. Now, more than a decade beyond my enrollment in the PhD program, I can reflect on my ongoing journey with a more critical eye, attempting to discern its meaning. I stand in wonderment at the outcome—the unimagined, expanding horizons of research and practice that are now accessible to me. A growing ability to question, and reflect, is a significant outcome of the HOD experience. Embracing new modes of understanding in the spheres of the phenomenological, the lifeworld, and the pre-phenomenological has transformed me. New capacities have emerged that had, until recently, seemed at odds with my programmatic training in the rule-based world of applied scientific method—my other realities of engineering and applied natural sciences. I find myself consciously "deprogramming" from my upbringing in the scientific method—aligning with Schutz's distinction between the scientific attitude and the natural attitude (Psathas, 2005). However, I may have unique vantage because of my capacity to "see" things from both perspectives, and (following Husserl) believe that science starts where phenomenology ends. I take an increasingly more reflective stance in my current work as a coach and organizational development consultant, catalyzed by my critical interest in addressing inequities faced by people in the world of work.

My foundation for research and practice has evolved toward a heuristic (Figure 4), patterned after Valerie's construct of *mindful inquiry* and resonating with the knowledge that it, in itself, is a separate creation attributed to surrender-and-catch. An evolving *transformative, critical, hermeneutic, phenomenology* is my guide. As a map, it forms a basis from which to consider the nature of helpful scientific frameworks, with epistemic blinders removed. The map also provides clues about the intellectual terrain that I continue to ponder. It is a foundation that acknowledges the kernel of engaging the world through the "limit concept" of *surrender-and-catch* (Nasu, 2007), the transformative power of phenomenology, and purposefulness revealed through the adoption of a critical standpoint—where my purposefulness is focused on positive change in self, as well as positive change in willing others, organizations, and community. The explication of the constructivist, developmental, potential of *action inquiry* (Torbert, 2004) is a cognitive driver—an epistemology, standpoint, heuristic, prompt, a reminder—to attempt to see the world synchronously, from first-, second-, and third-person perspectives, and to consciously seek ongoing transformation.

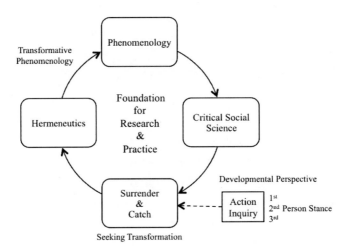

Figure 4: An evolving transformative, critical, hermeneutic, phenomenology is my guide.

In *Transformation in the Writing*, Wolff (1995) suggests that autobiography matters in assessing the veracity of his work. By giving the reader access to the development of his way of thinking, the reader might make a more informed assessment of his work. Wolff is not alone in recognizing the relevance of biography in comprehending a "scholarly life work", as revealed by Wagner who recorded aspects of the life of Alfred Schutz (Wagner, 1984). Encountering Wolff's poetic, autobiographical writings is a unique and interpersonal experience. Reading Wolff's biography (Psathas, 2003) is something akin to taking a deeper hermeneutic turn. His advocacy for the search for ineffable existential truth in the reduced phenomenological sphere is cogent. His commitment to his project of *surrender-and-catch* was dauntless. His "utmost test...the surrender to one's finding by another person" is a selfless and vulnerable stance (Wolff, 1995, p. 113). When Wolff asked of Simmel, "Who is this man? Does his life give insight into his significance? Is there a relation between a man's biography and his work?" he surmised that "once we are aroused to explore a life as a clue to mind, and a mind as a clue to its work, we become aware of our ignorance" (Wolff, 1950, p. xvii). In this awareness of our ignorance the opportunity for *surrender*—what Wolff (1976) refers to as *cognitive love*—emerges with the simultaneous opportunity for the *catch*. It is a space where we can become more aware of the subdivisions in the flux of our stock-of-knowledge that transition from a relatively small clear kernel of clarity and consistency, to ambiguity and vagueness, to the taken-for-granted realm with its blind beliefs, to complete ignorance (Wagner, 1970). The opportunity for the revelation of what Cardinal Nicholas of Cusa called *learned ignorance* (our self-awareness of our ignorance)—and through which Edward Harrison recognizes that all epistemologies are just another mask of the universe—takes us toward a more authentic pursuit of knowledge, with the inevitable acknowledgement of the ineffable nature of knowing (Harrison, 2003). Perhaps the Sisyphusic challenge of attempting to decipher the ineffable—what Philip Lewin (2011) calls "the darkness unobscured"—is, ultimately, the project that draws me back to the things themselves as a more authentic individual and schol-ar-practitioner.

After the Wildfire: A Lived Experience of Surrender-and-Catch

> Surrender-and-catch brings to light surrender's poten-tial—as a source for creative existential insight pro-vided by an opening to the transcendental capacity for meaning-invention. The catch of surrender comprises the new meanings that the surrender brings forth from immediate experience. (Backhaus, 2007b, p. 182)

As described previously, *surrender-and-catch* was invented by Wolff as a way of understanding and embracing the synchronous realm of ephemeral experience and serendipitous meaning-making under rad-ical conditions. *Surrender* is a unique experience born out of an extreme situation (Nasu, 2007). It is an experience both unpredictable and un-preventable and occurs outside of the limits of everyday experience. It involves the unintended "epoché of the natural attitude" in the absence of "received notions" (p. 138). Such situations can be described as "nonlinguistic or prelinguistic, prepredicative, prephenomenal" and as "an undifferentiated state in which anything can happen" (Wolff, 1995, p. xxi, 97 as quoted in Nasu, 2007, p. 138). Wolff also contends that the experience of *surrender* is accessible "for the radical human being" who is characterized by features of "maximum directness, directedness, im-mediacy, (and) freedom from the crutches of received notions" (Wolff, 1995, pp. 76-78, as quoted in Nasu, 2007, p. 139). The *catch*, in *surren-der-and-catch*, is the "invented" meaning that emerges from the radical experience (Backhaus, 2007b, p. 182) and involves "being thrown back on what a human being really is" (Nasu, 2007, p. 139). The following account describes my lived experience of *surrender-and-catch* that was catalyzed by a natural disaster (see Backhaus, 2007a; Backhaus, 2007b).

On May 1, 2016, the Horse River Wildfire ignited in the boreal forest approximately 15 kilometers southwest of Fort McMurray, located in remote northern Alberta, Canada. A "perfect fire storm" grew rapidly under the extreme weather conditions, characterized by temperatures exceeding 30°C, very low relative humidity, winds gusting to more than 70 kilometers per hour, and low moisture conditions in the forest because of poor snow pack the previous winter. By May 3 the fire had encroached on the city and surrounding communities, leading to the largest wildfire emergency evacuation in Alberta's history. More than 80,000 residents left the region that day, temporarily relocating to safe havens located to the north in the oil-sands work camps, south toward Edmonton and other communities, and onward to points across Canada. More than 2,400 homes and buildings were destroyed by the fire, and an additional 2,000 residents were displaced from their homes because of safety issues. Many of the oil sands operations were temporarily halted as a safety measure, and to accommodate the influx of evacuees. Over the following month, "The Beast" continued to spread across northern Alberta toward the Saskatchewan border. Enormous physical and financial resources poured into the region. Firefighting officials eventually declared the wildfire under control in early July, after it had burned 590,000 hectares. Reentry of displaced residents was permitted later that month. Remarkably, only two deaths were attributed to the fire and evacuation. The estimated cost to rebuild the affected communities was estimated at more than $9 billion. It will take years to determine the longer-term social, economic, and mental health impacts. Many individuals, families, extended families, and the community as a whole continue to experience the impact of grief and loss associated with the destructive event. Governments, agencies, and support workers will assist with recovery efforts for years to come. The source of the wildfire has been attributed to an unknown "human cause." Ineffective historical wildfire management practices and the role of global warming have also been implicated.

The Surrender Experience Befalls Me

The calls for evacuation started midday, starting with the neighbourhoods flanking the forest that now stand as mangled ashy skeletons—echoes of shattered life-worlds. I remember standing at the second floor office window gazing at the hellacious gray-orange billowing clouds that were rising to the heavens with a sense of wonderment of the power of Nature. Colourful clouds will never look the same way again. I could see the heat and smell the smoky uncertainty. I had experienced wildfires in other contexts and as I took in this vista I sensed the anxiety of others surrounding me, with openness—it was uncanny and surreal. I felt "neutral" to what might become, as if I was simultaneously observing and experiencing. It was strangely, synchronously, disorienting, and not disorienting, at the same time. I remember making a matter-of-fact statement to my colleagues that "if the fire crests the hill, I think that the city will be lost." (Excerpt from personal diary)

As the uncanny experience of *surrender* befell me, David Rehorick's phenomenological account of an earthquake experience mysteriously emerged into my consciousness (1986). I had not thought of his account for many years, and I was simultaneously surprised by my recollection and understood the significance of its emergence (which I will divulge later in this chapter). David's account records aspects of an unfamiliar and disorienting experience with a natural phenomenon, demonstrating the power of first-person studies to inform frameworks previously developed through the natural sciences. The account also illustrates the potential for life-saving insights that can be developed through human studies. In the face of the wildfire, I was able to bracket the immediate threat of the wildfire and *surrendered-to* my initial *surrender* experience.

I Surrender-to the Surrender Experience

A catalyzing memory, an origin, emerged while in that office, looking out of that window, in that moment, on that

72

day: a strange memory. An apparition appeared into my consciousness of David Rehorick's phenomenological study of his first experience with earthquake; an encounter with the unanticipated; from where, I do not know—a study, a human portrait, where social phenomenology, meets, and informs natural science; where Mercalli meets Richter. I wondered about the lifeworlds that were fracturing before my eyes in the face of a calamity of an emerging wildfire—a disaster. And I wondered how I might contribute to understanding and assist with helping others to heal, in the face of the likely loss and grief to come. And, more deeply, I wondered about how my naturalistic and phenomenological attitudes might anneal. I had experienced an "ah-ha" moment. (Excerpt from personal diary)

As I recognized my own *surrender* experience, I wondered if I was simultaneously experiencing and witnessing *surrender* by others on an unimagined city-scale. Later, I wondered what the unexpected outcome (my *catch*) was all about, or would be about. I also wondered about the *catch* of others, who may have lowered their taken-for-granted "shields" (Rehorick, 1986, p. 383), and I wondered about our collective *catch* that we might come to know. Different and ambiguous frames of reference emerged from my first-, second-, and third-person vantages. I wondered about the potential for learning and transformation that could be realized by so many people.

My own *catch* began to emerge from a "deeper" psychological place. David's phenomenological account of an earthquake experience was perfectly situated in my consciousness as a template to engage in social and natural science research associated with the wildfire. It was also a trigger in resolving a long-standing conflict within me that existed between the seemingly separate realities of my natural and social scientific vocations. The annealing of these separate realities was catalyzed in a wholehearted way, and my ongoing struggle to exist within this dichotomy began to dissipate in favor of a unity. I began to sense the emergence of my identity as a budding *applied social phenome-*

73

nologist—my *catch*—where first-person studies can inform the science that follows. This sense of emergence would continue to follow me as I experienced a sense of communion with fellow evacuees at the oil sands camps, the subsequent airlift to the south, re-entry into fire-ravaged Fort McMurray, and in my on-going work as an executive coach and organization development consultant with people in the community.

Meaning Making: I Realize the Catch

> But in that experience of immediate *surrender*, that instance, that moment, the insight, my *catch*, was an epiphany for me. It was a personal transformation as I embraced wonderment in the emerging experience of the wildfire "wilding" before me. My *catch*-in-that-moment was a synchronous realization that I had arrived, through the calamity, as a budding *applied social phenomenologist,* following in my mentor's footsteps; something that David had realized some three decades earlier. It was an actualization, a more robust emergence, a confirmation, a consolidation of the desire to experience, to observe, to share, to document, to make sense of the primordial, the non-sensical, and to link to the science that can follow—and, ultimately, a confirmation of the potential of *surrendering-to.* (Exerpt from personal diary)

The unexpected experience of *surrender* and the emergence of the *catch* of a phenomenological vocation from the "darkness unobscured" is an illustration of the ineffable nature of knowing—born out of an extreme situation, relationship, a philosophical foundation, a phenomenological attitude, and the subconscious. Through my experience of *surrender-and-catch*, an aspiration to seek additional "creative existential insight" has emerged. The allure of the possibility of a future unknown *catch* is apparent to me. Committing to adopting the attitude of a "radical human being," and selectively *surrendering-to* everyday encounters in the lifeworld, is an ambition. The sedimentation of aspects of my

74

lived experience of *surrender-and catch* continues, as I reflect and engage with a different way of being, "after the wildfire."

Epilogue

Phenomenology continues to have a growing influence on my life and work, and continues to emerge as part of the way that I engage in the world. I attribute my personal learning and transformation, through the HOD doctoral journey and beyond, in part to enduring "leregogic" encounters with my *mentor-strangers*. The lure of social phenomenology continues to strengthen as I "go back to the books on my shelf" physically, digitally, and imaginatively—holding hermeneutic dialogues with *strangers* new and old, that I meet again and again. My level of understanding develops with each turn. In *surrendering-to* David's and Valerie's invitation to create a chapter for their book, the *catch* of a phenomenological vocation became more apparent to me. The exploration of my experience with a wildfire is evidence of a restorative and transformative harvest that can occur through an embrace of the phenomenological domain. My lived experience of *surrender-and-catch* takes Kurt Wolff's construct further toward concreteness. My interest in the development and application of phenomenology toward the support of willing others to develop, learn, and transform—to *surrender-to*—has been reinvigorated. A type of *mindful inquiry* inspires me as a scholar-practitioner who acts within the helping professions of coaching, mentoring, leadership, and organization development. *Transformative phenomenology, mindful inquiry*, and *surrender-and-catch* will likely continue to offer a foundation for the pursuit of insight, akin to what Viktor Frankl (2006) believed can be realized through a scaffold of meaningful projects, the development of meaningful relationships, and through the discovery of the courage to *be*.

"Now in the next piece you'll see...that I am beginning all over again."

References

Backhaus, G. (2003). Vindication of the human and social science of Kurt H. Wolff. *Human Studies*, *28*, 309-335.

Backhaus, G. (2007a). Life after Kurt H. Wolff: A case study of surrendering-to-surrender. In G. Backhaus & G. Psathas (Ed.), *The sociology of radical commitment: Kurt H. Wolff's existential turn* (pp. 199-213). Lanham, MD: Lexington Books.

Backhaus, G. (2007b). Presuppositional surrender-to: Theoretical explication and a case study. In G. Backhaus & G. Psathas (Ed.), *The sociology of radical commitment: Kurt H. Wolff's existential turn* (pp. 181-198). Lanham, MD: Lexington Books.

Backhaus, G., & Psathas, G. (Ed.). (2007). *The sociology of radical commitment: Kurt H. Wolff's existential turn*. Lanham, MD: Lexington Books.

Barber, M. D. (2004). *The participating citizen: A biography of Alfred Schütz*. Albany, NY: SUNY.

Bentz, V. M. (1995). Husserl, Schütz, "Paul" and Me: Reflections on writing phenomenology. *Human Studies*, *18*(1), 41-62.

Bentz, V. M. (2002). From playing child to aging mentor: The role of *Human Studies* in my development as a scholar. *Human Studies*, *25*(4), 499-506.

Bentz, V. M., & Shapiro, J. J. (1998). *Mindful inquiry in social research*. Thousand Oaks, CA: Sage.

Boyd, R. D., & Myers, J. G. (1988). Transformative Education. *International Journal of Lifelong Education*, *7*(4), 261-284.

Brookfield, S. (1990). *The skillful teacher*. San Francisco, CA: Jossey-Bass.

Collins, R. (1994). *Four sociological traditions*. Oxford: Oxford University Press.

Cranton, P. (2006). *Understanding and promoting transformative learning: A guide for educators of adults*. San Franscisco, CA: Jossey-Bass.

Cranton, P., & Roy, M. (2003). When the bottom falls out of the bucket: Toward a holistic perspective on transformative learning. *Journal of Transformative Education*, *1*(2), 86-98.

Csikszentmihalyi, M. (1991). *Flow: The psychology of optimal experience*. New York, NY: Harper Perennial.

Dirkx, J. M. (2000). Transformative learning and the journey of individuation. *ERIC Digest*, no. 223.

Dirkx, J. M., Mezirow, J., & Cranton, P. (2006). Musings and reflections on the meaning, context, and process of transformative learning. *Journal of Transformative Education, 4*(2), 123-139.

Eriksen, E., & Weigard, J. (2003). *Understanding Habermas: Communicating action and deliberative democracy*. London, England: Continuum.

Frankl, V. E. (2006). *Man's search for meaning*. Boston, MA: Beacon Press.

Harrison, E. (2003). *Masks of the universe: Changing ideas on the nature of the cosmos* (2nd ed.). Cambridge, MA: Cambridge University Press.

Husserl, E. (1931). *Ideas: General introduction to pure phenomenology*. W. R. B. Gibson, Trans. Woking, England: George Allen and Unwin Ltd.

Lewin, P. (2011). *Commentary: The darkness unobscured*. 2011 Annual Meetings of the Society for Phenomenology and the Human Studies. Philadelphia, PA.

Marlatt, J. (2011). *When executive coaching connects: A phenomenological study of relationship and transformative learning*. Paper presented at the 2011 Annual Meetings of the Society for Phenomenology and the Human Sciences, Philadelphia, PA.

_____. (2012). *When executive coaching connects: A phenomenological study of relationship and transformative learning.* (PhD Dissertation) Fielding Graduate University, Santa Barbara, CA.

Marlatt, J., & Kyser, T. K. (2011). Paradigmatic shifts in the uranium exploration process: Knowledge brokers and the Athabasca Learning Curve. *Society of Economic Geologists Newsletter, 84*(January).

Maslow, A. (1999). *Towards a psychology of being*. New York, NY: John Wiley & Sons.

Mezirow, J. (1981). A critical theory of adult learning and education. *Adult Education Quarterly, 32*(1), 3-24.

_____. (2003). *Epistemology of transformative learning*. Retrieved from http://learningtheories.synthasite.com/resources/Mezirow_ EpistemologyTLC.pdf

_____. (2009). Transformative Learning Theory. In J. Mezirow, E. W. Taylor, & associates (Ed.), *Transformative learning in practice: Insights from community, workplace, and higher education*. San Francisco, CA: Jossey-Bass.

Mollering, G. (2001). The nature of trust: From Georg Simmel to a theory of expectation, interpretation, and suspension. *Sociology, 35*(2), 403-420.

Nasu, H. (2007). Scope and limits of Wolff's world of "Surrender." In G. Backhaus & G. Psathas (Ed.), *The sociology of radical commitment: Kurt H. Wolff's existential turn* (pp. 137-151). Lanham, MD: Lexington Books.

Natanson, M. (1973). *Edmund Husserl: Philosopher of infinite tasks.* Evanston, IL: Northwestern University Press.

Palmer, R. E. (1969). *Hermeneutics: Interpretation theory in Schleiermacher, Dilthey, Heidegger, and Gadamer.* Evanston, IL: Northwestern University Press.

Psathas, G. (2003). Kurt H. Wolff: A brief biography. *Human Studies, 26,* 285-291.

_____. (2005). The ideal type in Weber and Schutz. In M. Endress, G. Psathas, & H. Nasu (Ed.), *Explorations of the life-world,* (pp. 143-169). Rotterdam, The Netherlands: Springer.

Rehorick, D. A. (1986). Shaking the foundations of lifeworld: A phenomenological account of an earthquake experience. *Human Studies, 9,* 379-91.

_____. (2002). I/"Human Studies." *Human Studies, 25*(4), 467-71.

Rehorick, D. A., & Bentz, V. M. (Ed.). (2008). *Transformative phenomenology: Changing ourselves, lifeworlds, and professional practice.* Lanham, MD: Lexington Books.

Rehorick, D. A., & Taylor, G. (1995). Thoughtful incoherence: First encounters with the phenomenological-hermeneutical domain. *Human Studies: A Journal for Philosophy and Social Sciences, 18*(4), 389-414.

Rogers, C. R. (1961). *On becoming a person: A therapist's view of psychotherapy.* Boston, MA: Houghton Mifflin Company.

_____. (1985). Toward a more human science of the person. *Journal of Humanistic Psychology, 25,* 7-24.

Schutz, A. (1944). The stranger: An essay in social psychology. *The American Journal of Sociology, 49*(6), 499-507.

Schutz, A. (1945). The homecomer. *The American Journal of Sociology, 50*(5), 369-376.

Siljander, P., & Sutinen, A. (2012). Introduction. In P. Siljander, A. Kivela, & A. Sutinen (Ed.), *Theories of Bildung and growth: Connections and controversies between continental educational thinking and American pragmatism,* (pp. 1-18). Rotterdam, The Netherlands: Sense Publishers.

Stehr, N. (2007). How I came to sociology and who I am: A conversation with Kurt H. Wolff. In G. Backhaus & G. Psathas (Ed.), *The* sociology of radical committment: Kurt H. Wolff's existential turn (pp. 37-61). Lanham, MD: Lexington Books.

Stober, D. (2006). Coaching from the humanistic perspective. In D. R. Stober & A. M. Grant (Eds.), *Evidence based coaching handbook: Putting best practices to work for your clients*. Hoboken, NJ: John Wiley & Sons, Inc.

Torbert, W. R. (2004). *Action inquiry: The secret of timely and transforming leadership*. San Francisco, CA: Berrett-Koehler Publishers, Inc.

van Manen, M. (1997). *Researching lived experience: Human science for an action sensitive pedagogy*. London, Ontario: Althouse Press.

_____. (2016). *Phenomenology of practice: Meaning-giving methods in phenomenological research and writing* (J. Morse Ed. Kindle ed.). New York, NY: Routledge.

Wagner, H. R. (1978). Between ideal type and surrender: Field research as asymmetrical relation. *Human Studies, 1*(2), 153-164.

_____. (1983). *Phenomenology of consciousness and sociology of the life-world: An introductory study*. Edmonton, Canada: The University of Alberta Press.

_____. (1984). Schutz's life story and the understanding of his work. *Human Studies, 7*(2), 107-116.

_____. (Ed.) (1970). *Alfred Schutz:On phenomenology and social relations*. Chicago, IL: The University of Chicago Press.

Wolff, K. (1976). *Surrender and catch: Experience and inquiry today*. Boston, MA: D. Reidel Publishing.

_____. (1995). *Transformation in the writing: A case of Surrender-and-Catch*. Norwell, MA: Kluwer Academic Publishers.

_____. (Ed.) (1950). *The sociology of Georg Simmel* (1964 ed.). New York, NY: The Free Press.

Wood, M. M. (1969). *The stranger: A study in social relationships*. New York, NY: AMS Press.

About the Author

James Leonard Marlatt, PhD is an independent certified executive coach, organization development consultant, and mineral exploration management consultant. He holds a geological engineering degree from Queen's University and an MBA from Athabasca University. Prior to obtaining his doctorate in human and organizational systems from Fielding Graduate University, he was the director of global mineral exploration for Cameco Corporation, where he led the team that discovered the world-class McArthur River uranium deposit. He has facilitated research in applied earth science and has co-authored scientific publications. Dr. Marlatt is an expert consultant to the International Atomic Energy Agency, serving as a speaker, educator, and author. As a dual-careerist, he practices as an executive coach and organization development consultant to leaders and organizations across different business sectors. As a scholar-practitioner, he leverages insights from applied social phenomenology to assist with the positive transformation of willing individuals, teams, and organizations. Jim and his wife, Margaret, live in Kingston, Ontario, and are the proud parents of identical twin daughters, and many pets. Contact: jim@marlatt-consulting.com

CHAPTER 3
Leadership and the Lifeworld of Nelson Mandela:
A Hermeneutic-Phenomenological Inquiry

Shirley G. Knobel, PhD

Global Leadership and Organizational Development Consultant

Fielding Graduate University, Alumna

Abstract

My dissertation study on which this chapter is based examined the lifeworld of Nelson Mandela through a systematic exploration of the structures of everyday lived experience, helping us understand the complex structures of his lifeworld and how these influenced his choices and actions, and ultimately his destiny. This approach required a broad lens that includes three main concepts underlying the inquiry: leadership, lifeworld phenomenology, and hermeneutics.

In order to explore Mandela's lifeworld, I conducted a hermeneutic phenomenological analysis on a selection of Mandela's reflections, including letters written during his long incarceration on Robben Island in South Africa, where he spent 18 of his total 27 years in prison. He was allowed to write and receive only one letter every six months. These writings are regarded as descriptions of meaningful experiences as characterized by Alfred Schutz. The data is illuminated by being able to imagine a question that the text answers, a method developed by Hans-Georg Gadamer. In the initial analysis, five universal themes emerged that characterized Mandela's lifeworld, in addition to six key findings. My study provides new knowledge about Mandela's lived experience, how he interpreted his experiences, and how the structures of his lifeworld influenced his leadership. More broadly, my research calls for an understanding of the ties between one's lifeworld and the wider sociocultural and historical traditions within which lifeworlds become meaningful.

Keywords: Phenomenology, Hermeneutics, Leadership, Mandela, Lifeworld, Lived Experience, Schutz, Gadamer

A Window to Mandela's Lifeworld

My decision to conduct doctoral research in the latter part of my career was deliberate, aimed to enhance and enrich my understanding of human development, specifically leadership. Unlike traditional doctoral research, I wanted to connect my life, my work, and my research study, working from a foundation grounded in experience. My research question emerged from my lived experience of Nelson Mandela. I had the privilege of knowing him personally through the Nelson Mandela Children's Fund—a charity he established during his term of office as President of South Africa (1994–1999). I selected the lifeworld of Nelson Mandela as the subject of my PhD dissertation research because I believe he demonstrated an unparalleled ability to lead, reconcile, and transform a broken society (Knobel, 2014).

My research journey was not without challenges. For my original research study, I had planned to interview twelve participants who, like me, had either known Mandela personally or had experienced him as a leader who had influenced their lives. I set out on my pilot study with great enthusiasm. But the interviews that I conducted left me feeling disheartened. While interesting and reinforcing my preconceived notions of Mandela, they seemed to lack depth and made me feel that something important was missing. The interview questions called for thoughtful answers, and people were very open and willing to be interviewed. However, it was difficult to get beneath the surface of their obvious admiration for Mandela. I found it difficult to get a balanced view of how people remembered both the good and the not so good aspects of Mandela's leadership. In some of my interviews I thought I caught glimpses of the 'real' Mandela, but they were fleeting.

I believe this tendency came from the deep respect and affection that people hold for Mandela. He is greatly revered in South Africa as a leadership icon. Also, at the time that I was conducting my interviews in late 2012, people were aware of his frailty. While seemingly in good health when he celebrated his 94th birthday in July 2012, he had experienced a health scare a few months later and was hospitalized. He was subsequently discharged and recovered, but his health remained extremely fragile. I felt that the timing of my interviews might be the issue. I discussed this with my External Examiner (who was based in South Africa at that time) and he agreed that this might be the case. I decided to raise my concerns with my Supervisor and committee members. After discussions, we acknowledged the constraints that the timing of my research imposed on my original plans. Instead, we agreed that I would shift the focus of my dissertation research analysis to an in-depth study of a selection of texts chosen from Mandela's personal archives. These had been made available through the Mandela Centre of Memory in Johannesburg, a reputable source of Mandela's archived material. These excerpts from private letters, journals, and biographical texts clearly reflect the voice of Mandela himself, in all his humanity.

With this in mind, I flew to South Africa in late February 2013 to view the original archive materials. I spent a month immersed in research, visiting the Nelson Mandela Centre of Memory as well as the National Archives. My most paramount memory of this time was a hot and steamy day in early March 2013 when I was taken into the cool, rather homely archive room at the Centre of Memory in Johannesburg and shown the two notebooks containing Nelson Mandela's poignant drafts of letters that he wrote while incarcerated on Robben Island. During his time in prison, Mandela was limited to sending only one letter every six months. Even then he was never sure if his letters would reach their destination because of the censorship of the prison authorities. Nothing could have prepared me for that moment, seeing the books and knowing the circumstances in which they were used. I feel greatly privileged to have had access to these letters, written between 1969 and 1971, for my dissertation study. Mandela's personal reflections, captured in draft form in these modest exercise books during deeply contemplative moments, describe in his own voice his lived experience, and they provide a window to his lifeworld. I was also shown the manuscripts of Mandela's unpublished biography. The archive team was proud to showcase their book project called *Nelson Mandela: Conversations with myself*, which has its origins in the 2004 inauguration of the Nelson Mandela Centre of Memory and Dialogue. It was published in an effort to make accessible to the world some of the extensive material that makes up Nelson Mandela's private archive. I decided to cite the published material as much as possible in my scholarly work to bring further attention to the rich array of texts that the archive team continues to bring together so that they may conserve and protect them. Soon after returning from my research sabbatical, I was granted approval to commence with a hermeneutic-phenomenological research inquiry on the lifeworld of Mandela, using the Mandela texts as data.

Why Hermeneutic-Phenomenological Research?

It became evident early on that my research inquiry would require a multidisciplinary approach. I was inspired by Valerie Bentz and Jeremy Shapiro's (1998) book *Mindful inquiry in social research*, in which they encourage scholar-practitioners to blend professional practice with scholarly, scientific, and academic knowledge and discourse (p. 66). Bentz and Shapiro were first to raise my awareness to the importance of adopting a "phenomenological stance" in the study of human experience (p. 99). Through discussions and study under the guidance and mentorship of Professors Rehorick and Bentz, I learned about the concept of "lived experience," which invites us to look back and apprehend

84

a lived moment in time in order to extract meaning from it (Rehorick & Bentz, 2008, p.3). During my studies at Fielding, I was also introduced to the writings of Edmund Husserl, a champion of the phenomenological method, who gave us the concepts of "phenomenological reflection" (Husserl, 1976/1983, p. 114) and "lifeworld" (1954/1970, p. 122). He referred to this as the only real world, given to us through perception (1976/1983, p. 49). Both Husserl and William James (1890/2013) encourage us to search for what they describe as the paramount reality in the natural attitude, or the attitude of original natural life (Husserl, 1954/1970, p.281). Husserl raised a concern that in our quest for knowledge, the world has been seduced into believing we can reduce our understanding of lifeworld experiences to a mathematical construction. He asserts that when it comes to studying lived experience, we should focus on nothing but what we can make evident "by observing consciousness itself in its pure imminence" (1976/1983, p.136). Phenomenological research is the study of lived experience and recognizes that everything we know, we know through consciousness (Bentz & Shapiro, 1998). Hermeneutics is essentially the study of texts. Hermeneutic phenomenology is a human science which studies texts related to the lived experience of human beings (van Manen, 1990/2007, p.6). A hermeneutic-phenomenological inquiry into the lifeworld of Mandela allowed me to ask the question "what was this kind of experience like?" in an attempt to gain insight into the way Mandela experienced the world (Knobel, 2014).

The Importance of *Meaning* When Studying Lived Experience

Not all our experiences are meaningful. James (1890/2013) first referred to "the wonderful stream of our consciousness" which, he says, like a bird's life seems to be made of an "alternation of flights and perchings" (p. 243). He James suggests that we call the resting-places the "substantive parts" of our consciousness, while referring to the places of flight as the "transitive parts" or stream of thought. Henri Bergson

(1921/2012) provides us with a distinction between living within the stream of consciousness and living within the world of space and time. He contrasts the inner stream of duration (*durée*) as a continuous coming-to-be and passing-away of heterogeneous qualities with homogeneous time, which he describes as having been "spatialized, quantified, and rendered discontinuous" (p. 233). Bergson argues that we generally live and act outside our own person, in space, rather than duration. Of significant importance to our search for meaning is Bergson's insight that pure inner duration can only be reached by an act of deep introspection, which leads us to "grasp our inner states as living things, constantly becoming" (Bergson, 1921/2012, p. 231; see also Schutz, 1967, p. 51; Wagner, 1983, pp. 28-30).

In developing his theory of the understanding of meaning, and building on Bergson's (1921/2012) and James' insights, Alfred Schutz (1967) reminds us that lived experience has a temporal structure in that it can only be grasped reflectively. Meaning does not emerge in the stream of consciousness, but as the result of my explication of my past lived experiences, which I grasp reflectively. Schutz sees Husserl's phenomenology as providing a rigorous method for a descriptive analysis of what constitutes the world of everyday life in human experience; he contends that meaning only arises through an act of reflection (p. 47).

Wagner (1983), a student of Schutz, notes that intentionality of consciousness is a fundamental aspect of phenomenology, referring to intentionality as "the heart of consciousness" (Haddad, 2009, p. 194). Wagner shows how Schutz studies of consciousness help us reconnect scientific research to the reality of human experience, encouraging us to explore how our lifeworlds are constituted and organized (Rehorick & Bentz, 2008). Schutz draws on the work of Husserl, Bergson, and James, saying that in the process of living in the flow of duration, we encounter undifferentiated experiences that "melt into one another in a flowing continuum" (Schutz, 1967, p. 51). When I immerse myself in my stream of consciousness, I find that there are no clearly differentiated experiences; rather, I experience my duration as a temporally unidirectional, irreversible stream. Awareness of the stream of duration requires what Schutz refers to as a turning back against the stream, or an act of reflection or attention. It is this act of reflection that lifts the experience out of the stream of duration, modifying our awareness and making it a remembrance (Schutz, 1967). Consciousness remains a pure stream of duration without any discrete, lived experiences, unless we stop and reflect. Schutz (1967) defined the concept of a *meaningful lived experience* as a turning of attention to an already elapsed experience, "in the course of which the latter is lifted out of the stream of consciousness and identified as an experience in such and such a way and in no other (p. 215).

This is an important concept in relation to my study of the lifeworld of Mandela. It informed my strategy for the selection of texts for analysis from all the material on Mandela's leadership that was available for analysis. We know from Mandela's manuscripts that he valued the time he was able to spend in meditative contemplation, and that he believed such reflection helped him grow as a human being. This inquiry focuses on texts generated by Mandela, captured during deep contemplative moments. We can thus benefit from his self-explication of his lived experiences that he grasped in reflection. Bergson (2012) points out that the moments in which we are truly free and able to grasp our inner consciousness are extremely rare. Mostly we live outside ourselves, focusing on the external world. Schutz (1967) explains that the meaning I attribute to my own experience is often radically different from the meaning another person might attribute to the same experience. It is one thing to interpret my own experience but quite another to interpret the experience of someone else. Only when I begin to grasp the other person's point of view--"when I make the leap from the objective to the subjective context of meaning"— am I entitled to say that I understand the other person (Schutz, 1967, p. 217). This is another important concept that sets this analysis apart. By providing a phenomenological-hermeneutic "subjective context of meaning" perspective to the reading of the Mandela texts, the analysis brings insights to the surface that would not have emerged using an objectivist research methodology.

A Research Design for an Inquiry into the Phenomena of Lived Experience

It was the combined insights provided by the above scholars that led me to reframe my research question to "How did Mandela's lifeworld construct him as a leader?" and to focus my inquiry to understanding the phenomena of his lived experience (Knobel, 2014). I applied the Schutzian concept of *meaningful lived experiences* as a filtering mechanism to select texts for analysis (Schutz, 1967, p. 71). My strategy for choosing archival material for hermeneutical analysis involved searching for and selecting examples of significant life experiences that Mandela chose to reflect upon, and where his meditations and reflections had been captured in writing. While many manuscripts from the archives were part of the study, Mandela's prison letters are the most poignant. These texts are full of meaning, incorporating stocks of common knowledge and systems of typifications that reveal how Mandela made sense of his lifeworld, including his understandings, longings, hopes, and fears.

While Schutz's research was useful in selecting texts and in revealing the complex layers that make up the structures of lived experience, I was still unsure how to progress with an empirical analysis of the Mandela texts—until I was pointed in the direction of the epistemological theory of Gadamer. Gadamer's (1975/2012) hermeneutics provided a theoretical basis for researching lived experience, including the interpretation and understanding of everyday lifeworld phenomenon. He encourages us to approach hermeneutics in a way that recognizes the interpretation of texts as an experience of truth, one that not only needs to be justified philosophically but "which is itself a way of doing philosophy" (p. xxii). He argues that to truly understand the meaning of a text is to understand the text as the answer to a question (p. 368).

Contrary to the philosophy of science perspective—in which theoretical knowledge is derived from observing the world in such a way that the observer is no longer completely engaged in the world and where the acquisition of knowledge requires a point of view which stands outside the everyday lifeworld—hermeneutic-phenomenology is founded on the belief that the researcher is embedded in a context of explanation that influences the context of the data (Bentz & Shapiro, 1998, p.112; Polkinghorne, 1983, p.202). The great challenge for the researcher who applies phenomenology and hermeneutics to her study is that there is no clear methodology (Gadamer, 2004; Rorty, 1979; van Manen, 2007). The researcher has to find the most appropriate way of understanding the text while maintaining scholarly rigor. Gadamer points out that the hermeneutical experience applies its own rigor, which, he says, is that of uninterrupted listening. Gadamer notes that all speech and all texts are related to the art of understanding, and likens the hermeneutic experience to a conversation. Conversation may be viewed as a game in the sense that participants enter into something that has its own logic and includes them, while at the same time extending beyond them to develop in its own way. A genuine conversation is never the one that we intended to conduct; rather, it is more correct to say that a true conversation has a spirit of its own (Gadamer, 2004, p. 385). Gadamer encourages an attitude of openness coupled with curiosity in our dialogue with the text, which he characterizes as "playful seriousness" (Bentz & Shapiro, 1998, p. 113; Gadamer, 2004).

The Gadamerian Hermeneutic Circle of Understanding

Gadamer (2012) draws our attention to three levels at which the researcher demonstrates hermeneutic understanding (see also Rehorick & Bentz, 2008). By applying the Gadamerian hermeneutic circle of understanding as a framework to guide my analysis (Knobel, 2014, p. 76), I discovered a different perspective to Mandela's lifeworld and leadership that would not have shown itself simply within my own limited horizon. The nature of hermeneutic inquiry is dialogical in nature. The interpretive methodology that the study entails demanded openness to exploration and a freedom from the need for specific answers. The process of inquiry involved a fine-grained hermeneutic scrutiny of Mandela's reflections on his lived experience while searching for patterns of meaning. The process required that I return to the texts repeatedly, allowing insights to emerge before returning again, each time approaching the data with a more thorough understanding. At each turn my understanding was refined and corrected as fresh questions came to mind that could only be answered by revisiting the texts and the events studied, and by revising my earlier interpretations.

At Level 1, I began by looking for universal characteristics. In this iteration, I asked myself how traditions and culture appear to be operating as I searched the data for patterns and emerging themes. In the second iteration, at Level 2, I applied an attitude of openness coupled with curiosity in my dialogue with the text—entering into a fictionalized "conversation" with Mandela. Gadamer encourages us at this level to experience the other as a Thou, and to be prepared for and open to the other telling us something. At this level, I became increasingly aware of my own prejudice and bias as I struggled to allow the text to assert its own truth by imagining a question that the text answers. At Level 3 the researcher is encouraged to be open to transformation by directing her attention on the "things themselves," all the while guarding against arbitrary fancies and limitations imposed by imperceptible habits and thought. At this level, I frequently experienced unexpected flashes of insight.

By way of illustration, in a letter released to South African newspapers on June 26, 1961, Mandela wrote: "I will not leave South Africa, nor will I surrender. Only through hardship, sacrifice, and militant action can freedom be won. The struggle is my life. I will continue fighting for freedom until the end of my days" (Mandela, 1995, LWTF, p. 327). In my analysis of this text, at Level 1, I uncovered themes including an overarching sense of purpose, a life-mission, all-consuming passion, willingness to endure great personal suffering, and a call to militant action in the fight for freedom. At Level 2, the questions that tumbled from me included: "Why did you not leave South Africa even though you knew the danger you were in? Was it because the African National Congress (ANC) wanted you to stay in the country and you agreed? Or was this truly a personal choice? Oliver Tambo, your best friend had left and gone into exile in London—you missed him so much, why did you not follow? Was it because you felt that you could not serve your people adequately while in exile?" At Level 3, I realized that Mandela's sense of duty, or rather his sense of being called to a higher purpose, was at the heart of his decision to remain in the country. Knowing the possible consequences of his decision to remain, Mandela refused to leave South Africa to escape into exile or to give himself up, thereby in every sense living and breathing his fundamental belief that "the struggle is my life."

Excerpts from a Gadamerian Hermeneutic "Dialogue" with Nelson Mandela

It became clear when studying Mandela's prison letters that during this time there were strong spiritual, social, and political lifeworld dimensions influencing Mandela's choices and actions, some of which caused him considerable personal conflict and pain. What follows is an extract from my "hermeneutic-dialogue" with Mandela (Knobel, 2014, p. 126-32).

Q: "What saddened you most about being in prison?"

Mandela writes about the loss of his loved ones and of his heartache at not being able to pay his last respects to them in various drafts of letters to friends and family while in prison. He describes these as experiences that "eat too deeply into one's being, into one's soul," and goes on to compare the pain of loss with the pain inflicted by prison life, describing it as worse than the hard labour to which we are condemned, the coarse and tasteless menus, the grim and tedious boredom that stalks every prisoner and the frightful frustrations of a life in which human beings move in complete circles, landing today exactly at the point where you started the day before (Mandela, 2010, p. 172).

After his son Thembi's death, Mandela wrote to his second eldest son, Kgatho, in a letter dated 28 July 1969, reminding him of the heavy responsibility that he had to pick up on the death of his older brother. It was a plea for effort and discipline.

Q: "What lessons did you want to pass on to your children?"

Emerging themes are a belief in the rewards and benefits of discipline and hard work, and a belief in the importance of acquiring knowledge through higher education. Mandela writes, "The richest rewards are reserved for those who have undergone the most thorough training and who have attained the highest academic qualifications in their respective field" (p.173). Mandela believes in the value of leading an orderly and disciplined life. He pleads with his son to work hard and systematically in his studies, adding that "human beings like to be associated with a hardworking, disciplined, and successful person." He notes that "by carefully cultivating these qualities you will win yourself many friends" (p.173). Mandela encourages his son to "never allow yourself to be discouraged by difficulties or setbacks, and never give up the battle even in the darkest hour." adding, "To lead an orderly and disciplined life...to work hard and systematically in your studies throughout the year, will...bring you...much personal happiness" (Mandela, 2010, p. 173).

In a similar vein, in June 1969, Mandela wrote to his wife, Winnie, encouraging her never to give up.

Q: "What are your thoughts about honour?"

In a letter to his wife Winnie, dated 23 June 1969, Mandela writes,

Honour belongs to those who never forsake the truth even when things seem dark and grim, who try over and over again, who are never discouraged by insults, humiliation, and even defeat.... A new world will be won not by those who stand at a distance with their arms folded, but by those who are in the arena, whose garments are torn by storms and whose bodies are maimed in the course of contest (p. 175).

On discipline and dedication to a worthy cause, Mandela writes, "We should be ready to undertake any tasks which history might assign to us however high the price to be paid may be" (p. 175).

Q: "How were you able to face the possibility of execution with such courage?"

Mandela says, "for my own part the threat of death evoked no desire in me to play the role of martyr...[but] I was ready to do so if I had to.... But the anxiety to live always lingered (p. 175).

Q: "What are the values you hold most dear and that kept you going through the decades in prison?"

In a letter to Adelaide Tambo dated 31 January 1970, Mandela wrote about the difficulties of being in prison, cut off from all communication with his loved ones, saying that the human soul and human body has an infinite capacity to adapt (p.176). He writes, "I never dreamt that time and hope can mean so much to one as they do now" adding that "hope is a powerful weapon even when nothing else may remain" (p.177). He adds that his family have given him strength, commenting that he is a member of a large and broad family "tried and tested and who have triumphed over many difficulties" (p.177). This fact he says, "endows my spirits with powerful wings" (p.177). Themes of hope, the passage of time, and thoughts of family remain strong over the coming decades. Mandela expresses his love and concern for his daughters in a letter dated 1 June 1970, noting that the therapy of writing to his children "tends to calm down the shooting pains that hit me whenever I think of you" (p.181). He expresses a fervent hope that one day his letters might reach his daughters, saying that

> writing letters is the only means I have of keeping in touch with you and of hearing something about the state of your health, your school-work, and your school progress generally. Although these precious letters do not reach, I shall nevertheless keep on trying by writing whenever that is possible (p. 180).

On August 1, 1970, Mandela writes about the lack of honesty and honour demonstrated by prison officials who were censoring his letters. He refers to the prison authorities as the "remorseless fates" who "consistently interfere with my correspondence and that have cut me off from my family at such a critical moment" (Mandela, 2010, p.181).

Q: "What sustained you during these difficult years, when cherished beliefs were put to the test?"

In a letter dated 1 August 1970 to Senator Douglas Lukhele, Mandela recalls, "Throughout my imprisonment my heart and soul have always been somewhere far beyond this place, in the veld and the bushes." He talks of his love for his country village "with its open spaces, lovely scenery, and plenty of fresh air," adding that "I live across these waves with all the memories and experiences I have accumulated over the last half century" (p. 181).

Q: "This was a powerful letter with many fundamental beliefs and concepts shared. Would you say that these are the same beliefs that you hold dear today?"

Mandela writes,
the anchor of all my dreams is the collective wisdom of mankind as a whole. I am influenced more than ever before by the conviction that social equality is the only basis of human happiness . . . . It is around these issues that my thoughts revolve. They are centred on humans, the ideas for which they strive; on the new world that is emerging; the new generation that declared total war against all forms of cruelty, against any social order that uphold economic privilege for a minority and that condemns the mass of the population to poverty and disease, il-

literacy and the host of evils that accompany a stratified society (pp. 182-183).

Mandela's frustration at not being able to communicate with his loved ones becomes increasingly evident. However, he never allowed bitterness to completely overtake him and he never gave up, noting in a letter to his wife Winnie dated 1 August 1970 that "the records will bear witness to the fact that I tried hard and earnestly to reach you by writing every month. I owe you this duty and nothing will distract me from it." He expressed his belief that "there will always be good men on earth, in all countries, and even here at home" (p. 185), adding

> one day we may have on our side the genuine and firm support of an upright and straightforward man, holding high office, who will consider it improper to shirk his duty of protecting the rights and privileges of even his bitter opponents in the battle of ideas that is being fought in our country today; an official who will have a sufficient sense of justice and fairness to make available to us not only the rights and privileges that the law allows us today, but who will also compensate us for those that were surreptitiously taken away (pp. 183-184).

Q: "How did you stay positive over all these years?"

Despite everything that happened, Mandela wrote that he "lived in hope and expectation," saying that "sometimes I even have the belief that this feeling is part and parcel of myself. It seems to be woven into my being. I feel my heart pumping hope steadily to every part of my body, warming my blood and pepping up my spirits." He adds, "To a freedom fighter, hope is what a lifebelt is to a swimmer—a guarantee that one will keep afloat and free from danger" (p. 184).

Q: "While you were in prison, to whom did you turn when you were in need?"

Mandela acknowledges his indebtedness to his mentors, counsellors, and advisors, including Oliver Tambo, Walter Sisulu, Kathy Kathandra, and other friends from the broader community, saying,

Walter and Kathy share one common feature which forms an essential part of our friendship and which I value very much – they never hesitate to criticise me for my mistakes and throughout my political career have served as a mirror through which I can see myself. I wish I could tell you more about the courageous band of colleagues with whom I suffer humiliation daily and who nevertheless deport themselves with dignity and determination. I wish I could relate their conversations and banter, their readiness to help in any personal problem suffered by their fellow prisoners so that you could judge for yourself the calibre of the men whose lives are being sacrificed on the fiendish altar of colour hatred (p. 211).

Q: "What did you find out about yourself while you were in prison?"

Mandela confessed that after his release and in the midst of the demands of public life, he missed solitude and time to reflect. In a letter written in prison dated February 1, 1975, he writes,

Incidentally, you may find that the cell is an ideal place to learn to know yourself, to search realistically and regularly the process of your own mind and feelings. In judging our progress as individuals we tend to concentrate on external factors such as one's social position, influence and popularity, wealth and standards of education. These are, of course, important in measuring one's success in material matters and it is perfectly understandable if many people exert themselves mainly to achieve all these. But internal factors may be even more crucial in assessing one's development as a human being. Honesty, sincerity, simplicity, humility, pure generosity, absence of vanity, readiness to serve others—qualities which are within easy reach of every soul—are the foundation of one's spiritual life. Development in matters of this nature is inconceivable without serious introspection, without knowing yourself, your weaknesses and mistakes. At least, if for nothing else, the cell gives you the opportunity to look daily into your entire conduct, to overcome the bad and develop whatever is good in you. Regular meditation, say about 15 minutes a day before you turn in, can be very fruitful in this regard. You may find it difficult at first to pinpoint the negative features in your life, but the 10th attempt may yield rich rewards. Never forget that a saint is a sinner who keeps on trying. (pp. 211-212).

Q: "What did you find most challenging about these daily reflections?"

Mandela writes that reflecting on the past was far more difficult than thinking about the future. In a letter to a friend dated 8 July 1985 he wrote:

> How is your memory? It may well be that you no longer need it, with all the modern facilities which surround you—newspapers, good literature, archives, libraries, radio, television, videos, computers, and what have you. In my current circumstances, thinking about the past can be far more exacting than contemplating the present and predicting the course of future events. Until I was jailed I never fully appreciated the capacity of memory, the endless string of information the head can carry (p. 115).

Q: "Did you ever wonder if your cherished ideals would be realised in your lifetime? Did this worry you?"

In a letter dated April 1, 1985, Mandela writes about the importance of meeting expectations:

> The ideals we cherish, our fondest dreams and fervent hopes may not be realised in our lifetime. But that is besides the point. The knowledge that in your day you did your duty, and lived up to the expectations of your fellow men is in itself a rewarding experience and magnificent achievement (p. 243).

Themes that emerge are dutifulness and the importance of delivering against the expectations of others. Mandela was proud of his legacy and wrote, "If your knees are becoming stiff, your eyes dim, and your head is full of silver, you must take comfort in the knowledge that your own contribution is an important factor in this ferment" (p. 244).

A Merging of Horizons

The intention of this inquiry was to help develop a greater understanding of how our lifeworlds influence who we become, focusing in particular on the complex structures through which this world and our knowledge of it are constructed in our consciousness, not forgetting to take into consideration the sociocultural and historical traditions that give meaning to our world. Studying the reflections of Mandela's lived experiences using this model of inquiry rendered the texts meaningful to me in a way that has touched me deeply.

The inquiry places emphasis on the importance of deep contemplative reflection, recognizing that our personal growth and development is dependent to some extent on the attention we give to contemplative activities. It also recognises the extent to which each human being is embedded in his or her own lifeworld structures, and the role that our lifeworlds play in shaping who we become by focusing on the complex structures through which the world and our knowledge of it are constructed in our consciousness. Phenomenological and hermeneutic concepts helped me to show how, through reflection and explication, Mandela's lived experiences became meaningful to him. In the process of this inquiry, Mandela's experiences also became more meaningful to me.

Throughout my research, I was cognizant of the fact that it is impossible to approach a text in a value-free context because our search for knowledge will always be influenced by our culture and traditions. Gadamer (2012, p. 278) reminds us that prejudices constitute the historical reality of our being. Combining the Schutzian lens with the use of the Gadamerian hermeneutic circle of understanding helped me understand and articulate the lived experience of Mandela, while holding in awareness my own prejudices and biases. Our vantage point determines what we can see, hear, or experience, and relevance is the factor that determines what we choose to experience.

Phenomenological and hermeneutic concepts helped me to understand how Mandela's vantage point shifted from his early childhood years, through his experiences at university, and subsequently into adulthood and the political arena. The process highlighted the shifting relevance structures evident in his lifeworld and demonstrated how these influenced the constitution of his stock of knowledge and understanding. The inquiry recognizes that our stocks of knowledge are systems of typifications that help us communicate and make sense of our world. What we consider to be relevant is informed by our stocks of knowledge, which in turn is an accumulation of our typifications. My inquiry brought to light Mandela's passions and beliefs as well as his own prejudices and the constraints of his social circumstances, showing how these influenced his choices and actions. Every new experience is determined by means of a type constituted in earlier experiences and all experiences are grounded on relevance structures.

I discovered during this study that there were multiple typifications in Mandela's lifeworld. I was also reminded that throughout our lives there are potential trigger events that can stimulate or inhibit our growth and development. I was reminded that we only become aware of deficiencies in our stocks of knowledge if a novel or shock experience "explodes" the taken-for-granted nature of our experience, causing a "leap" from one finite province of meaning to another (Schutz & Luckmann, 1973, p. 24; Wagner, 1983, pp. 191-193).

Gadamer (2012) contends that hermeneutic understanding requires a three-way relationship in which one person comes to an understanding with another about something they both understand. As in play, this process of "coming to an understanding" rests on a mutual willingness on the part of the players to lend themselves to the emergence of something new, which Gadamer (2012) describes as the truth that emerges in conversation (p. xvii). The fundamental condition for truth's coming to light is not simply the result of a technique or method, something that the interpreter does, but is a result of something that "happens to us over and above our wanting and doing" (Howard, 1982, p. 122). I experienced this phenomenon when applying the circle of understanding framework to my analysis of the lifeworld of Mandela as a shift in my perspective, or what Gadamer describes as a *merging of horizons*, which enabled me to perceive Mandela's experiences from his point of view.

Gadamer would argue that I did not apply a method in my search for truth, but rather that the general characteristic of *Bildung*, or keeping myself open to what is other, led me to a deeper understanding of the lived experience of Mandela. What we encounter in our everyday lifeworlds does not only widen our horizons by adding to our existing stocks of knowledge. By changing our existing perspective, our everyday lifeworlds frequently provide us with a broader understanding of human life and culture and of our own limitations. This knowledge constitutes what Gadamer (2012) calls a "non-dogmatic wisdom" (p. xiii).

Unlike other leadership studies, this hermeneutic-phenomenological inquiry into the lifeworld of Mandela (Knobel, 2014) offers a holistic approach to the study of leadership, taking into consideration the lived experience of the leader, the context of his lifeworld, and the environment within which his leadership took place. In the field of the human sciences—and in particular human development and lifeworld phenomenology—the importance of reflection on how and why we think and act the way we do should not be underestimated. Overarching insights from my study now focus my attention and passion on two key elements for growing our understanding of ourselves and of others: the benefit of deep personal reflection, and the need for dialogue. These are not new concepts, but here I turn to Gadamer's (2012) view of dialogue. He reminds us that "the path of all knowledge leads through the question" (p. 357), and that to reach an understanding in a dialogue we need to be "transformed into a communion in which we do not remain what we were" (p. 371).

It is my hope that this dialogical inquiry into the *meaningful lived experiences* of Nelson Mandela (Knobel, 2014), captured in contemplative mode while he was in prison on Robben Island, not only reflects the personal change in my own growth and development as a scholar-practitioner in the field of leadership, but also brings new understanding to the lifeworld of Mandela, an extraordinary human being and iconic leader who made something miraculous happen in my country of birth.

References

Bentz, V. M., & Shapiro, J. J. (1998). *Mindful inquiry in social research.* Thousand Oaks, CA: Sage.

Bergson, H. (1921/2012). *Time and free will: An essay on the immediate data of consciousness.* Charleston, SC: Forgotten Books.

Gadamer, H.-G. (1975/2012). *Truth and method* (2nd ed.). (J. Weinsheimer & D. G. Marshall, Trans.). New York, NY: Continuum.

Haddad, D. B. (2009). Intentionality in action: Teaching artists phenomenology. In D. A. Rehorick & V. M. Bentz (Ed.), *Transformative phenomenology: Changing ourselves, lifeworlds, and professional practice.* Lanham, MD: Lexington Books.

Howard, R. J. (1982). *Three faces of hermeneutics: An introduction to current theories of understanding.* Los Angeles, CA: University of California Press.

Husserl, E. (1954/1970). *The crisis of European sciences and transcendental phenomenology.* (D. Carr, Ed., Trans.). Evanston, IL: Northwestern University Press.

_____. (1976/1983). *Ideas pertaining to a pure phenomenology and to a phenomenological philosophy.* (F. Kersten, Trans.). The Hague, The Netherlands: Martinus Nijhoff.

Knobel, S. G. (2014). *Becoming a leader: A hermeneutic phenomenological study of the lifeworld of Nelson Mandela.* (Doctoral dissertation). Available from ProQuest database (UMI 3615745).

_____. (2014). *Becoming a leader: A hermeneutic phenomenological study of the lifeworld of Nelson Mandela.* Overall Winner, Annual Student Research Colloquium, OD Network Annual Conference, October 25-28, 2014, Philadelphia, PA.

Mandela, N. (1994/2010). *Long walk to freedom.* London, England: Abacus.

_____. (2010). *Conversations with myself.* London, England: Macmillan.

_____. (2011). *Nelson Mandela By Himself: The authorized book of quotations*. Johannesburg, South Africa: Pan Macmillan.

Polkinghorne, D. (1983). *Methodology for the human sciences: Systems of inquiry*. Albany, NY: State University of New York Press.

Rehorick, D. A., & Bentz, V. M. (Ed.). (2008). *Transformative phenomenology: Changing ourselves, lifeworlds, and professional practice*. Lanham, MD: Lexington Books.

Rorty, R. (1979*). Philosophy and the mirror of nature*. Princeton, NJ: Princeton University Press.

Schutz, A. (1967). *The phenomenology of the social world*. (G. Walsh, Trans.). Evanston, IL: Northwestern University Press.

Schutz, A., & Luckmann, T. (1973). *The structures of the life-world*. R. Zaner & H. T. Engelbrecht, Jr. (Trans). Evanston, IL: Northwestern University Press.

van Manen, M. (1990/2007). *Researching lived experience: Human science for and action sensitive pedagogy*. London, Ontario, Canada: The Althouse Press.

Wagner, H. R. (1983). *Phenomenology of consciousness and sociology of the life-world: An introductory study*. London, Ontario, Canada: The University of Alberta Press.

About the Author

Shirley G. Knobel (also known as Lee), PhD is an accomplished organization and human development professional with a significant track record of achievements in strategy, coaching, and leadership development. Her background includes more than 20 years of experience working with individuals and multi-cultural teams around the world, helping to find solutions to complex and challenging issues. Shirley is a valued coach, mentor, facilitator, and trusted adviser to leaders in more than twenty countries. She has a bachelor's degree in Industrial Psychology from the University of South Africa (UNISA), and a master's degree and PhD from Fielding Graduate University's School of Human and Organization Development. She lives in London with her husband and family. Contact: sknobel@email.fielding.edu

CHAPTER 4

The Lifeworld of Sustainability Entrepreneurs:
A Schutzian Exploration of Women's Experiences

Jo-Anne Clarke, PhD

Director, School of Continuing Education + Professional Development

Alberta College of Art + Design

Fielding Graduate University, Alumna

Abstract

Drawing on my research with women sustainability entrepreneurs, this chapter illustrates how social phenomenology can be put into practice and used to explore aspects of the lifeworld that are sensed and conceptualized. I describe aspects of the process from preparation to analysis through a Schutzian lifeworld lens, with the hopes that others will use phenomenology as a means to explore social and ecological issues. From the findings, three ideal types are constructed to personify values of community, quality, connection, and environmental preservation. Together, they form a new general ideal type called the integrative entrepreneur.

Keywords: social phenomenology, Schutzian puppets, ideal types, sustainability, entrepreneurship, women entrepreneurs, integrative entrepreneur

Introduction

I have often felt that I did not choose phenomenology, and that it chose me. My first introduction to phenomenology was at a 2010 research workshop in Vancouver, British Columbia, facilitated by David Rehorick. David was a faculty member at Fielding Graduate University and well-known for his depth of knowledge about qualitative and quantitative research. I was a new student at Fielding, nervous about the start of my doctoral studies and eager to make my mark as an academic. David provided a historical overview of research, and shared his own story of becoming a social phenomenologist. None of my previous undergraduate or graduate research courses mentioned phenomenology and I remember thinking, "What is this phenomenology and why am I only hearing about it now?" Perhaps it was the anomaly that sparked my curiosity, or maybe it was David's enthusiasm that drew me in, but I left that weekend with a desire to learn more about this mysterious methodology. It was the start of what I would describe as a slow, percolating relationship that continued to mature throughout my doctoral studies, peeling away layers of my assumptions about the very nature of social research itself.

Inevitably I chose social phenomenology for my dissertation to study the experiences of six women who are running businesses that are environmentally, socially, and financially sustainable. In this chapter I share insights gleaned from putting social phenomenology into practice, including strategies and techniques I used to explore aspects of the lived experience that were intangible and relational, felt and sensed rather than conceptualized. Instead of explicating the details of my dissertation, here I will draw on aspects of the methodology and findings to illustrate my process of doing phenomenology. Learning how to *do* phenomenology is a bit of a misnomer because phenomenology is really a transformative process of *becoming* that commences long before crafting a research question or drafting a proposal. It begins with cultivating a phenomenological attitude or gaze.

Preparing for Phenomenological Research

One of the first things I noticed about phenomenology was its poetic language. Phenomenologists use words like "wonder" and "fascination" to describe their intellectual curiosity, infusing the research with an almost childlike playfulness. I found it refreshing to hear such terms used in academia, but I also wondered if it was naive. Could this really be scholarly research?

Having now studied phenomenology for several years and applied it to research, I can attest that it is scholarly. In fact, I would suggest that phenomenology is more rigorous than many research methodologies because of the demands it places on the researcher's self-awareness. As much as humanly possible, a researcher must try to be free from prejudicial suppositions so that she or he can reflect upon the everyday lived experience of human existence as it *is*, not as it is conceptualized. This demands an epistemological undressing of one's self; a willingness to be vulnerable and set aside one's presuppositions so that the essential nature of a lived experience can be unveiled in all its naked wonder.

Cultivating a phenomenological gaze is not easy, particularly as we grow older. Young children live in the present and are naturally curious about the world they encounter. By adulthood, however, our ability to see *what is* has been layered with mental constructs and social conditioning. Add in years of education in critical thinking and argumentation for academics, and our capacity for awe is diminished even further.

A phenomenological approach to research runs counterintuitive to positivistic undercurrents that are deeply embedded in our western worldview and academic traditions. For example, in my formative school years, research was only taught in science classes. I was trained to develop a hypothesis, set up an experiment with dependent, independent, and control variables, complete testing, and draw conclusions to either prove or disprove a theory. The researcher's role was to remain neutral and to collect data through observation. This was valid research.

At the graduate level, I learned about inductive approaches to research and qualitative interviewing. The researcher was no longer a neutral or passive player, but acknowledged as an active agent in the process. What a relief! I could metaphorically trade in my sterile lab coat for a button-down sweater that humanized the research experience for participants, and for me. Intuitively it felt right, but I was still confused about role expectations and boundaries. Was stating my biases up front enough? How did I know what my biases were? I was beginning to reflect on preconceived notions about what constitutes valid research. The net had widened but it was still intact.

At Fielding, I began reading phenomenological works, and was fortunate to have experienced mentors like Valerie Bentz and David guide me into what I can only describe as dense philosophical territory. They suggested readings that gave form to phenomenology without ever condensing it to a prescriptive methodology. Even with their expertise and guidance, I found it difficult to wrap my head around phenomenology and circled back, repeatedly, to select works by thinkers like Edmund Husserl, Alfred Schutz, and Maurice Merleau-Ponty. Ideas that made sense when I was reading were impossible to articulate later: I was adding to my knowledge but it felt like I was stripping away layers of illusion, leaving me untethered to a framework for academic research. Nevertheless, my language and writing started to change as my understanding evolved and new insights unfolded. It felt exciting, discomforting, and personal.

It was Merleau-Ponty (1945/1962) who criticized objectivist science as artificial and fragmented, arguing that we are not disengaged observers of the world but intimately involved in bringing forth a world that is intersubjective and shared. Phenomenology as a research domain is inseparable from ontology: it is philosophy, epistemology, and methodology all in one. I was drawn to phenomenology because it recognizes and validates non-cognitive ways of knowing that are often dismissed, if not negated, in academia. The phenomenologist sees the concrete and measurable aspects of this world, and then directs her gaze

106

to what is not immediately apparent. It means tuning into sensual, emotional, relational, and felt aspects of the lived experience that are often taken for granted because they are implicit in the human experience. The phenomenological researcher does not assume the stance of a detached observer, but lives with the phenomenon as an engaged beholder.

I would argue that learning how to engage with the phenomenon—to grasp what lies below the surface—is the single most challenging aspect of a phenomenological research practice. It requires giving up the intellectual safety of prescriptive models, freeing oneself from rationality, and attending to other aspects of knowledge that are sensed and felt (van Manen, 2007). It is precisely this capacity to access and capture the dynamic nature of lived experience that sets phenomenology apart from other research methodologies. It also helps to explain why phenomenology is not commonly taught in undergraduate or graduate classes, for it is much easier to teach step-by-step methodology than it is to help students develop their emotive modalities of knowing (ibid).

In my case, I credit years of practising meditation and an early career in social work for predisposing me to phenomenology. Social work deepened my empathic listening and exposed me to lived experiences that were very different from mine. Meditation taught me to detach from ideas and ego, and to gaze upon things from an outsider's stance while remaining connected and engaged in the world. Although I cannot claim it is required to practise phenomenology, I highly recommend a regular contemplative practice such as meditation or yoga as one way to nourish a phenomenologist's gaze.

Doing Phenomenological Research

Although there are no "fixed signposts" (van Manen, 1997, p. 29) to phenomenological research, there are methods and strategies that one can use to move from thinking about phenomenology to applying it in research (see Rehorick & Bentz, 2008, for a variety of research methods). Phenomenological research starts with identifying a question or topic that deeply interests you (van Manen, 1984, p.43).

My interest in sustainability entrepreneurship was driven by concern about the impact of business on the environment, and a long-standing belief that we need models of business that are more egalitarian and environmentally responsible than what currently exist. As a woman, I was curious about the life experiences of other women and what they might contribute to the scholarly discussion about sustainability and leadership. I wanted a methodology that would harness subjective experiences of participants as well as the intersubjective world of shared meaning. A Schutzian lifeworld approach was the logical choice.

Husserl (1970) introduced the concept of the lifeworld (*Lebenswelt*) to denote the everyday experiences we take for granted as common reality, but it was Alfred Schutz who developed it more fully as a means to contemplate the intersubjective realm of ordinary human experiences (Rehorick & Bentz, 2008; Wagner, 1983). At this point, it might be useful to provide a brief overview of Schutz's framework before I share details of my research design and findings that I believe will provide value to the reader.

Schutz's Lifeworld Structures

Schutz (1932/1967) understood that we take in the world in culturally bound ways (the world intended) and we socially act upon (intend upon) the world. He called this everyday life our paramount reality, acknowledging there are multiple realities at play that give structure and meaning to our lives. To manage in this complex lifeworld, we create typifications of familiar constructs that helps us to orient to everyday life and engage with others (Schutz, 1970a, 1970b; Schutz & Luckmann, 1974). Typifications are "socially constructed abstractions and simplifications" that are "not invented by us but by the discourse communities who use them" (Bentz & Shapiro, 1998, p. 50). Over time, these typifications accumulate into what is referred to as stocks of knowledge, which shape what we see as relevant and attend to. Rehorick & Bentz (2008) explained it this way:

> What we see as relevant is shaped by our personal stock of knowledge, an accumulation of our typifications. In turn, our typifications are formed by what is relevant to us, and relevancy is shaped by our tacit awareness of what we think we should be doing with our lives, moment to moment and situation to situation. (p. 18)

To understand how relevancies shape our lifeworlds, Schutz distinguished between intrinsic relevancies which stem from our interests (proactive) and imposed relevancies which force themselves on our attention (reactive). According to Schutz, there are three kinds of relevancies: topical or thematic, interpretative, and motivational. Topical or thematic relevance is when I can no longer take something for granted and it becomes a topic of interest worthy of further attention or investigation. Interpretive relevance follows topical relevance: Now that I have identified a problem or topic, I seek an explanation by relating it to a larger scheme of reference. Topical and interpretive relevancies become motivational relevances when something has to be done about the topic (Wagner, 1983, pp. 69-71).

Here we see a direct connection to motives and the will to act. For example, one of my research participants developed an extreme allergy to chemicals that forced her to quit her job and recuperate at home. She spent her summer avoiding public parks, lawns, and even street boulevards that were sprayed with pesticides because they made her ill. Her freedom to enjoy the outdoors was no longer a given, which prompted her to investigate further. What started as a personal health problem (topical relevance) spurred her interest in learning more about chemical pesticides (interpretive relevance), which eventually led to starting an eco-friendly landscaping business and inventing her own compost tea fertilizer spray (motivational relevance).

From a lifeworld perspective, motives can be understood as the meaning one attaches to lived experience and action. Schutz differentiated between *in-order-to* motives, which are future and goal-oriented, and *because* motives, which can be understood in terms of actions of the past. The two types of motives are inextricably linked in a cyclical and temporal relationship. Typifications reveal what we see as relevant, which in turn is shaped by our stocks of knowledge and motives (Schutz, 1970a, 1970b; Schutz & Luckmann, 1974). It is the social phenomenological researcher's task to explicate typifications, motives, stocks of knowledge, and underlying relevancies so that we can better see and understand structures of lifeworld that shape our everyday actions.

Gathering Descriptions

A phenomenological study begins with rich description of the lived phenomenal experience itself. How the researcher gathers this data may differ from inviting participants to write personal accounts, to artistic expressions and, of course, qualitative interviews (Rehorick & Bentz, 2008).

In social phenomenology, interview questions are designed to elicit descriptive answers that will elucidate lifeworld structures about how research participants typify and make meaning of their lived experiences. The focus is on the phenomena as experienced rather than as conceptualized. Soliciting meaningful phenomenological descriptions is highly dependent upon the ability to build quick rapport and on the nature of the questions asked (Gadamer, 1960/1975). For example, in my study of women sustainability entrepreneurs, I wanted to know more about how each participant typified her business. I asked questions like: How would you describe your business? Who is your typical customer? How do your competitors look at you? To learn more about their motives and relevancies, I asked: What inspired or motivated you to start a sustainable business? Reflecting back on the start-up phase, what stands out for you? What challenge or obstacles did you encounter? What support did you receive? I inquired about each woman's background growing up, roles models and early influences, and invited conversation about what sustainability means to them (see Clarke, 2015). Regularly using a prompt like "Can you describe what you mean or give me an example?" kept the focus of the interview on description and personal narrative.

The types of questions to ask seem fairly obvious now, but it was not immediately clear to me when I first designed the study. I was worried about choosing the right questions—another reminder of my own typifications about how to do proper scholarly research. Gadamer (1960/1975) describes the interview as "a process of coming to an understanding" (p. 385), which demands an openness of heart and mind, a state of presence, and the rigor of "uninterrupted listening" (p. 465). I started to meditate before each interview so that I could quiet my own inner dialogue and listen attentively. Getting centred beforehand allowed me to listen and follow the conversation rather than guide it.

Attending to the Non-Verbal

At Fielding, students complete a pilot study to test out their research design and make adjustments prior to commencing with the full dissertation. During the pilot study, I toured the participants' work sites and was immediately taken with the aesthetics. The spaces reflected each woman's personality and what was meaningful to her. Serendipitously I was enrolled at the same time in a writing phenomenology course with Valerie Bentz, in which we were asked to write descriptive protocols. I chose to describe my first interview and what emerged was a portrayal of lived or felt space. Lived space (spatiality) is one of four existential themes that phenomenologists use to assist with reflective analysis. The others are lived relation (relationality), lived body (corporeality), and lived time (temporality) (van Manen, 1997).

To capture the sensory aspects of participants' work environment, I decided to take photographs and to write first-person protocols describing my impressions of their lived spaces. These additional sources of data provided important clues about participants' values and how this manifested in their business design and work culture. The photographs provided a visual representation of lived space, and the first-person protocols situated my reactions and observations as a source for further reflection.

For readers who may be concerned about anonymity, it should be noted that participation in this study was not anonymous. Participants signed release forms granting permission to use photographs, names, and details of their business practises in publications. These are unique businesses in Calgary, Alberta, Canada, and it would have been impossible to describe them in any detail without disclosing participants' identities. My committee members agreed that removing identifiers would dilute descriptions that are essential to phenomenology and restrict the potential benefit of the research to others. Including photographs enlivened the data and enriched understanding of each participant's lifeworld. It is a research practise I would encourage others to use, if appropriate, as a means to explore aesthetic dimensions of their research question.

The Importance of Transcription

With phenomenological research, conceptual analysis is about opening up to a range of provisional meanings, not to create categorical statements but to understand the experiential structures that make up that lived experience (van Manen, 1984, p. 20). For me, the in-depth analysis began with the transcription process.

At the time, I was suffering from a shoulder injury that prevented me from typing at length. I contemplated hiring transcription services to expedite the process, as many researchers do, but opted to use dictation software (Dragon Naturally). The software slowed the recorded interviews down to a snail-pace, and I repeated each statement into a microphone and the software transcribed my words into a document format. It was painfully time-consuming, but a critical part of the reflective analysis particularly for an auditory learner like me.

I became intimate with every nuance of the conversation including the tone, pace, inflection, emotion, and spaces between the words. Reading through the transcribed interviews later was like listening to a radio drama whereby each woman narrated her own story. I could recall non-verbal gestures and subtleties of the conversation that, I believe, were only available to me because I had listened to the conversation slowly and repeatedly. Themes like community, education, values, family, and personal connection readily emerged from the data as I highlighted phrases and made notes in the margins.

This initial categorization into themes came easily but it lacked depth. A critical turn of analysis occurred when I started to look at the data through a Schutzian lens.

Analysis through a Schutzian Lens

The second stage of analysis involved deeper consideration of the themes as typifications, relevancies, motives, and stocks of knowledge.

Typifications. The purpose of the research was to better understand the everyday, ordinary experiences of women sustainable entrepreneurs. I started by building a profile of each participant and her sustainable business practises, and then teasing out typifications from the descriptions. To illustrate, I discuss some of the most interesting findings that I deem relevant for future research, beginning with typifications and stocks of knowledge.

The participants exemplified the typifications of an entrepreneur as someone who is ambitious, determined, a risk taker, and innovative. It is interesting, however, to notice how much these women identified as atypical or "other" to their conventional competitors and peers. For example, when asked to describe how competitors viewed them, they struggled to put this into words. Trusha, a study participant, said: "I have no idea. I am pretty sure a lot of them don't even know I exist." In a similar vein, Laureen remarked: "I honestly don't know that. Well, wait a minute…I think sometimes they probably think it's a little weird" (Clarke, 2015, p. 114). The interviewees situated themselves as members of the broader sustainability community, but placed themselves on the fringe of their respective industries as "other" to the norm.

The vantage point of other was, at times, compounded by gender. Some interviewees felt they were taken less seriously in business and typified by others as naive or incapable because they are women. Differences in how they were treated spanned from personal interactions to systemic barriers including limited access to capital equity. Indeed, financial support was one of the biggest barriers the participants faced—a finding that is well-supported already by research literature (Alsos, Isaksen, & Ljunggren, 2006; Orser, Riding, & Manley, 2006). Typical of women entrepreneurs generally, the study participants invested their personal savings, or relied on help from family and friends, to get things started. How this affects the sustainability or growth of business is an important topic worthy of future research.

How is sustainability entrepreneurship different from a conventional business start-up? Entrepreneurship is typically associated with economics, specifically wealth creation, job creation, and economic growth (Spencer, Kirchhoff, & White, 2008; Tilley & Young, 2009). When asked to describe their business, the interviewees typified them as environmentally and socially conscious, emphasizing the importance of attributes like "quality," "craftsmanship," "high grade," and "premium" services (Clarke, 2015). Several women talked about job creation as a means to support the local economy but, in general, there was very little discussion about economics or economic growth. Instead, they describe their businesses as mission driven, that mission being to leave the world better than they found it.

Stocks of knowledge. What happens when the stocks of knowledge in the social world are inadequate or incongruent with one's lived experience? In general, participants did not find conventional business books, programs, or networking events with other entrepreneurs particularly useful or reflective of their experiences. They learned through trial-and-error, building new stocks of knowledge based on their personal experience.

Formative experiences as children and family were strong influencers on their values, which have informed their choices in business. For example, one participant recalled childhood memories of playing outside in her neighbourhood until dark. As an adult, the value of community still lives strongly in her desire to turn her business into a "community hub" for neighbours and friends (Clarke, 2015). Another participant described growing up in a small community where everyone knew one another. Today, she strives to restore personal connection between her customers and the artists designing her products. Across the board, relationships with others and the environment were relevancies that motivated them to take action and try something different.

Motives and relevancies. For many entrepreneurs, the motivation to start a business stems from an opportunity and desire to make money. This was not true for the study participants, who were predominantly motivated by personal connection, personal struggle, and search for meaning. In fact, when asked what motivated them to start a business, none of the participants talked about the opportunity to make money. They want their businesses to be financially viable; however, their motives reflected a personal connection to interests, values, and lifestyle. For example, one participant's decision to open a health food and organic grocery store stemmed from her child's health issues and food allergies. Eating a more natural diet became part of her family's lifestyle and eventually their family business. Several participants left high-paying, demanding careers in search of a more balanced lifestyle and meaningful work. They turned personal hobbies like gardening, sewing, and cooking into viable businesses.

These are just some of the examples from the larger study, but they illustrate how the researcher digs below the descriptions to examine the underlying structures of the lifeworld. In Schutzian terms, imposed relevancies such as health issues shape our beliefs and motivate action. A personal interest in cooking is clearly a *because* motive, while the desire to offer a tasty product that supports sustainable farming is an *in-order-to* motive. At the macro-level, the interviewees were motivated to act because of a desire to change how businesses operate. In this sense, their individual motives cannot be understood as separate from the sphere of we-relations and social meaning.

Intersubjectivity. Schutz (1967) assumed the fundamental structure of reality is not private but intersubjective from the very beginning. To help us understand this more fully, he differentiated between a thou-orientation and we-relations. A thou-orientation begins when a person becomes aware of another human being and ascribes consciousness to that other person. This may be one-sided as in the case of direct observation. We-relations refer to two people who are aware of one another and interact, even briefly. This occurs through dialogue but it may also be grasped through subtle body movements. Schutz illustrates this idea with an example of two people watching a bird in flight. Each person's lived experience of that moment will be different, however, in that moment the two people have "grown older together" (p. 165). The essence of the social world, then, is its commonness or shared meaning that we co-create through we-relations. We act within the lifeworld but also upon it (Schutz & Luckmann, 1974, p. 6).

Intersubjectivity showed up repeatedly in the language that participants used to describe their lived experiences, their values, and their leadership. For instance, even though only two of the women are co-owners of their businesses, all of the participants consistently used inclusive language like "we," "our," and "us." We-relations were so embedded in their psyches that, at times, I had to ask if there were more partners involved in the business. These women operate their businesses from an intersubjective consciousness of relationships and connection to other people and to the environment. Themes of connection, community, and care for others (including the Earth) dominated the interviews and were reflected in their lived spaces as well as their conversation. Their vision of business success is not competitive; it is cooperative and inseparable from the world around us.

Schutzian Puppets

The initial analysis was an iterative journey of moving back and forth between the interview transcripts, photos, my reflections, and the research literature. At some point in the process of reading and writing, I realized that I was creating typifications of typifications,—what Schutz referred to as puppets or ideal types of the woman sustainability entrepreneur.

Few typologies of the sustainability entrepreneur exist in the research literature and, of those that do, none of them accurately reflected the experiences of the women I interviewed. Constructing ideal types draws attention to features of the lifeworld that are relevant to participants' experiences. Using Schutz's (1964) technique of puppet creation, research participants become "actors on the social stage" (p. 17), performing typical acts that are selected by the interpreter and personified. The first step is to establish typical acts of the phenomenon under study, and then to ascribe typical motives (because and in-order-to motives). Schutz called these typical acts course-of-action motives, and they should remain constant regardless of the individual or type of business. For example, a typical act that was common to all participants in this study was efforts to reduce consumption and waste because of concern for the environment. The next step is to ask who would typically perform these acts, and then to construct a personal ideal type.

To develop personal ideal types, I organized the course-of-action types into groups, and then played with the themes using imaginative variation. Imaginative variation is a technique often used in phenomenology to shift one's attention from facts toward meaning (Moustakas, 1994, p.98). By varying the frames of reference and asking questions from divergent perspectives, the structural essence of the experience is revealed. What I was looking for was the "again and again" character that is typical, homogeneous, and repeatable (Schutz, 1967, p. 184).

During the process, three puppets emerged: Ms. A.L.L. Green, Ms.

117

Carin Relationship, and Ms. I.N. Tentional. These puppets characterize some of the less tangible but meaningful aspects of sustainability entrepreneurship and the particular contributions that women have to offer.

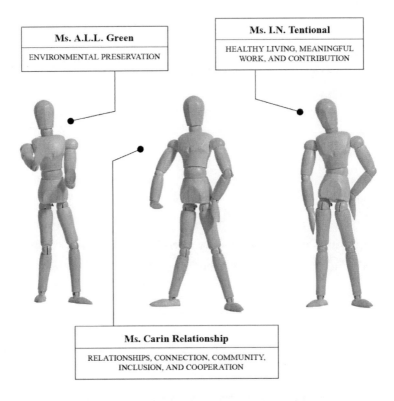

Figure 1. Schutzian puppets from the research

Ms. A.L.L. Green personifies concern and care about the environment. She is the voice that asks, "How will this impact the environment?" whenever a business choice or decision is made. Ms. Carin Relationship represents a leadership style that is relational, inclusive, and cooperative. Ms. I.N. Tentional personifies participants' commitment to their beliefs, values, and a purposeful life. Each puppet represents separate themes that emerged from the research but, like siblings, they are intimately related. The final stage of analysis was to create a general ideal type that embodies all three puppets as parts of one whole. I named this new ideal type the integrative entrepreneur (Clarke, 2015).

Integrative Entrepreneur

Ideal types draw attention to features of the phenomenon that the researcher deems significant (Psathas, 2005, p. 165). Schutz (1967) called it a "frozen cross-section of consciousness" (p. 190) that is always determined by the point of view as the observer. The power of the ideal type is that it creates a persona that can now enter our language for further discussion, research, and debate. For instance, my choice to study sustainability and women was driven by ethical concerns about environmental devastation, and a long-standing belief that we need new models of business that are more egalitarian and environmentally responsible than what presently exists. My research describes a new way of doing business and a new characterization of entrepreneurship.

Language has a powerful effect on our social, collective consciousness. The integrative entrepreneur typifies many of the characteristics of a conventional entrepreneur, but there are some major differences. The integrative entrepreneur is driven and ambitious but not by profits and personal gain. Her actions are motivated by personal connection, relationships, and an ethic of care that extends to others and the environment we share. As a leader, she seeks to create an inclusive organizational culture where staff members, suppliers, and customers feel respected and appreciated. Her business decisions are vetted through an ecological lens first; environmental sustainability is not a "nice to do" but a business driver. She leads from integrative values of conservation, cooperation, quality, and partnership (Capra, 1996).

People who do not necessarily connect with conventional models of entrepreneurship may see themselves reflected in this new ideal and use it to typify themselves. If enough people typify themselves as an integrative entrepreneur, it becomes part of our stock of knowledge, shifting social norms, expectations, and actions. Whether this happens or not, the construct of an integrative entrepreneur enters our discourse and can now be examined critically by others.

Phenomenology is Never Done

Phenomenology is not something that a person is ever done with. It cultivates a capacity for wonder that, once ignited, continues to infuse how we take in and act upon the world around us. Although my doctoral studies are finished, my relationship with phenomenology continues to mature as I do. I am more likely to ask questions than to have the answers, and more comfortable with noticing rather than drawing a conclusion. I am more patient with process and infinitely more patient with myself.

The resounding appeal of social phenomenology, for me, is how it blends wonder with pragmatism. There is great creative potential in this coupling, for wonder fuels the imagination and pragmatism makes it happen. Currently I work in an art and design institution where I witness and experience this dynamic at play on a daily basis. Cultivating imagination is embedded in the curriculum and pedagogical practice. Much like the participants in this study, it can be difficult to describe because this type of learning does not fit into typifications of academia and scholarship. Yet what I see happening is nourishing the capacity for wonder, and it has sparked my interest in the transformative potential of creative practice.

Creativity goes well beyond artistic talent and skill. I am interested in how creativity, as a phenomenon, can help us to find innovative solutions to pressing social and environmental problems. Practicing phenomenology cultivates a mindfulness that allows the researcher to reach beyond prescription to description. It is this capacity to see, to clearly describe *what* is, and to live with a phenomenon in its most natural state that makes space for new ideas to emerge. We are all makers—each one of us is intimately involved in bringing forth a world and, as such, responsible for that creation.

References

Alsos, G. A., Isaksen, E. J., & Ljunggren, E. (2006). New venture financing and subsequent business growth in men- and women-led businesses. *Entrepreneurship: Theory & Practice, 30*(5), 667-686.

Bentz, V. M., & Shapiro, J. J. (1998). *Mindful inquiry in social research.* Thousand Oaks, CA: SAGE.

Capra, F. (1996). *The web of life: A new scientific understanding of living systems.* New York, NY: Anchor Books.

Clarke, J. (2015). *The integrative entrepreneur: A lifeworld study of women sustainability entrepreneurs* (Doctoral dissertation). Retrieved from ProQuest Dissertations & Theses Open (ISBN 3700410).

Gadamer, H. (1960/1975). *Truth and method.* New York, NY: Seabury Press.

Husserl, E. (1970). *The crisis of the European sciences and transcendental phenomenology: An introduction to phenomenological philosophy.* (D. Carr, Trans.). Evanston, IL: Northwestern University Press.

Merleau-Ponty, M. (1945/1962). *Phenomenology of perception.* (C. Smith, Trans.). New York, NY: Humanities Press.

Moustakas, C. (1994). *Phenomenological research methods.* Thousand Oaks, CA: SAGE.

Orser, B. J., Riding, A. L., & Manley, K. (2006). Women entrepreneurs and financial capital. *Entrepreneurship Theory and Practice, 30* (5), 643-665.

Psathas, G. (2005). The ideal type in Weber and Schutz . In M. Endress, G. Psathas, & H. Nasu (Ed.), *Explorations of the lifeworld: Continuing dialogues with Alfred Schutz,* (Vol. 53, pp. 143-169). Dordrecht, South Holland: Springer Netherlands.

Rehorick, D. A., & Bentz, V. M. (Ed.). (2008). *Transformative phenomenology: Changing ourselves, lifeworlds, and professional practice.* Lanham, MD: Lexington Books.

Schutz, A. (1964). *Collected papers II: Studies in social theory. Vol. II.* (A. Brodersen, Trans.) The Hague, The Netherlands: Martinus Nijhoff.

_____. (1932/1967). *The phenomenology of the social world.* (G. Walsh & F. Lehnert, Trans.). Evanston, IL: Northwestern University Press.

_____. (1970a). *On phenomenology and social relations.* R. M. Zaner (Ed.). Chicago, IL: University of Chicago Press.

_____. (1970b). *Reflections on the problem of relevance.* R. M. Zaner (Ed.). Chicago, IL: University of Chicago Press.

Schutz, A., & Luckmann, T. (1974). *The structures of the lifeworld.* (R. M. Zaner & H. T. Engelhardt, Jr., Trans.). London, England: Heinemann.

Spencer, A. S., Kirchhoff, B. A., & White, C. (2008). Entrepreneurship, innovation, and wealth creation. *International Small Business Journal, 26*(1), 9-26.

Tilley, F., & Young, W. (2009). Sustainability entrepreneurs: Could they be the true wealth generators of the future? *Greener Management International, 55,* 79-92.

van Manen, M. (1984). *"Doing" phenomenological research and writing: An introduction.* Edmonton, Alberta, Canada: Publication Services for Department of Secondary Education, Faculty of Education, University of Alberta.

_____. (1990/1997). *Researching lived experience: Human science for an action sensitive pedago*gy (2nd ed.) London, Ontario, Canada: The Althouse Press.

_____. (2007). Phenomenology of practice. *Phenomenology & Practice, 1*(1), 11-30.

Wagner, H. R. (1983). *Phenomenology of consciousness and sociology of the life-world: An introductory study.* Edmonton, Alberta, Canada: The University of Alberta Press.

About the Author

Jo-Anne Clarke, PhD is the Director of Continuing Education + Professional Development at the Alberta College of Art + Design where she develops educational programs for visual artists, designers, and makers of all types. She has a Bachelor of Arts in Psychology and a Masters in Continuing Education from the University of Calgary. At Fielding, she earned her PhD in Human and Organizational Systems with a focus on social phenomenology and sustainability entrepreneurship. Contact: jo.clarke@shaw.ca

CHAPTER 5

Understanding Patients' Experience of Heart Attack: Phenomenological Lessons for Nurses and other Practitioners

Carol G. Laberge, PhD, RN

Provincial Executive Director, Cardiac Services British Columbia

Adjunct Professor, University of British Columbia, Okanagan

Fielding Graduate University, Alumna

Abstract

My research applies phenomenology to nursing research. I employed a blended hermeneutic-phenomenological and narrative inquiry method to explore ten patients' heart attack experience treated with primary percutaneous coronary intervention (PPCI). The qualitative interpretive analysis approach that I used revealed nine meaning structures, with three overarching themes. These characterized the individual patients' journey from the onset of heart attack, through coronary medical intervention, to follow-up care in rural communities. My original poetic compositions capture the emotional and expressive meaning of each patient's journey. The study offers understanding around the shared meaning practitioners and patients make of an acute illness experience, and the emotional expression that plays a central part.

Keywords: phenomenology, heart attack, primary percutaneous coronary intervention, lived experience, poetic composition, nursing research

The Treatment of Heart Attacks Using Primary Percutaneous Coronary Intervention (PPCI)

As a cardiac scrub nurse working in a large-scale cardiac catheterization laboratory, I witnessed many heart attacks that were treated using Primary Percutaneous Coronary Intervention (PPCI). I also assisted the cardiologist in threading the wires and balloon up into the heart, allowing for opening of the blocked artery—ultimately the cause of the heart attack. While monitoring patient well-being, including patient vital signs, I often found myself wondering what the patient was thinking and experiencing while lying on that cold hard table, undressed, exposed, and vulnerable. A heart attack of any sort is a life-threatening event.

In search of answers, I attended conferences that addressed cardiac care. It immediately became evident that nursing knowledge in this area was still greatly influenced by traditional medicine, which uses a positivistic paradigm valuing objective as opposed to subjective meaning (Playle, 1995, p. 979). This is a tension I found disconcerting.

My nursing philosophy was and remains that, in order to care for people in a patient-centered manner, one has to understand the experiences of the patient by pushing toward a holistic nursing approach that includes subjective understanding. Medicine focuses on the "illness-cure model" based in objective evidence through random control trials (Playle, 1995). I did not question the utility of this model as it is imperative in creating evidenced-based best practice standards and treatment therapies. Other nurse researchers shared my concern regarding the lack of a holistic lens on the patient (Benner & Wrubel, 1989; Parse, 1990; Playle, 1995; Watson, 2004). Time and time again, I would see patients leave the cardiac catheterization laboratory thinking they had been "fixed." Indeed, it was true the mechanical piece was fixed, but what about the patient's conscious subjective understanding of the experience? This concern resonated deeply with me.

Collectively, these experiences inspired my doctorate journey at

Fielding Graduate University—to collaboratively explore with patients the illness experience through a methodology that delves beneath the concepts of psychology and the scientific objective model. As a novice nurse researcher, I sought to move toward a more holistic nursing approach with an emphasis on restoring and maintaining an individual's health and well-being that would unveil basic human truths. After all, it is well understood that nurses are able to provide holistic care to patients by understanding the circumstances of their experiences (Benner & Wrubel, 1989; Parse, 1990; Watson, 2004).

To further my journey, I participated in several Fielding Graduate University research and practice sessions pertaining to the qualitative research process. This included forms of interpretive inquiry, which provided a valuable foundation. In addition, I learned the complexities associated with qualitative interpretive inquiry. The importance of methodology design, along with rigor, credibility, and trustworthiness, was an intricate process. I read about phenomenology and was intrigued by the deep connection to consciousness and objects in the world. Having decided to explore further the area of phenomenology, I reached out to Valerie Bentz and David Rehorick, both considered leading experts in the field.

In my preliminary studies, I learned that one has to differentiate between philosophical underpinnings of phenomenology and phenomenology as a methodology. On one hand phenomenology is considered a philosophy; on the other, it is a research methodology geared toward achieving a deeper understanding of the human experience. Past researchers asserted that nursing had misconstrued the fundamental tenets and key concepts of phenomenology while practicing it as a research methodology (Crotty, 1996; McNamara, 2005; Paley, 1997). In order to achieve a quality study, I would have to clearly differentiate between the philosophical and methodological underpinnings to address the concerns raised by these researchers.

Through attendance at several phenomenology sessions, it became apparent that a blended phenomenological research approach based on the philosophical writings of Edmund Husserl, Martin Heidegger, and Hans-Georg Gadamer would help unveil a deeper shared meaning of the patient experience. Further, with Valerie's and David's guidance, my study would address previous concerns in the literature regarding nursing's misconstruction of the tenets and concepts of phenomenology.

Unravelling Phenomenology

Phenomenology is the study of the individual's lifeworld as it is experienced rather than as it is conceptualized, categorized, or theorized. It aims for a deeper understanding of the meaning of everyday experience; the ultimate goal of phenomenological research is to fulfill our human quest to become more fully aware of who we are (van Manen, 1990). Anne Flood (2010), stated "the primary stance of phenomenology is to elaborate basic human truth" (p. 7). It seemed to me that phenomenology naturally lent itself to the field of nursing research, given that a nurse's role is to focus on the lived experience of health and illness in a patient's lifeworld, particularly in stressful situations (Benner & Wrubel, 1989, p.xi).

Previously, nurse researchers had considered the question as to whether phenomenology is epistemology (knowing) or ontology (being) (Koch, 1995; Walters, 1995). Spending time at the Fielding research intensives taught me the important difference between the two: It is the type of question one asks to drive the inquiry. Depending on the philosophical underpinning used for a research design, one could privilege either the epistemological perspective rooted in Edmund Husserl's writings on knowing, or the ontological perspective of Martin Heidegger, who was concerned with modes of being of persons in the world.

Paley (1997) notes that phenomenology finds its roots in the early writings of Husserl, who first elaborated phenomenology as a philosophical approach for studying the essential structures or *essence* of human experience. More specifically, phenomenology focuses on constructs that make up consciousness by using first-person characterizations that entail the concept of *intentionality*—the direction of mind toward objects that are differentiated from the subject and therefore become descriptive content of reality (Koch, 1995). Further, Tina Koch (1995) maintained that Husserlian phenomenology retains elements of objectivism that make a basic metaphysical or epistemological distinction between subject and object. What is "out there" (objective) is presumed to be independent of "us" (as subjects), and knowledge is created when a subject represents objective reality. Therefore, Koch contended that Husserlian phenomenology emphasizes *intentionality*—that is, an analysis of the subject and object. The object appears through consciousness with an emphasis on *bracketing out* by reduction of any pre-understandings affiliated with the prior experience of the subject.

Husserl described the process of phenomenological reduction as one of placing the natural attitude toward the world in brackets, or *bracketing out* pre-suppositions or pre-understanding of the world that exist prior to description (Walters, 1995, p. 792). Therefore, the hallmark of Husserlian phenomenology is the "matter of describing" lived experience of an event in which the subject is detached from and living amidst a world of objects (ibid.). In line with this philosophical tradition, an emphasis on description that depends on subjective, first-person accounts formed the core of my study with the intention of eliciting the lived experience of heart attack treated with primary percutaneous coronary intervention (PPCI) as described by those who embody the event and its aftermath.

Husserl introduced the concept of the lifeworld to encourage a return to the phenomenon as they occur in everyday life. He posited that *lived experience* is accomplished by stepping outside of our *natural attitude* or everyday experience for the purpose of examining relationships within our consciousness through intentionality. This idea is based on the assumption that consciousness is the one thing of which we can be certain and, therefore, the "building of knowledge should start with the conscious awareness" (Koch, 1995, p. 828).

In contrast, Heidegger (1962) emphasized *being-in-the world* as an ontological foundation of understanding that cannot be bracketed in any meaning-making operation since it exists as a pre-structure or pre-understanding. Meaning is located in the co-constitution between the individual and situation; in other words, the individual is seen to both constitute and be co-constituted by the situation. Perception of meaning follows from the belief that experience involves linguistic, social, and cultural patterning. Furthermore, an emphasis on language as imbuing and constituting experience is central to this approach (Munhall, 1994).

Consequently, for Heidegger, meaning is created in the very transaction that occurs between a person and situation in which she acts, so that individuals and world are viewed as co-constituting one another (Walters, 1995). Further, there is an indissoluble unity between person and world that means they cannot be separated (Koch, 1995). Such situations are what comprise life, and Heidegger argues that we learn how to handle ourselves in a great many circumstances without any special kind of knowledge (Grondin, 1995). He considered the attempts of Husserl to understand *being-in-the-world* as flawed precisely because Husserl conceptualized human reality as an object. On the other hand, Heidegger referred to human existence as *Dasein,* or being-there "*in our average everydayness,*" by emphasizing *situatedness.* Being in the world, we necessarily become socialized in ways that influence coping skills, moods, and possibilities.

The tension between Husserl and Heidegger caught my attention because in practice the Heideggerian orientation acknowledges that I (as researcher), together with the patient participants, necessarily carried our pre-understandings of what it is "to-be-in-the-world" into the meaning-making interaction in this research (Koch, 1995). Understanding patients' meaning-making entailed asking questions about the experience that supported their interpretation of events, and our combined backgrounds, expectations, and frames of meaning shared the act of understanding. Consequently, interpretive claims made from a set of prior structures could not have been bracketed out. The context for the co-constitution of life events in my research was the past and present of patients' experience of heart attack treated with PPCI, together with my experience as a reflective expert practitioner.

My attraction to Heideggarian phenomenology, with Heidegger's two essential notions of the historicality of understanding and the hermeneutic circle, were important concepts in the practice of phenomenology as an expert reflective practitioner. Heidegger used the term pre-understanding or *historicality* to claim that humans must necessarily bring to every situation a story from their past which constitutes the pre-understanding of *being-in-the-world* (Heidegger, 1962). This pre-understanding cannot be eliminated or bracketed out, as Husserl suggests doing (Koch, 1995). Heidegger's phenomenology resonated with me as the novice nurse researcher.

While Heidegger saw the hermeneutic process as cycles of interpretation that situate our pre-understandings, Gadamer (1972/1989) believed that the task of hermeneutics was to clarify understanding by sharing common meaning. He reconceptualised the task of the hermeneutic circle as an iterative process that would yield understanding of a whole reality by virtue of exploring the details of existence. Gadamer viewed understanding as linguistically mediated through conversations with others in which reality is explored and an agreement is reached that represents a new understanding by means of a "conversation with a purpose." He extended the understanding of the ontological structure of the hermeneutic circle by claiming, "we must understand the whole in terms of the detail and the detail in terms of the whole" via shared common meaning (pp. 291-292).

For this reason, I chose hermeneutic phenomenology to explore with patients a deeper understanding of their experience. Hermeneutic phenomenology recognizes that each person involved in an experience brings pre-understanding, prejudices, motivation, and tradition to the dialogue where shared meaning is constructed inside a hermeneutic circle and pre-understandings and prejudices are operative (Gadamer, 1989). Gadamer argued that human beings share a commonality of pre-under-standing through traditions brought to the project of understanding that must necessarily be continuously transformed through experiences in the world. By recognizing one's prejudices, the possibility of opening existing horizons to create new understandings arises (Gadamer, 1989). In hermeneutics, if the meaning is to be understandable, it must embody significance and apply to each person's life (see also Grondin, 1994).

On the basis of this philosophical tradition, my research methodology utilized a narrative inquiry approach. Furthermore, a blended hermeneutic phenomenological approach offered me an opportunity as the nurse researcher to enter into the hermeneutic circle with patient participants in order to acquire a deeper shared understanding of how patients created meaning from the experience of a heart attack treated with PPCI. The hermeneutic task was to claim the meaning that emerged from the hermeneutic circle through narratives with the participants to answer the research question: What is the experience and meaning-making of rural community people who experience heart attack, which is treated with PPCI?

Linking Hermeneutic Phenomenology and Nursing Science

Nursing science is concerned primarily with the well-being of humans (Benner & Wrubel, 1989). Daily, nurses are faced with their own lived reality of "being-in-the-world" as well as that of their patients. Munhall (1994) argued that the everyday perceived world underlies scientific explanation. Because human experience is the focus of concern in nursing practice, it was necessary to employ an appropriate means of describing and interpreting human lived experience in nursing practice and research.

The philosophical underpinnings of hermeneutic phenomenology are applicable to nursing research because of the need for nurses to understand the situation of those who live through disease processes experienced in a time of illness. This continues to be important to develop a level of understanding to assist nursing interventions in a hospital setting that will fulfill the needs of any patients not only throughout their treatment but also following discharge.

Using the hermeneutic-phenomenological approach, I explored with ten patients living in rural communities their experiences of heart attack treated with PPCI. During that time, my professional role was Director for a growing rural cardiac program. I conceived that this research could benefit both patients and clinicians. Through the literature review process, I also knew that phenomenology and hermeneutic phenomenology alike were gaining growing recognition by other nurse researchers as a useful approach for the study of nursing practice (Benner, 1984; Benner & Wrubel, 1989; Munhall, 1994; Oiler, 1982; Parse, 1990; Watson, 2004). These researchers offered an interesting, diverse approach to phenomenology and hermeneutic inquiry that did not necessarily align with Gadamer's philosophical approach to hermeneutics, since they tended toward a more rigid methodological technique.

My hope was to create a more personalized approach by combining hermeneutics and phenomenology, creating a possibility for expanding the concept of *text* to include the patient participants as well as the researcher's observations, alongside scholarly literature. This would be the description of how meaning-making is achieved through the hermeneutic circle, a specialized dynamic that includes the participants, researcher, and scholarly literature (Grondin, 1995). Hermeneutic phenomenology recognizes that everything is an interpretation of what we know or believe our "horizons" to be, and that there is no single truth to be uncovered. Gadamer (1989) describes this co-constitution of meaning as the "fusion of horizons." A transformation of meaning occurs in the intersection of one's own horizon, prejudices, pre-understandings, effective history, and tradition with others who are centrally involved in the dialogue about a mutual event or concern. This transformation promotes discovery of meaning embedded within an experience as interpreted by those who experience it in *dialogue* with the researcher. As the researcher, I interpreted an understanding of the meaning of the experience through participants' narrative based on accounts within the context of my professional knowledge, prejudices, traditions, and scholarly literature.

In Gadamer's (1989) view, the possibility that someone else may be "right" is one of a series of possibilities that form the essence of hermeneutics. Through dialogue and questioning of study participants' reports, I was able to gain an understanding beyond the boundaries of the beliefs at that time. Philosophical hermeneutics aided in developing the conversation and was the most important principle (Grondin, 1994). As the conversation explicated new ideas between me as the researcher and each participant, a transformation in meaning influenced the original boundaries of our respective beliefs, producing fresh insights. Understanding the situation that occurred through language (Mitchell, 1994) with the principle goal of ensuring that the voice of the "other" was heard (Risser, 1997).

Blending Hermeneutics and Phenomenology through Narratives

The qualitative approach adopted for this research acknowledged and supported an interactive process between me, the research interviewer, and the participants through the medium of narrative inquiry. Polkinghorne (1988) maintained that narrative inquiry is the basis for practitioners' work, and that eliciting and interpreting the meaning in stories will help us to understand others much better (p. xi). Riessman (2008) describes the goal of narrative inquiry as generating a detailed account of an experience rather than general statements (p. 23).

I reviewed the literature on illness experience, guided by the key thinkers who maintained that storytelling is a rich way to explicate meaning and understanding from experience (Becker, 1997; Broyard, 1992; Frank, 1991, 1995; Kleinman, 1988; Morris, 1998; Sontag, 1978;

Zaner, 2004). I also reflected on hundreds of conversations I had with patients in my nursing career. It became clear to me that narrative inquiry would be a means to explicating the human truths that I sought to understand.

Arthur Frank (1995) contended that if illness obscures the individual's destination in life by disrupting the worldview, then narrative attempts to repair the damage by redrawing the map and highlighting new destinations. Narratives are embedded in our memory and, when given voice, can aid in a sense of coherence because the voice expresses the body. According to Arthur Kleinman (1988), "Illness narratives edify us about how life problems are created, controlled, made meaningful" (p. xiii). Gaylene Becker (1997) contended that narrative organizes the disruption often associated with illness; illness narrative expresses body aches and pain. David Morris (1998) argued that narratives bring suffering out of silence and into the awareness of others; the narrative gives voice, which can both encourage dialogue and provoke dissent. Susan Chase (2005) asserted that "narrative is retrospective meaning-making—shaping the order or ordering of past experience" and that "the purpose of a narrative is to understand the actions of oneself and others in order to organize events and objects into a meaningful whole" (p. 656). While Jean Clandinin and Jerry Rosiek (2007) suggested that beginning with a respect for ordinary lived experience, the focus of narrative inquiry is not only on valorizing of individual's experience but also an exploration of social, cultural and institutional narratives within which individual's experiences were constituted, shaped, expressed and enacted narrative inquirers study and individual's experience in the world, and through the study, seek ways of enriching and transforming that experience for themselves and others (p.42). Whitsitt (2010) asserted that, "the action inherent in the narrative prompts insights on the part of the storyteller" and/or the listener that can lead to change at personal and social levels (p.120). The narrative is an oral or written story that emerges from fieldwork, interviews, natural conversations, or writing.

133

Simply put by Clandinin and Connelly (2000), "Narrative inquiry is a way of understanding experience" (p. 20).

According to Max van Manen (1990), phenomenological human science is discovery that seeks to know what a certain phenomenon means and how it is experienced. The way to do this is to fend off any tendency toward constructing a predetermined set of fixed procedures, techniques, or methods because there are no "fixed signposts" for this kind of exploration (p. 29). The method is created as a means of responding openly to the research question. In Gadamer's (1989) hermeneutics, conditions for understanding "do not amount to a 'procedure' or method which the interpreter must of himself bring to bear on text" (p. 295). Therefore, hermeneutic phenomenology does not prescribe rigid method, which further appealed to me as a reflective expert practitioner and researcher.

Because of the congruence between hermeneutic phenomenology, understanding, meaning-making, and narrative inquiry, asking patient participants to illuminate their individual reflective thought through narrative stimulated understanding and meaning-making of lived experience (Becker, 1997; Broyard, 1992; Frank, 1991; Kleinman, 1988; Morris, 1998; Sontag, 1978; Zaner, 2004).

Hermeneutic Phenomenological Analysis

Forms of textual analysis in hermeneutics have contributed to important ideas in narrative inquiry. A good narrative analysis prompts the reader to think beyond the surface of the text toward a deeper meaning by moving from the surface of what is narrated into the essence and underlying meaning of stories. Catherine Riessman (2008) stated, "Narrative analysis interrogates intention and language— *how* and *why* experiences are storied, not simply the content to which language refers" (p. 11). Van Manen (1990) asserts that explication of meaning-making is a complex process that is neither simple nor one-dimensional. Making something of a text or of a lived experience by interpreting its meaning is a process

134

of insight or "discovery of disclosure" that is not so much rule-bound as it is a process of specialized "seeing" (p. 79).

Therefore, the hermeneutic phenomenological analysis process was understood in the context of the participants' and the researcher's co-constitution of "being-in-the-world" that we entered when we joined the hermeneutic circle. Gadamer's (1972/1989) key concept of *Bildung* (openness-to-meaning) underpinned my approach to analysis. The structure of *Bildung* allowed for openness by virtue of embracing more historical points of view. Weinsheimer (1985) maintains that in *Bildung* one "leaves the all-too-familiar and learns to allow for what is different from oneself" (p. 70). In other words, *Bildung* asserts that one's self is open to what is other. As the nurse researcher, I was left open to what was "other" in the participants' view by detaching to the extent possible from immediate desires and purposes. Being aware of my bias was crucial to understanding the phenomenon being explored because "working with appropriate projections, anticipatory in nature, to be confirmed by the things themselves, is the constant task of understanding" (Gadamer, 1972/1989, p. 267). In this way, the text (or content of the interview) presented itself in all its "otherness." In order to maintain and openness, I created a flowchart of "turns of data"

(see Figure 1 below)

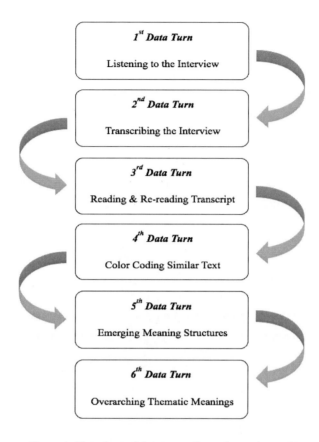

Figure 1. Flowchart of data turns: Toward meaning making

In keeping with the concept of *Bildung*, and considering van Manen's advice on seeing, I was open to participants' narratives as they revealed something new about the nature of experience as seen through their eyes. According to Gadamer (1972/1989), understanding consists not only of *Bildung*, but also "fore-projection" or early ideas and understanding that emerge as to what had been unveiled within the hermeneutic circle. In an attempt to understand the narrative of another, it was important for me to move from the whole of the narrative to its parts, and then to return to the whole again in order to capture the dimension and relationship of meaning. When analyzing the narratives, I considered how the "fore-projections" are constantly revised in the hermeneutic circle as new meanings emerged from the narratives, constituting the movement of understanding and interpretation (Gadamer, 1972/1989).

According to Clandinin and Connelly (2000), "A narrative researcher must read and re-read the field notes in order to construct a chronicled or summarized account of what is contained within different sets of text" (p. 131). I read and reread the interview manuscripts and listened to the audio-taped version several times. This was part of the turns of data analysis and afforded a continuing dialogue with the texts in an attempt to understand what was there, and then to use these insights to further explore meaning in an iterative manner. I looked for what van Manen (1990) describes as "structures of meaning" (p. 101) or what I termed as meaning structures. Through this process, I continued to journal my thoughts, assumptions, and reflections in order to identify co-constructed meaning structures, moving toward a fusion of horizons between myself as the nurse researcher and the participants. Van Manen refers to this process as "working at mining meaning from the text" (p. 86). Spending time at Fielding's qualitative interpretive analysis workshops, it became clear that, in order to track the meaning structures, color coding would become part of the interpretive role. I did this by drawing on my experiential and professional knowledge, taken in the context of pre-understanding and prejudices identified in prior journaling and color coding themes that fell into a meaning structure.

What emerged through the data analysis were nine meaning structures and the three overarching thematic meanings that reflected the participants' original comments and my analytic interpretation. This included a recollection of what I learned through the process of initial notation. In addition, the participants' original words and my analytic interpretation was achieved through an exercise of *Bildung* which included, "keeping oneself open to what is other to another, more universal point of view...embrac[ing] a sense of proportion and distance in relation to itself, and hence...rising above itself to universality" (Grondin, 1995, p.119). Throughout this process of analysis, I maintained awareness of the notion that prejudices are expectations or projections about the whole that must be continually revised as more parts of the whole come into view. Gadamer (1972/1989) asserts that understanding involves discriminating among prejudices by questioning beliefs about our own understanding, thereby becoming prepared for the text to say something unexpected (Weinsheimer, 1985). In this respect, I was conscious of my years of experience as a critical care nurse with experience primarily of the biomedical model.

Adequate rigor is another important consideration in a blended phenomenological hermeneutic inquiry that needs to be in accordance with the established standards for qualitative research (Creswell, 2009). Attention to rigor was a key point at the Fielding research and practice sessions I attended, as it is critical to establish integrity of the data and research findings. In my study, I achieved this by tracking the course of emergent understandings that evolved from beginning to end via the journaling process. Munhall (1994) suggests incorporating excerpts from the original transcripts in the findings to allow the reader to follow the course of analysis and the evolution of the meaning structures (p. 187).

According to van Manen (1990), for human science in general and hermeneutic phenomenology research especially, "Writing is closely fused into the research activity with reflection itself" (p. 125). Writing places thought on open paper by externalizing what in some sense might be internal. Writing the interpretive analysis of the texts into the nine meaning structures and then three overarching thematic meaning patterns became part of the process of re-writing, rethinking, reflecting, and recognizing (van Manen, 1990, p.131). In many ways, the reflective journaling and analytic writing was a hermeneutic phenomenological process itself. The object of human science research is essentially a linguistic project in itself that seeks to make some aspect of our lived experience understandable and intelligible. "Writing separates us from what we know," van Manen explains, "and yet it unites us more closely with what we know" (p. 127). This concept of analysis aided me in mining my and the participants' minds in search of new meaning that tied us more closely with what we knew.

Unveiling Shared Meaning through Poetic Composition

The research findings and insights from the ten individual interviews are displayed below as meaning structures in the order in which they emerged through my poetic compositions. Poetic composition is "a way to transcribe the content of the interviews in poetic form" (Kennedy, 2009, p. 1421). Corrine Glense (1997) asserts that poetic composition provides a third voice "that is neither the interviewee's nor the research-er's but a combination of both" (p. 215). This in turn allows for a power-ful tool for displaying participant voices that embraces the open, active co-construction of the researcher (Brady, 2000; Glense, 1997). During each of the individual interviews, as I allowed myself to completely em-bed in the phenomenological hermeneutic process, I was deeply struck by how each individual participant shared statements that I interpreted as being very powerful. I could not get some of their statements out of my head. I could feel the intensity of what the experience of having had a heart attack treated with PPCI meant for them. For this reason, I want-ed to find a way to arrange the statements matching the meaning struc-tures. The poetic compositions following each of the meaning structures are verbatim statements from each of the individual transcripts, then arranged by me the researcher into a poetic composition.

Meaning Structure 1: Operating in a Fog

 Horrible things happen

 Woozy, light-headedness

 Shortness of breath

 Lead one to operate in a fog

 Broken heart, mended heart

 You learn to live with it!

Meaning Structure 2: Disbelief and Trust

Remembering dignity

Expose my body, expose my heart

But don't expose my soul

I'm not dead yet!

A wonderful job done with a slab of meat

I'm fortunate to be alive

Meaning Structure 3: Impact on Heath Restoration

Two companions, life and death walk together

Impacts on life make one walk like Ox

In death, I realize, I walk alone

The sugar-coated pills, make me a medical marvel

Meaning Structure 4: Knowing Versus Not Knowing

Damaged animals in a cage

Illness infects my heart

Disease caged in my heart

Illness belongs in a cage

Meaning Structure 5: Taking Stock and Realization

Live forever?

Shuffle the deck

Dodge the bullet

I have to!

Meaning Structure 6: Advocating Follow-up Care

Hanging around

Quit smoking

Why no withdrawal symptoms

One drug replaces another

Still hanging around trying to find out

Meaning Structure 7: Transforming Lifestyle Pattern Change

Anything can happen to anybody

Become a better person

Be lucky, be fortunate

Make a succession plan

Sooner rather than later

Meaning Structure 8: Appreciating Luck

Luck, what is luck?

Luck is to be alive and see another day?

There is no life without luck,

There is no luck without life.

Meaning Structure 9: Living with Cardiac Health in Rural Areas

Once healthy

Now health challenged

Facing my health in rural areas

Still like roughing it!

After each interview, participants were asked if telling their story was helpful. Most confirmed that having someone to tell their story to was therapeutic. One participant replied that even after a period of time he was still figuring things out.

Poetic Composition

Figure it out

The little man on your shoulder,

Reminds you everyday

In never goes away.

Viewed more holistically, the nine emergent meaning structures can be expressed as three overarching thematic categories. This revealed a pattern within the experience and meaning of a heart attack followed by PPCI treatment for rural living people. The three emergent themes were: 1. Cardiac Disease and Rural Living, 2. Impact on Health Restoration, and 3. Emotional Expression of the Experience.

Blended hermeneutic phenomenology may be seen as one of the many research approaches under the umbrella of qualitative inquiry. This journey taught me the approach may be used when the researcher is attempting the project of understanding everyday experience and meaning-making as expressed by individuals such as the patients in my study. Hermeneutic phenomenology is being utilized more by nurse researchers when there is no significant clarity about a particular experience, no established understanding, or when the researcher wants to question a prevailing understanding of a particular human experience through narrative (Pratt, 2012). Hermeneutic phenomenological methods may not be appropriate when the researcher is trying to compare situations in order to predict or control, as seen in the "illness-cure model," because hermeneutic phenomenology examines the individual experience of consciousness, meaning-making, and understanding.

Ending One Journey and Beginning Another

Throughout my experience as a scrub nurse, I often felt tension and unease when listening to practitioners speak about patient- and family-centered care. I realized this was because practitioners rarely actively listened to the patients concerns or asked patients questions about their experiences. Once I learned about phenomenology, I knew I could employ research methods used in the field to better understand the patient lived experience. This was something I had wondered about for many years in my nursing career. My research enabled me to understand the parts of a patient's combined conscious experience of a heart attack treated with PPCI.

Since completing my doctoral studies, I have reflected on my journey and incorporated many principles of phenomenology and hermeneutics into my personal and professional life. The experience allowed me to combine my expertise in cardiac care with qualitative research methods, where I could further contribute to patient lived experience in the nursing literature. Interacting with other budding phenomenological researchers was a conscious experience, allowing me to realize ideas deeply rooted in my conscious perceptions and knowing.

From a professional perspective, my research gave me exposure in the nursing field across Canada. In 2012, I was fortunate to present my work at the Canadian Cardiovascular Nursing Congress meeting in Toronto. Nurse researchers from across Canada were in attendance and many had questions regarding the methodology used in my dissertation. Drawing upon my training at Fielding, I was able to navigate delicate questions with confidence and ease. Moreover, my research further provided me a chance to collaborate with a local university and create a nursing research interest group focused on patient-centered cardiac care. Additionally, I have supported and mentored other novice nurse researchers in qualitative interpretive inquiry, nurses who also have an interest in phenomenological methods relevant to their areas of study. Specifically, one student studied patient's interpretation of risk factors and Atrial Fibrillation, a malfunction in the heart's electrical pathway. Understanding patient experience in this area is important because there is no cure for Atrial Fibrillation, only management of the symptoms.

Further, my study of phenomenology has influenced my current teaching philosophy, which I actively apply to my leadership and management courses delivered to graduate nursing students. My graduate school experience has also made me a better leader. My career has steadily progressed since completing my studies and I have progressively moved up to more senior leadership positions. I owe this to my understanding of phenomenology, in knowing that each of us experiences our conscious world in different ways, and listening to each other is an important part of achieving a shared understanding. My perspective is that it is a privilege and honor to lead people in organizations, particularly in healthcare where people and patients are the focus. Phenomenology has helped me understand who I wanted to be and am as a leader.

Phenomenology also brought new meaning in personal relationships. My children were young at the time of my dissertation process, so I was able to apply some of my learning in raising my children. For instance, phenomenology influenced our dialogue with respect to their progress in school and development of their core values. Close friendships were also strengthened because of my phenomenological awareness. Visiting with close friends has so much more meaning since finishing my doctorate journey because I can see and share in their worlds as they do. One example is of a friend losing her mother. I could understand her loss because I too had lived that experience with my mother, which might not have happened prior to learning about phenomenology.

Phenomenology and hermeneutics also influenced my perspective on society. Daily, I remind myself that the conscious experience and how we see ourselves in the moment can affect those around us. Learning phenomenology facilitated my realization that we share meaning and understanding in different ways because we each experience our conscious life worlds differently. This causes me to reflect back to van Manen's (1990) simple but profound statement, "There are no right answers." It is how we share and understand the meaning of our conscious world that is important. This statement has resonated with me ever since, and I am comforted to know there are always new truths to be unveiled through shared conscious meaning.

Learning about phenomenology and hermeneutics was no easy feat. It was like learning a foreign language embedded in difficult concepts. I am grateful to David and Valerie, who had the ability to teach and translate the philosophical underpinnings of very difficult subject matter. This was a phenomenological experience in itself. As phenomenological professors, they possessed the skills to successfully lead us through intensives, an experience I will never forget. Once I grasped the idea whether phenomenology is epistemology (knowing) or ontology (being), and the difference between the two, it is really the type of question one asks that drives the inquiry. This helped me frame where I wanted to drive my research. Further understanding that phenomenology can be either thought of as a philosophy or a methodology was a pinnacle moment in my learning process. It was refreshing to know that phenomenology did not fit the biomedical model I had worked in for so many years. Working with Valerie and David provided me a rich opportunity to learn and advance phenomenology as a research methodology, which will further enhance the shared understanding of the patients' conscious experience.

References

Becker, G. (1997). *Disrupted lives: How people create meaning in a chaotic world*. Berkeley, CA: University California Press.

Bestul, M. B., McCollum, M., Stringer, K. A., & Burchenal, J. (2004). Impact of critical pathway on acute myocardial infarction quality indicators. *Pharmacotherapy*, *24*, 173-178.

Benner, P. (1984). *From novice to expert: Excellence and power in clinical nursing practice*. Menlo Park, CA: Addison-Wesley.

Benner, P., & Wrubel, J. (1989). *The primacy of caring*. Menlo Park, CA: Addison-Wesley.

Bentz, V. M. & Shapiro, J. J. (1998). *Mindful inquiry in social research*. Thousand Oaks: CA, SAGE.

Brady, I. (2000). Anthropological poetics. In N. K. Denzin & Y. S. Lincoln (Ed.), *Handbook of qualitative research* (2nd ed.), (pp. 949-979). Thousand Oaks, CA: SAGE.

Broyard, A. (1992). *Intoxicated by my illness and other writings on life and death*. New York, NY: Ballantine Books.

Chase, S. E. (2005). Narrative inquiry: Multiple lenses, approaches, voices. In N. K. Denzin & Y. S. Lincoln (Ed.), *The SAGE handbook of qualitative research* (3rd ed.), (pp. 651-679). Thousand Oaks, CA: SAGE.

Clandinin, D. J., & Connelly, F. M. (2000). *Narrative inquiry: Experience and story in qualitative research*. (F.M. Connelly, Trans.). San Francisco: Jossey-Bass. Inc.

Clandinin, D. J., & Rosiek, J. (2007). Mapping a landscape of narrative inquiry: Borderland spaces and tensions. In D. J. Clandinin (Ed.). *Handbook of narrative inquiry: Mapping a methodology* (pp. 35-75). Thousand Oaks, CA: SAGE.

Creswell, J. (2009). *Research design: Qualitative, quantitative, and mixed methods approaches*. Los Angeles, CA: SAGE.

Crotty, M. (1998). *The foundations of social research: Meaning and perspectives in research*. Thousand Oaks, CA: SAGE.

Flood, A. (2010). Understanding phenomenology. *Nurse Researcher*, *17*(2), 7-15.

Frank, A. (1991). *At the will of the body: Reflections on illness*. New York, NY: Mariner Books.

———. (1995). *Wounded storyteller: Body illness and ethics*. Chicago, IL: University of Chicago Press.

Gadamer, H. G. (1972/1989). *Truth and method* (2nd rev. ed.). (J. Weinsheimer, & D. G. Marshall, Trans.). New York, NY: Continuum.

Glense, C. (1997). That rare feeling: Re-presenting research through poetic transcription. *Qualitative Inquiry, 3*, 202-221.

Grondin, J. (1994). *Introduction to philosophical hermeneutics*. New Haven, CT: Yale University Press.

———. (1995). *Sources of hermeneutics*. New York, NY: SUNY.

Heidegger, M. (1962). *Being and time*. (J. Macquarie & E. Robinson, Trans.). New York, NY: Harper & Row.

Kennedy, B. L. (2009). Infusing participants' voices into grounded theory research: A poetic anthology. *Qualitative Inquiry, 15*, 1416-1433.

Kleinman, A. (1988). *The illness narratives: Suffering, healing, and the human condition*. New York, NY: Basic Books.

Koch, T. (1995). Interpretive approaches in nursing research: The influence of Husserl and Heidegger. *Journal of Advanced Nursing, 21*, 827-836.

Laberge, C. G. (2012). *The experience of heart attack: Individual accounts of primary percutaneous coronary intervention survivors*. (Doctoral dissertation). Retrieved from ProQuest Dissertations and Theses database. 3503952.

McNamara, M. S. (2005). Knowing and doing phenomenology: The implications of the critique of "Nursing Phenomenology" for phenomenological inquiry: A discussion paper. *International Journal of Nursing Studies, 42*, 695-704.

Mitchell, G. J. (1994). Discipline-specific inquiry: The hermeneutics of theory-guided nursing research. *Nursing Outlook, 42,* 224-228.

Morris, D. B. (1998). *Illness and culture in the post-modern age*. Berkley, CA: University of California Press.

Munhall, P. (1994). *Revisioning phenomenology: Nursing and health science research*. : Crocket, TX: Publications Development Company.

Oiler, C. (1982). The phenomenological approach in nursing research. *Nursing Research, 31*, 178-181.

Palys, T. (2003). *Research decisions: Quantitative and qualitative perspectives* (3rd ed.). Toronto, Ontario: Thomson Nelson.

Paley, J. (1997). Husserl, phenomenology and nursing. *Journal of Ad-*

vanced Nursing. 26, 187-193.

Parse, R. (1990). Parse's research methodology with an illustration of the lived experience of hope. *Nursing Science Quarterly, 3*(1), 9-17.

Playle, F. (1995). Humanism and positivism in nursing: Contradictions and conflicts. *Journal of Advanced Nursing, 22*(5), 979-984.

Polkinghorne, D. (1988). *Narrative knowing and the human sciences.* Albany, NY: SUNY.

Pratt, M. (2012). The utility of human science in nursing inquiry. *Nurse Researcher, 19*(3), 12-15.

Riessman, C. K. (2008). *Narrative methods for the human sciences.* Thousand Oaks, CA: SAGE.

Risser, J. (1997). *Hermeneutics and the voice of the other: Re-reading Gadamer's philosophical hermeneutics.* New York, NY: SUNY.

Sontag, S. (1978). *Illness as metaphor.* New York, NY: Vintage.

van Manen, M. (1990). *Researching lived experience: Human science for an action sensitive pedagogy.* New York, NY: SUNY.

Walters, A. J. (1995). The phenomenological movement: Implications for nursing research. *Journal of Advance Nursing, 22*, 791-799.

Watson, J. (2004). *Caring science as sacred science.* Philadelphia, PA: F. A. Davis Co.

Weinsheimer, J. (1985). *Gadamer's hermeneutics: A reading of truth and method.* New Haven, CT: Yale University Press.

Whitsitt, D. R. (2010). Illness and meaning: A review of select writings. *Journal of Humanistic Psychology, 50*, 108-113.

Zaner, F. M. (2004). *Conversations on the edge: Narratives of ethics and illness.* Washington, D.C.: Georgetown University Press.

About the Author

Carol Laberge, PhD has worked in healthcare since 1983, maintaining various nursing roles with an emphasis on cardiac and critical care. In 2012, she obtained a PhD in Human Development from Fielding Graduate University. Carol is passionate about patient- and family-centered care with attention to a patient's experience with acute illness. Resulting from these pursuits, in 2015 she accepted the British Columbia (BC) Quality and Safety Council award for leadership, having co-designed a new cardiac surgery program. She has held many senior leadership positions in healthcare and is currently the Provincial Executive Director with Cardiac Services, BC, Canada. She is also a mother of two grown children and lives with her husband in Vancouver, BC. Contact: cglaberge@shaw.ca

CHAPTER 6
Re-Placing Myself: Perspectives on the Experience of Work/Home/Life Place

Lori K. Schneider, PhD

Fielding Graduate University, Alumna

Abstract

Completing one's dissertation research and earning one's PhD, while substantial accomplishments, take on different significance when viewed from the larger places in which one dwells in life. In this chapter, I revisit the ways in which my graduate studies and my mentors have shaped the person I continue to become. I begin by placing myself in the story: considering the love of and sensitivity to place that I have felt since childhood. Next, I place myself as a scholar, with a review of my scholarly development and how I found my way to and through the dissertation process. My dissertation—a hermeneutic phenomenological exploration of how remote workers in global corporations experience local place—became a profound engagement with Martin Heidegger's writings about place. Then, I discuss how I "re-placed myself" after the dissertation, enlarging my sense of place through learning to live in two homes. I consider how I "moved to and through new places" in the process of learning to run, caring for my husband during his terminal illness, and then running and writing my way through the places of my grief. Finally, I reflect on dwelling in life as place and on the importance of phenomenology in the life that I lead today.

Keywords: Dwelling, global, Heidegger, home, local, phenomenology, place, remote work, running

Introduction: Placing Myself in the Story

Several years ago, I completed my dissertation (Schneider, 2009), a hermeneutic phenomenological exploration of how remote workers in global corporations experience local place. At that time, it seemed to be a definitive statement, but now I view it in the context of the person I have become.

Fielding faculty tell incoming students that "you don't get a PhD, you become one." They invite us to think deeply and explore widely across the social science disciplines and cultures of inquiry before selecting a research topic and finally developing a substantive, incisive dissertation question. We are encouraged to bring our identity—who we are and whom we hope to become—into this learning process.

Like many Fielding students, I came to my doctoral studies convinced that I knew who I was, what I wanted to study, and how I would research it. I was a confident, successful career professional who held well-honed views concerning leadership theory. Yet, to my surprise, my preconceived notions of scholarly discipline were uprooted on the first day of orientation. As an introvert who worked at home alone, I was disturbed by everything from the too-close arrangement of the chairs to the too-exuberant urging of Fielding faculty to share my hopes and dreams. In the midst of the cacophony I gravitated to the one faculty member present who exuded a quiet calm and talked about philosophy. I took a leap of faith and asked Valerie Bentz to be my mentor; she graciously agreed.

Although I had no idea at that time, my story of coming-to-be as a phenomenologist and a scholar had begun long before I met Valerie. My choice of dissertation methodology would eventually be determined by the research question that I asked and the way that I asked it. However, those things themselves arose from deep within my personal history and my natural way of relating to the world. I cannot remember a time when I did not approach my own experience through a reflective, interpretive lens, essentially narrating my life even as I lived it. I tell myself about my experiences as I am having them. The stories I tell myself then reverberate, as I remember and re-tell them to myself.

I remember bodily-and-emotion-laden sensory images: the breathless joy of examining a bright-yellow, bitter-tasting, just-picked dandelion in my back yard; the spongy, squishy feel of grass under my bare feet as I ran as fast as I could, arms and legs flailing; the soft-firm touch and black-coffee breath of my mother holding me close as she explained that our cat Cookie was not going to return. In those same moments, I also remember imagining that I was on a "nature walk" through my backyard. I remember pretending, as I ran, that I was a horse. I remember imagining that I was playing with Cookie, even as I struggled to understand that she was gone forever.

All of these memories are grounded in places. I can take myself in my memory to virtually every square inch of the back yard where I picked dandelions and ran around in circles. I can see and smell and feel the sofa that my mother and I sat on, and I can place it along with all the other furniture in a room that I have not seen in fifty years.

The ideas of place, sense of place, and being in a place hold a fascination for me. Both my parents had a strong sense of place, but in different ways. My mother had no sense of direction; she got lost if she drove around the block the wrong way. Yet when we stood in front of the farmhouse in Wisconsin where she had grown up, she told us that north was over there by the barn, while the fence was to the west. She had no trouble navigating when she was back in her home place. Although she never felt fully at home in California, she planted lilacs as a reminder of home. Furthermore, she made sure that her children became as familiar with our back yard as she was with her childhood farm.

My father, on the other hand, had lived in many places as a child and had no sense of being embedded in a place, although (perhaps because of this) he possessed an uncanny sense of direction. As an adult, he made a home and stayed there. Although he stubbornly rooted himself in this place, he was also a keen traveler who showed us much of the United States on our vacations. Part of my sense of place is a sensation of a road continually unwinding and opening toward the horizon.

I married a restless man who never stayed content in one place for long. We moved approximately every two and a half years, buying and selling ever-larger houses. Each time he insisted that this was *the* perfect house. I would try to settle in and make it a place that felt like home to me. Each time, just as I grew attached to that place, he became discontented and persuaded me to move again. I would feel heart-wrenched over leaving this place that I had, once again, managed to make "feel like home."

Most of our homes were situated in extraordinary places. We had a home on a golf course, with expansive green views in the middle of the city. We lived on a densely-treed half acre adjacent to National Forest. We lived 5,000 feet high on the edge of a mountain, looking straight down at thousands of houses and, on the occasional clear day, looking southwest one hundred miles to the ocean. As I began my dissertation research, we were living on a bluff top, precariously perched fifty feet above salt water yet in a place so beautiful that the risk felt almost worthwhile. Within each home, I learned to create personal places: a corner, a window, a room, sometimes just a chair that was *my place,* zealously guarded and not to be disturbed by anyone.

While I have always felt the weight of this personal history with respect to place, I had not fully acknowledged its significance in my life, nor was I aware of how much phenomenology has had to say about the experience of being in a place. At Fielding, I would learn that phenomenology concerns itself with lived experience and employs a careful discipline of close observation and thorough description in order to gain understanding of and insights about a phenomenon of interest. As Max van Manen (1997) noted, phenomenology focuses on the "four fundamental existentials of spatiality, corporality, temporality and relationality" (p. 102), with spatiality defined as *lived space* or *place*. Yet phenomenology has taken two distinct approaches to an understanding of lived experience. Edmund Husserl and those who follow his example, such as Don Ihde (1986) and Clark Moustakas (1994), tend to focus on phenomenological method. We observe an object from a particular place, at a particular angle or perspective, focusing first on this aspect and then on another. In contrast, Martin Heidegger and his follows have tended to discuss phenomena more metaphorically, with careful attention to the hidden, forgotten meanings of words and the fine distinctions between concepts. Heidegger's own writings, especially his later essays such as "Building Dwelling Thinking" (1971), focused explicitly on place, with many helpful examples of and distinctions between the concepts of home, place, work place, and experiences of being in a place. As a result, contemporary scholars who study phenomenology of place, such as Jeff Malpas (1999) and Robert Mugeraurer (1993), follow Heidegger's approach to phenomenological thinking.

None of the foregoing would have been interesting to me as I began my studies at Fielding. My graduate study and the things that I have learned since then constitute a full personal transformation from a would-be "expert" to a scholar/philosopher. This transformation has been an iterative process of reflecting on my values and passions while also engaging deeply with phenomenology as research method and, ultimately, as a life practice.

In the following sections, I first discuss "placing myself" as a scholar, the process of working through my graduate studies and completing my dissertation. Second, I consider "re-placing myself" immediately after the dissertation, because of life events that caused me to rethink my conceptions of home and place. Third, I describe "moving to and through new places" in life, real and metaphorical places that challenged me to develop new strengths, essentially redefining my life philosophy in terms of the trail unfolding before and behind me. Finally, I reflect upon dwelling in life as place and upon the broader ways in which phenomenology informs and enriches my life.

Placing Myself as a Scholar

I spent my entire career working in the information technology industry. As an employee working for a large global corporation, I was expected to do its bidding at whatever cost to other aspects of my life. At the age of 39, I was forced to accept a job assignment that required an unmanageable commute of more than two hours each way. After fourteen hellish months of this, my husband and I made the difficult decision to move from our home high up on the mountainside and into an extremely ordinary condo in the city.

To soothe my broken heart, I took a few "fun classes" at a local university. These few classes multiplied and eventually led to a master's degree in Organizational Leadership. This achievement revitalized my career and rekindled a nearly forgotten dream of earning my PhD. Throughout my life, I have been proud of my intellect, my rationality, and the ways I have used these talents to set and achieve goals. Yet one life goal, that of earning a PhD, had been set aside for my career. I regretted that, and I began looking for a path to achieving it.

Fielding's learner-focused, virtual approach to doctoral studies held promise as a place where I might fulfill my dream while still working. Fresh from my master's program and full of ideas, I came to Fielding determined to find "truth" that would have real-world consequences. For my planned doctoral research, I envisaged a rigorous, large-scale survey study that would find a correlation between personality type and leadership style. I thought I knew what the answers would be and what I needed to study to get to those answers.

Yet from the beginning, Fielding's faculty challenged me to rethink my preconceived ideas. I experienced a series of shocks to my identity and my beliefs about the world. For example, I learned about personality theories that posited that the "I" is a construct; that who "I am" is fluid and changing over time and place. My rational self struggled when I was asked to listen and respond to parts of myself that I had pushed firmly to back corners: What am I feeling now, what is that tension in my body and where does that come from? I resisted: how is any of this relevant to what I want to research?

As I delved into the study of research methods, I experienced a profound epistemological crisis. If, as the postmodernists say, no truths are final—if truth is tentative, theoretical, and rests on prior knowledge that is ultimately not empirical—then how could I know the "truth" about anything? How could I construct a survey that would not presuppose the answers I hoped to find? I suddenly doubted that anything was real, much less researchable. A wise professor told me that I had to take something on faith or that I would be unable to research anything.

According to Valerie Bentz and Jeremy Shapiro (1998), given that the social science researcher cannot avoid bringing her self into the research, then she *must* bring herself, along with her values, experience, and assumptions, *while making these as explicit as possible*. But how could I do such "subjective" research and convince the corporate Vice President who was approving my tuition reimbursement that my efforts or results had any validity? Whatever topic I chose to research, I knew that the setting would have to be in or directly applicable to my workplace.

In the interest of making progress toward my degree, I set aside both my epistemological crisis and my concerns about workplace relevance. I spent some time studying ecological theories. This action was a conscious attempt to *ground myself* in something. In reading about mountains and rivers and ways of being on the earth—and in simultaneously putting my feet to the ground and walking mountain and beach trails near my home—I understood. I reconnected with my childhood "nature walks" and grasped that if a tree falls in the forest without humans to hear it, it indeed makes a sound as it reaches the earth, and through its death a chain of interconnected organisms will live their own life cycles

155

and nurture the next generation of trees. That cycle recurs whether or not we are around to call the tree a Douglas fir, clear-cut its brethren, or destroy its ecosystem. The world exists as undifferentiated phenomena, but it surely exists. It is merely our perception of it that we construct. The earth is real, and so am I. My lifetime of accumulated place experiences, with their layers of sensory and emotional significance resting upon real locations, is real and it matters.

With this insight, my uncertainty about myself and the world vanished. I realized that something about "being in a place" or "sense of place" was so integral and important to me that I needed to understand it intimately and embrace whatever it might teach me. When I discussed this interest with my mentor, Valerie, she described it as a "very phenomenological topic," but I did not see the connection until she guided me to hermeneutic phenomenology.

My initial reading about hermeneutic phenomenology revealed that it makes explicit the idea that we all have our unique experiences of reality. It claims that together, through sharing our perspectives, we can arrive at an increasingly rich interpretation of reality—always subject to additional interpretations, yet combining the richness of one's personal lived experience with the activity of collaboratively making sense of one's experience in the context of others' experiences. I read a few papers early on that demonstrated the potential of hermeneutic phenomenology to describe and synthesize the perspectives of multiple individuals in order to reach a deeper understanding of a phenomenon. In particular, Turner's (2003) explication of hope as seen by Australian youth provided a glimmer of what a hermeneutic phenomenological research method might look like in practice, while Rehorick's (1986) account of his and his students' experience of an earthquake demonstrated the power of phenomenological writing to capture the range of emotions and sensations associated with an unfamiliar phenomenon.

As my studies continued, I learned that phenomenology was originally founded upon Edmund Husserl's (1999) assertion that one can access the experience of consciousness and an understanding of the essence of "things in themselves" by "bracketing" one's awareness and focusing first on one aspect of one's experience, and then another. Martin Heidegger (1962) added a hermeneutical or interpretive dimension to phenomenology, drawing on his interpretation of ancient texts and obscure etymologies in order to tease out concealed meanings and bring unknown or forgotten truths to light. Hans-Georg Gadamer (2004) went further still in incorporating hermeneutics into phenomenology, writing of the *horizon* or vantage point, which can be broadened by other perspectives ("fused" with other horizons) through encounters with others (texts or humans) or with additional experiences over time.

As a research method, hermeneutic phenomenology requires ongoing, careful reflection on the researcher's own assumptions, biases, and personal experiences with respect to the phenomenon under investigation. It also requires similar reflection and interpretation on the part of the research participants. The interpretive process involves multiple interactions between researcher and participants and an explicit construction of a reality that incorporates the multiple perspectives of all participants. While de Sales Turner (2003) served as an example, van Manen (1997) provided a step-by-step procedure for how to conduct hermeneutic phenomenological research.

Although this way of approaching an inquiry was intriguing, I needed to hone my fascination with place experience down to a dissertation question that not only had substance and intrinsic interest for me, but relevance and potential value in my workplace. I also needed practice in "doing" phenomenology; that is, closely observing phenomena that interested me, identifying and bracketing my assumptions or preconceptions regarding those phenomena, and writing detailed descriptions or protocols about them.

Without yet knowing where my inquiries might lead, I plunged into David Rehorick's and Valerie's workshops on reading and writing phenomenology. As I began to engage with Husserl and Heidegger, I was startled by my vivid recollections of my first encounter with Heidegger. During my undergraduate study years before, I had taken a "philosophy of poetry" course. I had no background in philosophy, but I wrote poetry and I wanted to understand the thought processes behind writing and reading poetry. As it happened, the essays in Heidegger (1971) had only recently become available in English. In that long-ago class, I had read "The Origin of the Work of Art," "Language," and "Poetically Man Dwells." Furthermore, I was intrigued enough that I had gone on to read "Building Dwelling Thinking" and others on my own. During a bleak, lonely period as a young adult, I had found joy in Heidegger's descriptions of remote, beautiful places like the mountain "hut" to which he retreated to write. I had forgotten these things—but David and Valerie encouraged me to remember, and to explore more deeply.

Given an assignment to write phenomenological protocols, I bombarded David with words. I wrote exhaustive phenomenological protocols describing nearly every place I had ever worked, focusing on how each workplace looked, sounded, smelled, and so forth, and on how each place made me feel. I thought about the circumstances in my work life that had led me to the fortunate position of being able to work from home for the large global corporation where I had spent much of my career. Specifically, I thought about the moment a few years prior—when my husband had lost his job and we were trying to decide what to do next with our lives—that I realized that because I was already working from home, *I could live anywhere.* Beginning at that moment, we had made a series of decisions that led us from southern California to western Washington state.

As I reflected upon that insight, I realized that my life had changed as a result of working remotely for a global corporation, and that the nature of that change was related directly to a *shift in my lived experience of place.* I wondered whether other remote workers had felt a similar shift in their place experience. I also wondered how they and I mentally navigate through a workplace that is simultaneously global (with direct

engagement with colleagues in other parts of the world) and local (situated within one's home/neighborhood/community). With that, I had my
dissertation question: *How do remote workers in global corporations
experience and interpret local place?*

To situate the question in its scholarly setting, I included in my
initial literature review a survey of the literature in several divergent
areas. First, I looked at phenomenology of place and other approaches
such as geography and environmental studies to understand the experience of place and "sense of place." Edward Relph (2000), Yi-Fu Tuan
(1990), and John Jalbert (2006) provided good examples here. Second,
I considered the nature and processes of globalization from economic
(for example, Bhagwati, 2004), cultural (such as Shiva, 2005), social
(Giddens, 2003; Friedman, 2005), and corporate (Cavanagh & Mander,
2004) perspectives. Third, I reviewed the existing research on remote
work. These sources (such as Crandall & Gao, 2005) typically took the
perspective of the corporation, examining the effect of remote working on worker productivity and return on investment. However, a few
researchers (including Steward, 2000; Tietze & Musson, 2002) considered subjective phenomena such as remote workers' lived experience of
time, which were directly relevant to the phenomenon I wished to study.
My engagement with each of these bodies of literature was ongoing because of the iterative nature of hermeneutic phenomenological research.
In addition, I later reviewed the literature on architectural theory as it
has been influenced by Heidegger, and closely examined selected writings of Heidegger himself. I thus returned several times to the literature
in order to more deeply understand and interpret what my research participants were telling me.

For my dissertation research, I worked with eight research participants, all of whom were full-time remote workers for global corporations (defined as a U.S.-based corporation with decentralized operations
in at least three countries and more than 1,000 employees world-wide)
who had worked from home for between three and twelve years. Six

people worked for the same corporation as I did; I received approval from my management to do research in my work place.

I conducted my research via a series of extended, open-ended telephone interviews, held individually with each participant. I began by asking all participants to recollect and describe a place or places that held particular personal meaning for them. I asked them to describe their home offices in great detail, focusing on sights, sounds, and other sensory impressions, along with the ways they structure or organize their offices to be conducive to work and supportive of their needs. I asked them to situate their offices within their homes, considering details such as the threshold between "work place" and "home place." They discussed their interactions with distant work colleagues. They described their communities and the ways in which they participate in local events, inside and outside of work. Finally, I encouraged them to provide photographs showing any aspects of their home offices, homes, or communities that were special to them; about half of the participants did send photos.

I audio recorded our conversations and had them transcribed. Then I wrote lengthy individual summarized descriptions, drawing on each participant's words to describe his or her lived experience of the remote global/local work place. Each person reviewed, edited, and approved this summarized description. In essence, I worked with each participant to write a phenomenological protocol.

I then reviewed the individual descriptions as a whole, interpreted what I was reading, and identified common themes. I wrote descriptions of each theme, again drawing on the words of individual participants and incorporating my own insights into place experience. Each participant reviewed and approved the consolidated thematic descriptions. This phase of the research was recursive; each revisit incorporated and enabled deeper hermeneutic interpretations.

Concurrent with the interview and interpretation process, I continued to reflect upon my own place experiences. I also engaged more deeply with Heidegger's (1971) essay "Building Dwelling Thinking" and the remarkable influence it had had on architectural theory. This influence had begun almost immediately after Heidegger's 1951 lecture—given in Darmstadt, Germany, to an audience of architects and engineers—that would later become "Building Dwelling Thinking." Heidegger's ideas were taken up quickly by the architect Alvar Aalto (Petzet, 1993) and then by others. This influence has extended to contemporary architects such as Peter Zumthor (2006) and Michael Benedikt (1987), whose work has drawn directly on Heidegger's ideas about authentic dwelling and who have written about architectural theory in explicitly phenomenological language.

Ultimately, because Heidegger's writings about place are often viewed as entangled with and tainted by his brief alignment with the Nazi party in mid-1930s Germany, I wrestled with Heidegger's attachment to his home town of Messkirch, his feelings about his country, and his relationship to his own two homes. I found parallels between his background and my own (my mother's family were farmers originally from near Messkirch). I concluded that, while Heidegger exhibited poor political judgment, his sense of place was probably fundamental rather than an intentional idealogical glorification of the "homeland" on his part. At Heidegger's core, it seems, he actually was the sturdy peasant who hiked for many miles on his favorite trails through the mountains.

Throughout my dissertation process, Valerie (my committee chair) and David (my de facto research mentor) encouraged me to reach further toward a mastery of phenomenological concepts and methods with respect to understanding the lived experience of being in a place. They repeatedly nudged me toward broader horizons of insight and interpretation. While such work is never "complete," I eventually developed a model of place experience that identified five themes and afforded limited generalizations.

First, *the threshold between work and home* concerned how remote workers manage the threshold or transition between their home/work places and their home/work lives. Several research participants used a visual boundary ("when the office door is closed, Dad is at work"), while others preferred a more fluid threshold and shifted seamlessly from home to work modes throughout the day.

Second, *creating spaces for interaction at work* addressed how remote workers manage task-related and social interaction with colleagues and how they collaborate at a distance. Because the research participants all worked in high technology industries, all were proficient with messaging systems, online meeting spaces, and other means for creating a container for work-related interaction. They used a variety of methods for informal social interaction, including casual texting, occasional visits to a central office, and regularly-scheduled meetings with colleagues for coffee. Some occasionally felt lonely, but all found ways to create interaction spaces.

Third, *the remote worker in the community* dealt with the relationship between remote workers and the broader local places beyond their home offices. Working from home frees up time formerly spent commuting and makes it possible to spend more time in one's local community. Several research participants reported doing more with their families, beginning an exercise program, or participating in community volunteer or political activities. All expressed a greater appreciation for their local community as a result of spending more time in it.

Fourth, *place as an opening of possibilities and choosing of alternatives* highlighted the experience of remote workers who have chosen, moved to, or created a place that expresses who they are and how they want to live, unconstrained by physical ties to a centralized work place. Several research participants, including myself, chose to relocate to another state or (in one case) another country to improve their quality of life and the way they wished to live. Everyone mentioned ways in which they had subtly or substantially reorganized or redesigned their home offices or entire homes to serve their personality and needs at work and at home.

Finally, *work place in the context of the remote worker's life* considered how the home work place fits within the individual circumstances of the remote worker's life. Some participants appreciated that working remotely allowed them to live near family members or in places with good schools. One person had relocated at his employer's behest, and then began working from home; he felt no attachment to his current location but was not yet ready to decide where he wanted to live next. Others, nearing retirement, were in the process of making that decision.

The first two themes were shared by all of the research participants, although managed differently by each. These themes have appeared in prior research on remote work, often expressed in negative terms. For example, Anita Greenhill and Melanie Wilson (2006) argued that remote working creates role conflicts that contribute to poor work/life balance, especially for women. Cecily Cooper and Nancy Kurland (2002) described professional and social isolation as a significant problem for remote workers. Yet all of my research participants skillfully managed the threshold and described no significant problems with work/life balance or isolation.

In contrast, the themes of place within community, place as possibility, and place within life context suggested three possible ways of experiencing and interpreting place in general; that is, they suggested something unique that my research had revealed. Focusing, therefore, on these themes, I developed a three-fold model, representing three facets of place experience that I designated as CENTER, SETTING, and SOURCE. This three-facet model is not hierarchical; each facet contains, reflects, and tends toward the other two. An individual's primary orientation to place may change over time and in different contexts.

CENTER is a view of place experience and interpretation in terms of being grounded in history and relationships, or rooted in a home place or *community*. This facet is based on the participants' descriptions of the experience of working/living in a home community, where they had lived most or all of their lives and had chosen to remain near family and friends.

SETTING is a view of place experience and interpretation in terms of life *context*, or the activity, convenience, or purpose that take place within a place. This facet is concerned with a utilitarian approach to place: some participants were required to live near a former employer, had chosen a neighborhood with good schools, or had prioritized some other life purpose over their place experience per se.

SOURCE is a view of place experience and interpretation in terms of *possibility*, generativity, inspiration, or transcendence. This facet is a creative approach to place experience, an active place-making by an individual who envisions an ideal place and chooses or arranges her surroundings to inspire, nourish, or transcend limits. Several research participants described place-making as an invitation to create a desired life, calling upon places as sources for development.

While this model and the insights that it generated arose direct-ly from my repeated engagement with the research participants, in the background I continued to examine my personal place experience through my ongoing dialogue with Heidegger's later essays. I began to converse with Heidegger almost as a research partner. The concept of the fourfold of earth, sky, mortals, and divinities became critical to my understanding. I saw that the homes my husband and I had chosen were, whenever possible, oriented to the *sky*, perched on the edges of things and featuring views that we looked out upon but did not participate in. They were in beautiful SETTINGS (locational contexts in which we lived our lives), or I lived in them as SOURCES of aesthetic inspiration (we loved the beautiful views from safely behind the glass walls of our homes), but they lacked a CENTER, a sense of rootedness in the *earth* or connection to community. In one of our homes, our commute had been so long that our few hours at "home" were primarily devoted to sleep. We passed through our small mountain town each morning and evening, almost as tourists, with no relationship to other *mortals* who lived there, and no sense of the history (*divinities*) that had taken place

164

there.

With this realization and after much discussion with my husband, it was I who insisted, this time, that we move. We sold the waterfront house and bought an architecturally interesting house in the center of town. Although its large windows and skylights face the *sky*, this house sits firmly grounded on the *earth* of its location within the grid of the city's streets. I feel the presence of *mortals* and *divinities* (the community and its history) here, in the way its room configuration and usage served the evolving needs of its original architect-owner and now serves the ways in which I dwell within it.

Re-Placing Myself After the Dissertation

I finished my doctoral studies with a depth of self-awareness and self-efficacy that I never imagined possible at the time I had begun. Yet I had also learned that there will always be further questions and new challenges. I had already taken on one new challenge before completing my dissertation. I had begun to run. However, learning to run was a long, slow process for me, and did not become a priority until later.

Of more immediate concern after my graduation, my restless husband revealed that he was struggling to cope with Pacific Northwest winters. While he loved our home during most of the year, he could not bear living here through another cold, damp winter. Over the next several months, he campaigned to convince me to purchase a second home: a condominium in the southern California desert. I finally agreed, on the condition that we choose an architecturally interesting mid-century modern home. By agreeing to this purchase, I committed myself to developing a new conception of "home." I would have to become what is commonly called a "snowbird," or a seasonal migrant who uproots oneself from a northern home each winter and travels to reside in a warmer place for months at a time.

In grappling with this initially unpleasant idea, I began to think of it in terms of *platiality*. According to Una Chaudhuri (1997), platiality in the context of the theatre acknowledges that not only does each play have a setting, but the setting becomes a real place in itself. The stage is not merely a place for performance "but a place to *be*, a fully existential arena" (p. 10). Perhaps I could play myself on a different stage for a few months a year. Perhaps I could even work from the stages of two different home offices.

Taking platiality as the set of qualities that identify a place and make that place a specific, personal place for me to be, I expanded that concept, calling it *bi-platiality*: the lived experience of dwelling in two places, each with its unique platial qualities. To make sense of my imperative to become bi-platial, I drew directly on my dissertation research method and the insights that I had gained about my personal platial experience. I reflected deeply, writing a series of phenomenological protocols. I considered the process of coming to feel "at home" in two homes. I explored the process of developing a sense of place in two very different communities. I considered what it is like to work from home in two different homes, drawing not only on my own experience but that of Heidegger, who wrote in both his city home and his mountain "hut." Finally, I related all of these perspectives to the CENTER/SETTING/SOURCE model of place experience.

These two homes from which I worked could not have been more different. In my Pacific Northwest office, I sat comfortably on the bottom floor of a multistoried house in the center of my small town, looking out my window at the flowers in the courtyard. I could feel the weight of history and the lightness of the house soaring above me. When I walked upstairs, I could admire the view of the county courthouse and its chiming clock, the harbor and strait with ships from all over the world coming and going, and further across the strait to Canada.

In contrast, my desert home was on a busy street, with a constant roar of traffic. I looked out my window at a small patio with a few languishing succulents. The condo's strong horizontal lines and flat roof created a sense of hunkering down against the heat, noticeable even in the winter. The only way to see the horizon was to walk through the front door and out to the street. Yet during the time I lived and worked there, I came to appreciate the beauty of the desert and the interesting history of the town in which we lived. I learned to value the fact that I lived lightly there, free from most of my treasured "things" that were temporarily left behind. Although I worked in that home, it did feel at times as if we were there on vacation.

Heidegger's similar experience of living and working in two homes—his grand house in Freiburg and the mountain "hut" at Todtnauberg that he used as a writer's retreat—helped me accept my bi-platiality. Heidegger's poem-essay, "The Thinker as Poet" (1971), can be read as an attempt to capture the inner significance to him of the hut in its mountain setting. It was a place that comprised "the core of philosophy 'up there,' a palpable veracity that outreached irrelevances he perceived in life 'below'" (Sharr, 2006, p. 73). He seemed to have felt more at home psychologically in the hut, yet he chose to live most of his life in Freiburg. In my terms, he used the hut as a SOURCE of inspiration, the place he went when he needed to devote large blocks of time to focused work, while his city house served as CENTER and SETTING, suited to his status as a philosopher and scholar.

Given these perspectives, I saw that my husband's seasonal affective disorder had driven him to seek a second home/place as a SETTING that would improve his mental health, whereas I desired a home/place that could serve as both SOURCE of inspiration and CENTER within in my community. As a result of my reflections during my dissertation writing, I had come to experience my Pacific Northwest home/work place as a SOURCE of creativity and growth that was also embedded in the CENTER of the small town where I wanted to become a full member of the community. In contrast, the desert home/work place was only a SETTING in which I must spend time against my wishes.

Although I was now expected to leave my Pacific Northwest home for a few months each year, I realized that I could grow to love and feel at home in any number of places, and that by recalling a loved place, I could be there at any moment. Heidegger (1981) expressed this idea when he reflected on a pathway in his birthplace of Messkirch:

> When the puzzles crowded into each other and there seemed no way out, the pathway was a help. It quietly escorts one's steps…. Time and again when my thinking is caught…I go back to the trail traced by the pathway through the fields. (p. 69)

Like Heidegger, I could revisit a place in memory; I could "place" myself there when I needed to. While in my desert office, I could summon the sensation of walking through a mountain meadow and draw comfort from knowing I would return to that place soon. Surprisingly, I could enjoy a similar imaginary experience, sitting in my Pacific Northwest office and revisiting the stark beauty of the desert.

In this respect, I came to view the experience of place as SOURCE as inherently *multi-platial* or *trans-platial*—a sense of place as it affects the mind. Precisely because I have lived in many places and thought deeply about their meanings to me, my "sense of place" has become flexible and expansive enough to encompass many meanings. I have learned to get what I need from the places in which I find myself.

Moving to and through New Places

This transcendent quality of multi-platiality had still more to teach me. I would learn my next lessons about my lived experience of place while running. The call to run had come from deep within me while I was in the midst of my dissertation writing. I had taken a break on a sunny summer morning to stand by our local trail and watch people running our hometown half marathon. I knew nothing about running other than my childhood memories, but I was stirred by these passing runners wearing numbers on their chests. They were simultaneously in a beautiful place and moving through it, in a heroic way that celebrated both the place and themselves. I recalled that a Fielding alumna had advised me to pick a short-term goal upon which to focus immediately after completing my degree, in order to prevent post-degree "let-down" and possible depression. Standing by that trail, I decided to run a half marathon.

This was an odd, almost impossible choice of goal. At the time, I could not walk comfortably due to marginally-successful bunion surgery followed two years later by a broken bone in my left foot. I had gone to a physical therapist, who had fitted me with a custom orthotic. When that did not help, she shrugged and commented that I would probably never walk without pain. I chose not to accept this diagnosis. I started running because I wanted to rediscover my early memories of running, and because of a feeling that I had places that I wanted, and perhaps needed, to go.

The process of becoming a runner unfolded very gradually for me. I bought a treadmill and walked many miles on it before finally breaking into a tentative trot. I ran and walked many more miles on the treadmill before I felt brave enough to run outside on a trail. Much of the time I had formerly devoted to my doctoral studies, I now devoted to running. Because of inexperience and lack of coaching, I injured myself and missed the half marathon I had registered for, yet after my recovery I returned to running. During our first winter in the desert, I even learned to run on city streets at dawn before the temperature became too warm.

Then, shortly after our return from the desert the following spring, my husband was diagnosed with lung cancer. I became his cheerleader and caregiver, while also working full time for a manager who demanded superhuman efforts as payback for the time I had been distracted by dissertation writing. My only respite, the place and time I created for myself, was running. By that time, I was finding significant psychological benefits from running, and I sensed that running would carry me through the difficult months ahead.

I am not the first runner to realize that running changes a person. The lived experience of running has been described phenomenologically. Jeremy Wisnewski (2007) learned to run as a phenomenological experiment to determine whether creating a new type of relationship with his body-as-runner would, as Maurice Merleau-Ponty had maintained, create a shift in his perception and understanding of the world. At first, he could only run well if he occupied his mind with something, anything but thinking about running. As he gained confidence and skill, he began to think about nothing—he simply ran, fully absorbed in the runner's world.

What sort of place is this runner's world? When I moved from my home treadmill to a waterfront trail, I discovered a new world. Up close to the strait, I saw ships, waterfowl, and other people coming and going with passing days and seasons. I started to find and name places along the trail. At first I could only run to "that tree," but soon I was marking "two miles out" and "half a mile to the finish line" as places on my running map.

As my husband's disease took its inevitable course over the next ten months, I began to write about running. I would come home from a run exhausted, help my husband in any way I could, and then wring out my emotions with words on the screen. I had again registered for a half marathon, and while I seldom had time for the long runs required to be fully ready to run 13.1 miles, the running I was able to do gave me time alone to process what was happening to us. In the final weeks of my husband's life, I recruited friends to stay with him while I ran. My friends' support enabled me to complete that half marathon; my husband died four days later.

After his death, I spent many hours running and writing. Running gave me time to think, places to cry, and freedom to grieve. Phenomenological writing and reflection helped me make sense of my life. Both gave me places and moments of beauty and joy in the awareness that I, at least, still lived. While I ran, I could enjoy every second, every step, without worrying about what had been or what might be. I could be fully inside of the experience of be-here-now, and that could be enough. I could simply be in the world:

170

> My eyes and mind took in every detail, every rock and root, every ridiculously green tree, shrub, and patch of moss in my surroundings…. I was in a flow state; I was in running nirvana…. That was me out there dancing on the trail, bounding from step to step, feeling the lightness in every cell of my body. (Schneider, 2013, p. 13)

As I repeatedly ran and then wrote about my experiences and thoughts while running, I saw that my grief would be "a long, wrenching process of false starts [and] bad steps…the only way…[to] keep going is to keep telling myself, 'one step at a time. One foot in front of the other'" (Schneider, 2013, p. 8). Running literally grounded me in a sustainable place: "The physical act of putting one foot in front of the other allows me to suspend…the emotional imperative to take steps toward thresholds" (p. 9).

Eventually I did cross those thresholds. As Heidegger (1981) said, "the call of the pathway awakens a sense which loves the free and open and, at the propitious place, leaps over sadness and into a final serenity" (p. 71). As time passed, mile markers (both real and metaphorical) approached and then faded behind me. I found my way, and I found my place. "It's such a relief to feel…a semblance of solid ground beneath my feet. And the beginnings of a way forward" (Schneider, 2013, p. 10).

Running occurs in places; the runner travels in, through, and to places. Sometimes the running place is a gestalt in which I experience being in that place: an immersive impression of a shimmering green and blue world. At other times a run is not a single place, but a series of *places that I run through*:

> This little rise, that turn and the way it reveals a different view… all become etched in my memory until I could run them in my dreams. I no longer have to look at my watch to know how far I've run; the trail tells me where I am. (Schneider, 2013, p. 15)

As I run in and through places in and around my community, I see them in new ways. In terms of place as CENTER, SETTING, and SOURCE, I have become more grounded, more rooted, in my community as a CENTER of my place experience. Places such as the grocery store, a row of restaurants, our city pier, and a public restroom all look different and mean different things when approached on foot from what they do from a car.

As a runner, I prefer not to experience place primarily as SETTING—for its utilitarian purpose only. Running on a treadmill is not very enjoyable; a high school track is only slightly better. I would rather run in natural environments than on city streets: "Yet during a race I appreciate the utilitarian value of the aid stations…[and] each finish line is a setting that I savor" (Schneider, 2013, p. 17).

Running has most dramatically sharpened my experience of place as SOURCE. The places I have run to and through have inspired me and offered moments of transcendence. My experience of running through grief serves as the basis of a subtle change in my philosophy of life. As I did with my two home offices, I call upon my memories of a much-loved running trail as sources of strength. I have gained the ability to travel to, through, and beyond the darkest places, by attending to and caring for my physical and mental states. I now live my life moment by precious moment, one step at a time.

Conclusion: Dwelling in Life as Place

As the places and times of my doctoral studies at Fielding recede further behind me, I continue to reflect upon my experiences of being in a place. Guided by Valerie's and David's mentorship, and enriched by Heidegger's ideas, I have extended my thinking to new places as I approach, examine, and interpret new horizons of life experiences.

One of the significant gifts of my dissertation research was a heightened appreciation of architectural theory. I now have words to describe the sensation of walking into a built place and glimpsing what the architect saw and intended me to see: the way the light reflects around a room at different times of the day and year, or the way a walkway leads to a doorway, simultaneously obscuring and teasing what lies across the threshold. These insights have made *my* special place, my home, all the more meaningful to me. This home is truly *my* home, the place where I have now lived for nearly a decade—longer than anywhere else in my adult life. With no one urging me to uproot myself, I have become fully settled in this place.

Yet with passing time, new interests, and new relationships, the places within my home have become transformed. My home office is now a home brewery and bicycle garage; my late husband's TV room is slated to become a taproom. I now share my home with a partner, who has brought his own ideas about how to dwell within these walls. It is not entirely coincidental that he is an architect. As we subtly negotiate our respective place-making, I learn from his technical perspective on structural space while I teach him the phenomenological concepts of lived place that were not emphasized in his long-ago architectural curriculum.

As I have spent more time in my community, I have gained a broadening circle of new friends. On any night, I can walk into a certain local tavern and see friends. I call it "the living room;" it is, metaphorically, a cozy extension of my home, a place where my friends and I can sit a while and talk over a local craft ale. We discuss politics and the weather, as people do in taverns; sometimes we venture into philosophy. This place looks shabby to first-timers, but what I see there is my cherished, layered memory of many happy occasions and the anticipation of future such times.

I have brought my training as a phenomenological researcher to my new interest in brewing and judging beer. Through sensory training I learned to describe in great detail what I see, smell, taste, and feel as I approach and then taste a beer. As a certified beer judge, essentially what I do is write brief protocols describing beers that are presented to me for evaluation.

Beyond the insights into lived experiences that phenomenological research and writing have provided, a phenomenological perspective continues to shape my experience of life in general. In addition to "becoming a PhD," I have become a phenomenologist. I live more intentionally now. My focus is different: more discerning and at the same time more open, more receptive. My goals are simpler, yet larger in some ways. While running still brings me the greatest joy, I have added other types of daily physical activity. I have become an endurance cyclist, completing several multi-day tours and seeing the road unwind before me from another new perspective (higher than the view from on foot but still much more detailed than the view from a car). I take long hikes in our local mountains, no longer content to observe the view of wilderness but actively placing myself in the middle of it. I have returned to the daily practice of meditation after a lapse of more than thirty years. Through all of these transformations, I have reached a place of comfortable bodily presence—a sense of "at-homeness" in my body that I had lost somewhere in the process of leaving childhood behind. I am becoming a whole person.

With passing time, the places in which I dwell continue to grow layers of meaning and reveal new perspectives on my life. I shape and respond to places based on these lived meanings. I treasure the places that have shaped me as my life has taken place within them. As I re-place myself, my places continue to re-place me.

References

Benedikt, M. (1987). *For an architecture of reality.* New York, NY: Lumen Books.

Bentz, V. M., & Shapiro, J. J. (1999). *Mindful inquiry in social research.* Thousand Oaks, CA: SAGE.

Bhagwati, J. (2004). *In defense of globalization.* New York, NY: Oxford University Press.

Cavanagh, J., & Mander, J. (2004). *Alternatives to economic globalization: A better world is possible.* San Francisco, CA: Berrett-Koehler.

Chaudhuri, U. (1997). *Staging place: The geography of modern drama.* Ann Arbor, MI: The University of Michigan Press.

Crandall, W. R., & Gao, L. (2005). An update on telecommuting: Review and prospects for emerging issues. S.A.M. *Advanced Management Journal, 70*(3), 30-37.

Cooper, C. D., & Kurland, N. B. (2002). Telecommuting, professional isolation, and employee development in public and private organizations. *Journal of Organizational Behavior, 23*, 511-532.

Friedman, T. (2005). *The world is flat: A brief history of the twenty-first century.* New York, NY: Farrar, Strauss and Giroux.

Gadamer, H. (2004). *Truth and method* (2nd ed.). (J. Weinsheimer & D. G. Marshall, Trans.). New York, NY: Continuum.

Giddens, A. (2003). *Runaway world: How globalization is reshaping our lives.* New York, NY: Routledge.

Greenhill, A., & Wilson, M. (2006). Haven or hell? Telework, flexibility, and family in the e-society: A Marxist analysis. *European Journal of Information Systems, 15*, 379-388.

Heidegger, M. (1962). *Being and time.* (J. Macquarrie & E. Robinson, Trans.). New York, NY: Harper & Row.

_____. (1971). *Poetry, language, thought.* (A. Hofstadter, Trans.). New York, NY: HarperCollins.

_____. (1981). The pathway. (T. F. O'Meara & T. Sheehan, Trans.). In T. Sheehan (Ed.), *Heidegger: The man and the thinker* (pp. 69-72). Chicago, IL: Precedent Publishing.

Husserl, E. (1999). The basic approach of phenomenology. In D. Walton (Ed.), *The essential Husserl: Basic writing in transcendental phenomenology* (pp. 60-85). Bloomington, IN: Indiana University Press.

Ihde, D. (1986). *Experimental phenomenology: An introduction.* Albany, NY: SUNY Press.

Jalbert, J. E. (2006). Lifeworld cartography: Echoes, footprints, and other guideposts to the self. In G. Backhaus & J. Murungi (Ed.), *Ecoscapes: Geographical patterning of relations* (pp. 181-203). Lanham, MD: Lexington Books.

Malpas, J. E. (1999). *Place and experience: A philosophical topography.* Cambridge, England: Cambridge University Press.

Moustakas, C. (1994). *Phenomenological research methods*. Newbury Park, CA: SAGE.

Mugeraurer, R. (1993). Toward an architectural vocabulary: The porch as between. In D. Season (Ed.), *Dwelling, seeing, and designing: Toward a phenomenological ecology* (pp. 103-128). Albany, NY: SUNY.

Petzet, H. W. (1993). *Encounters and dialogue with Martin Heidegger, 1929-1976*. (P. Emad & K. Mary, Trans.). Chicago, IL: The University of Chicago Press.

Rehorick, D. A. (1986). Shaking the foundations of lifeworld: A phenomenological account of an earthquake experience. *Human Studies, 9*, 379-391.

Relph, E. C. (2000). Geographical experiences and being-in-the-world: The phenomenological origins of geography. In D. Seamon & R. Mugeraurer (Ed.), *Dwelling, place and environment: Towards a phenomenology of person and world*. Malabar, FL: Krieger Publishing.

Schneider, L. K. (2009). At home in the global work place: Remote workers' experience of local place in global corporations. (Doctoral dissertation). Fielding Graduate University, Santa Barbara, CA. UMI No. 3357415.

_____. (2013). "Re-placing" myself one step at a time: Grief, running, and transformation. Presented at Society for Phenomenology and the Human Sciences (SPHS) annual conference, Eugene, OR, 2013.

Sharr, A. (2006). *Heidegger's hut*. Cambridge, MA: Massachusetts Institute of Technology.

Shiva, V. (2005). *Earth democracy: Justice, sustainability, and peace*. Cambridge, MA: South End Press.

Steward, B. (2000). Changing times: The meaning, measurement, and use of time in teleworking. *Time and Society, 9*(1), 57-74.

Tietze, S., & Musson, G. (2002). When "work" meets "home:" Temporal flexibility as lived experience. *Time and Society, 11*(2/3), 315-334.

Tuan, Y. (1990). *Topophilia: A study of environmental perceptions, attitudes, and values* (2nd ed.). New York, NY: Columbia University Press.

Turner, dS. (2003). Horizons revealed: From methodology to method. *International Journal of Qualitative Methods, 2*(1) Winter, 2003.

van Manen, M. (1997). *Researching lived experience: Human science for an action sensitive pedagogy* (2nd ed.). London, Ontario, Canada: The Althouse Press.

Wisnewski, J. J. (2007). The phenomenology of becoming a runner. In M. W. Austin (Ed.), *Running and Philosophy: A marathon for the mind* [Kindle version] (pp. 35-44). Retrieved from amazon.com.

Zumthor, P. (2006). *Thinking architecture* (2nd ed.). (M. Oberli-Turner & C. Schelbert, Trans.). Basel, Switzerland: Birkhauser Publishers for Architecture.

About the Author

Lori K. Schneider, PhD, originally from southern California, vowed as a teenager that she would someday move to a small town in a cooler and greener place. As an undergraduate studying linguistics at the University of California, Los Angeles, she spent a year at the University of Edinburgh, Scotland. There, she demonstrated her California accent in phonetics class, developed a taste for real ale, and learned to love short, damp winter days. Upon her return to the United States, she leveraged her language-learning ability into a 35-year career in information technology. Her expertise included operating systems, utilities, information security, and technology policies. After earning an MA in Organizational Leadership at Chapman University in Orange, California, she shifted her career focus to learning and development. She became one of the first employees in her corporation to work full time from home. This innovation enabled her to move, with her late husband, to a small town in western Washington State. She then went on to earn an MA and PhD in Human and Organizational Systems at Fielding Graduate University in Santa Barbara, California, and completed her career as an executive coach. She now spends her time running, cycling, brewing beer, and hiking the mountain and beach trails of Olympic National Park. Contact: drloriks@gmail.com

CHAPTER 7
The Experiences of Heideggerian Hermeneutical Methodology: Round Dance of Servanthood, Philosophy, and Myself

Ayumi Nishii, PhD

Fielding Graduate University, Alumna

Abstract

In this chapter, I reflect on my experiences of working on a dissertation study that used a Heideggerian hermeneutical methodology, on the subject of servanthood in servant-leaders. With this methodology, researchers fuse the horizon of texts (data) with philosophical thoughts and the researchers' fore-structure (pre-understandings and perspectives based on them). During my interpretive process, the voices from the servant-leaders (15 study participants) and philosophers' thoughts started to closely intertwine and mirror each other, as if they were doing a round dance of three with me. The round dance was particularly eminent with the themes of *eros* (aspiration toward the ideal; Plato), *philia* (friendship; Aristotle), *I-Thou* (Martin Buber), and *authenticity* (Martin Heidegger). My reflection touches on these themes from the study by describing the study participants' experiences and my interpretive work, as well as their influence on me as a researcher, an aspiring servant-leader, and as a person. I also discuss my thoughts on knowledge and knowledge creation as a part of my learnings from the hermeneutic study.

Keywords: Heidegger, hermeneutical methodology, phenomenology, hermeneutics, servant leadership, servanthood

Introduction: The Beginning of the Journey

How about "the experiences of leading"? One of the workshop attendees at the Institute for Heideggerian Hermeneutical Methodologies popped up with this suggestion when I was telling the group that I needed to come up with a new research topic and question. It was the beginning of my journey with my dissertation and the methodology.

I knew I wanted to do a dissertation on servant leadership because its leadership philosophy of serving others and higher purpose deeply resonated with me. It is a concept since ancient times, and Robert Greenleaf (1970/2008) coined the term *servant leadership* in his essay, *The Servant as Leader*. It has been enthusiastically embraced among leaders, practitioners, and scholars who resonate with it. Despite the popularity, however, other people think it is too ideal or not appealing because of the connotation of being a servant or even a slave. I thought it would be meaningful to work on this subject for my dissertation since I have a strong interest in it.

Prior to attending the five-day Institute workshop, I had done a preliminary literature review and developed a research question about servant-leaders' foresight. But my dissertation chair wisely suggested my reconsidering this direction because of the challenges of finding instances of this phenomenon. This suggested change came just a couple of days before the trip to Indianapolis to attend the Institute at the School of Nursing in Indiana University.

The timing was not a problem because I was not planning to use the Heideggerian hermeneutical methodologies for my dissertation. The purpose of attending the workshop was to satisfy my personal interest. I took a phenomenology course at the beginning of my doctoral program, and it opened my eyes toward phenomenology, especially Heidegger's philosophy. After completing the course, I continued to study Heidegger through self-paced coursework, and my appetite to learn his thoughts was growing.

People say everything happens for a reason. Maybe it is true. During the literature review on foresight, I came across a dissertation that used a Heideggerian hermeneutical methodology, and I read about the Institute in the author's study on nurses' intuition. I immediately looked it up on the internet and found out that the workshop was not only offered to the public, but also scheduled one week before the servant leadership conference I was committed to attend in the same city. I was too curious about the methodologies rooted in Heidegger's philosophy to pass up this coincidental opportunity.

During the week at the Institute I had mixed experiences, from being overwhelmed with the philosophy and the methodology, to being excited, inspired, and awed. At the same time, I was totally confused and lost about what I should do with my research question. On the last day of the workshop, each participant talked about her dissertation or research status. After hearing my distress about my research question, one of the students suggested, *How about the experiences of leading?*

I had not thought about such a fundamental question regarding servant leadership, but she had a good point. Phenomenology, especially a Heideggerian approach, pays attention to mundane experiences that people have in their daily and practical lives. It appreciates the subtle and nuanced experiences that are often overlooked, and it tries to illuminate what is taken for granted in larger contexts. I left the Institute and went home to California with this small seed of thought. It was the beginning of the journey.

My hermeneutic process was listening to and dialoguing with the study participants' voices (data); it was also a "converging conversation" (Diekelmann & Diekelmann, 2009), in other words, the "fusion of horizons" (Gadamer, 1960/2004) among the data, philosophical and non-philosophical accounts on the emerging themes, and my own experiences and biases (*fore-structure* in Heidegger's term). In addition, I realized during the interpretive process that philosophers' thoughts and the experiences of servanthood from my study participants were closely intertwined and mirrored each other, and this in turn influenced me as a researcher and as a person, which I had not anticipated. It was as if they were doing a round dance with me. In the discussion below, I will reflect the round dance, along with my experiences of and learnings from the Heideggerian hermeneutical study, which I titled, *Servanthood as Love, Relationships, and Power: A Heideggerian Hermeneutic Study on the Experiences of Servant-Leaders* (Nishii, 2017).

Fore-Structure

I wrote that the beginning of the journey started at the Institute, but it is actually not accurate. My journey had already begun a few years prior to the Institute because my experience there was not free from my historicity, my experiences of servant leadership as well as Heideggerian philosophy. Heidegger (1927/2008) considers that human ("Dasein") understanding has a close relation to temporality; a person's past experiences influence the way one understands now and the future—and conversely the future influences the now and the past. The new experience will feed into the hermeneutic circle. He calls this structure *fore-structure* (pp. 191-195). Fore-structure consists of *fore-having* (practical familiarity, past experience, or background), *fore-sight* (perspectives that come from fore-having), and *fore-conception* (anticipated or projected understanding, something we grasp in advance). Below, I discuss my ties to servant leadership and Heideggerian philosophy. This provides the context for subsequent reflections on what I learned from my research.

Servant Leadership

My professional background is in human resources, training, and organizational development in the corporate world, and I first encountered the term of *servant leadership* more than fifteen years ago. This paradoxical term caught my eye, but I did not pay close attention. In fact, I was rather appalled with the term, thinking that someone tried to sell a leadership methodology by having a unique and catchy name. I also did not find anything new in the idea of leaders serving others. Therefore, I did not bother learning what it was, and I even had forgotten about it. Several years ago, however, I was requested to accompany a client to the annual Greenleaf Servant Leadership Conference, which was my re-encounter with the concept of servant leadership.

Contrary to my low expectation, the experience of the conference—listening to keynote speakers and participating in various sessions, visiting servant-led companies as case study tours, and meeting leaders and participants who aspire to be servant-leaders—turned out to be full of excitement. I had never felt so welcomed, accepted, and connected to the other participants and speakers at any conference. They reminded me of the people-oriented leaders, managers, and colleagues I had known in the past. Moreover, being surrounded by so many of service-oriented people at one place was a profound experience. I thought, *Who are these people? I want to know more about them!*

Since then, I have developed networks with servant-leaders through the conferences and other various occasions. I also immersed myself with literature and workshops on the subject.

Heidegger's Philosophy

I did not have any scholarly background in philosophy, and I had never been interested in studying it. Therefore, when I took the phenomenology course, I was nervous: even the terms "phenomenology" and "hermeneutics" sounded very intimidating. To my surprise, one of the readings of the very first week—Heidegger's (1951/1971) short essay, "The Thing"—captivated me, leaving me both puzzled and excited. At that time, I did not understand the essay fully but I was attracted to Heidegger's poetic and enigmatic expressions. More importantly I sensed a glimpse of what I knew from ancient Asian thought in his writing. Both the poetic expression and the resemblance to the Asian culture were not something I had anticipated from my initial image of Heidegger. As I progressed in the course, I was more and more intrigued by the Heideggerian approach to phenomenology, which lets things themselves appear and tries to observe phenomenon without the subject and object separation.

I read some of Heidegger's original works and various secondary literature, but the several books by Gen Kida were most important for me to get into the notoriously difficult philosophy of Heidegger. Kida was a well-respected Japanese scholar on Western philosophy, who had a special interest in phenomenology, especially in Heideggerian philosophy. He tackled the challenge of constructing the unwritten part of *Being and Time* by reviewing the Western philosophers before Heidegger and perusing Heidegger's works. Kida (1983, 1996, 2000) posits that the concept of nature that the Japanese have held since ancient times provides a useful perspective to understand Heidegger's thoughts, especially the notion of Being.

In his magnum opus, *Being and Time*, Heidegger (1927/2008) tries to overcome (or *deconstruct*, in Jacques Derrida's term) the ontological tradition that originates in Plato and Aristotle. This is the dichotomous apprehension of essentiality (*essentia*: what it is, what-ness, the precursor of idealism) and actuality (*existentia*: that it is, that-ness, the precursor of realism). Both consider the human being as a super-naturalistic existence who conceptualizes Being in a super-naturalistic manner. Heidegger argues that Plato and Aristotle distorted the question of Being; that is, they considered Being as a static *idea* or producedness focused on the present, not dynamic, temporal existence. This distortion has been carried over throughout the philosophical tradition.

Heidegger claims that the ancient Greeks (prior to Socrates, Plato, and Aristotle) were living harmoniously with nature, which they called *physis* (Kida, 1983, 1993, 1996, 2000; Moran, 2000). For them, *physis* meant something alive, self-producing, self-becoming, self-ending, and organic in nature, and all beings self-emerge there. For ancient Greeks, *logos* equated to *legein*, meaning collecting or collection of all beings

183

(Heidegger, 1956/2003; Kida, 1993, 2000). The ancient Greeks lived in harmony with *logos*, and in this harmony a question of existence or essence had never been posed. For them, Being (existence) was beyond the dichotomous understanding of *what* it is and *that* it is; instead, it had an organic, self-emerging nature. In this paradigm, humans do not possess the ultimate superiority to other beings (all life, nature, all things), and they exist relatively to others in a whole big system. There is no subject and object separation; humans (or any other existents) harmoniously exist as a whole. Kida (1983, 2000) postulates that Heidegger had another axiom in his mind when he called for the deconstruction of metaphysics: to understand Being based on *physis*, the nature and world pre-Socratic philosophers lived in. Kida sees a parallel between the experience of *physis* for the ancient Greeks and the experience of nature for the Japanese.

Contemporaries of Heidegger, such as Karl Jaspers, Rudolf Otto, Max Scheler, and Martin Buber, were introducing the ancient Asian concepts to European philosophical circles. Heidegger also had a strong interest in the ancient Asian thought (May, 1996; Parks, 1996). I was intrigued that Heidegger painstakingly examined the Western philosophical tradition and argued for the deconstruction of the tradition within the Western philosophical lineage instead of promoting something new from outside, that is, Eastern thoughts. My interest in Heidegger's philosophy grew, even though his thinking was not easy to digest.

This was my context when I attended the Institute for Heideggerian Hermeneutical Methodologies the first time. For the next three years, I kept going back to the Institute and participated in the workshop focused on philosophy (Institute for Hermeneutic Phenomenology, a four-day workshop). I studied philosophy and hermeneutics with nurse education researchers. The world of servant leadership and the world of hermeneutics were separately creating hermeneutic circles in my experience until the beginning of the dissertation journey.

The Study on Servanthood in Servant-Leaders

After the initial Institute, I did a thorough literature review on servant leadership. Although the literature is rich in the attempt to define the concept and explore relationships with other leadership concepts, I wanted to know what the experience of "serving" entails for leaders.

Interpretive research with the Heideggerian approach aims to examine shared meanings in people's contextual practices and uncover and illuminate the taken-for-granteds in everyday practice (Benner, 1994; Diekelmann & Ironside, 1998). Researchers who choose to take this approach tend to "relish nuances, appreciate differences, embrace ambiguity, and seek uniqueness in contextualized lived experiences" (Wojnar & Swanson, 2007, p. 178). This is in contrast to the descriptive and eidetic Husserlian phenomenology that looks for patterns and universal essential structure of phenomena. The Heideggerian approach was a good fit for my inquiry because I wanted to understand the mundane nature of servanthood in leaders and what is hidden behind it.

I set a research question, *How do servant-leaders who have line responsibilities experience servanthood in organizations?* I then collected narrative data from face-to-face interviews with 15 other-nominated servant-leaders in the United States. These participants worked in various types of institutions (such as corporations and government) with various work responsibilities (such as manager or CEO). Throughout the interpretive (data analysis) process, I *dwelled* (Heidegger, 1952/2008) and *played* (Gadamer, 1960/2004) with the data. Instead of a mechanistic process of coding, I took a more organic process of *naming*. Heidegger believes "the essence of poetry is understood as *naming*, bringing something to revelation in language" (Moran, 2000, p. 218; italics in original). I reflected on my own experiences and fore-structure while having dialogues with the participants' stories; I named themes or any pointers that I felt calling my gaze and contemplation. Concurrently I read widely from pertinent philosophical and non-philosophical ac-

185

counts on emerging possible themes, and they provided deeper or new perspectives to understand the data.

As my hermeneutic circle "circled" and went deeper, themes started to emerge, and three larger themes started to form. It was as if I began to recognize three constellations after gazing at numerous random stars in a dark sky. Prior to recognizing the constellations, I tried to play with the possible themes by typing them on small pieces of papers and moving them around on a large table to try to make sense of it. At this point I had many possible themes and I had a hard time seeing a structure. Juggling the themes (concepts) was a stimulating and satisfying experience, but I stopped the process as I realized that it was more of a conceptual and analytical exercise; it moved me away from the participants' experiences themselves. Heideggerian hermeneutical researchers assume that understanding is deeply informed by experiences (Heidegger, 1927/2008; Smythe, 2011). Therefore, I took a further step of engaging with the data by crafting short stories from the data, and included it in the iterative process of playing, naming, writing, and reading.

Heidegger (1927/2008) suggests interpretation is understanding phenomena with "the structure of *something as something*" (p. 189; italics in original) and the as-structure helps to illuminate the salient facets of the phenomena. As such, I captured the emerging themes in the as-structure and named the three constellations as follows: Servanthood as Love and Care, Servanthood as Relationships and Connections, and Servanthood as Power. Once I was conscious of these themes, I adjusted the research question to *How do servant-leaders who have line responsibilities experience servanthood as love, relationships, and power?*

The Experiences of Servanthood as Love, Relationships, and Power

These three constellations and their sub-themes are captured in Figure 1, but unlike the appearance of the figure that each item is in silos, the three constellations and their sub-themes are interrelated and mirror each other. I now briefly summarize each constellation and offer my synthesizing thoughts.

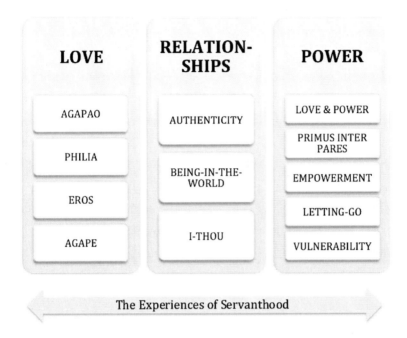

Figure 1. Three constellations of the experiences of servanthood.

Servanthood as Love and Care

"Servant leadership is, I think, primarily about love when you really boil it down." This comment from one of the study participants succinctly summarizes the sentiment that all the study participants hold. For the study participants, servanthood is based on their deep love toward others (including self in a non-egotistic way) whether they use the term of *love* consciously or not. They engage with other people with humanistic love, and develop it through interactions. For them, love is not just sentiment; it is action.

Servant leadership as a virtuous theory of *agapao* as moral and humanistic love is well established and embraced in the literature (Winston, 2002; Patterson, 2003, 2010), but the other facets of Greek love helped me highlight the elements of love as equal partners (*philia*), acceptance of others as a whole person (philia), love of wishing one's well-being and growth (philia), aspiration toward the ideal (*eros*), seeing possibilities in others (eros), and altruism (*agape*).

Servanthood as Relationships and Connections

"When caring, you hear, you feel a human connection. You feel a spiritual connection with another person." As one of the participants expressed in this remark, loving and caring are closely related to the experiences of relationships and connections with others. And the relationships include the one with self. The word *authentic* has a root in the Greek *autos*, that means "self, etc." (Inwood, 1999, p. 23). The experiences from the study participants indicated that their aspiration to serve others is genuine, and they *own* this value. Authenticity as ownedness (Heidegger, 1927/2008) is a facet of the study participants' relationships to self and others.

Because the participants are other-centered, they have high awareness about their relationships and connections with others. They consider others as equal human beings, and engage with others as *I-Thou* instead of *I-It* (Buber, 1923/2000). "I love helping people. What it comes down to is our relationships…. I look at everybody as a person, holistically. They're not the job they have to do." This remark came from a study participant who is naturally good at making connections with others, but even other participants who are not naturally good at connecting with people realize how precious relationships and connections are.

Servanthood as Power

"When you take care of the person as a whole, they produce better and more work because they want to. They want to follow someone who they know they can trust, and that cares about them." This remark epitomizes how the study participants recognize and appreciate the integrative power, power from love. The integrative power is not a conventional form of power in organizations such as winning power-games or monopolizing power for selfish reasons.

The unconventional power experienced by the study participants is not limited to the integrative one. They consider themselves as first among equals (*primus inter pares*) and they lead as well as follow. The concept of empowerment has been popular in organizations, but this concept assumes that the hierarchical power as empowerment can mean bestowing power from the have to the not-have. But the study participants consider that their staff and frontline employees have the power, and the leaders' job is to support them. Participants also experience letting go—or *surrender-and-catch* in Kurt Wolff's term (1976)—and vulnerability as strength.

Servanthood as Love, Relationships, and Power

In the acts of love, relationships and unconventional power, one of the things I saw is that the study participants dare to dwell in paradoxes. They walk on the "narrow ridge" in Buber's (1938/2014, p. 184) expression, meaning that they cope with uncertainties and polarities without ignoring or escaping from the reality of paradoxes or contradictions (Friedman, 2002, Chapter 1). They give their followers what colloquially is often called "tough love." The "tough" aspect of this experience is not only for the followers, but also for the servant-leaders. They empower or liberate their followers in the form of *leap-ahead care* (Heidegger, 1927/2008, pp. 158-159; Tomkins & Simpson, 2015) by letting the followers find solutions themselves so that they can grow.

Secondly, servanthood is not a static endpoint. Even the study participants who are considered as role models of servant-leadership feel a constant dilemma between the ideal and their own shortcomings (or selfishness). It is a constant movement toward the ideal, and it is a journey. Heidegger (1927/1962) considers the nature of Being as temporal and organic movement. Likewise, the servant-leaders are always *be-*

coming servant-leaders.

Lastly, servanthood as love, relationships, and unconventional power parallels with what Joyce Fletcher (1999) calls *relational practice*; how women work. A feminist scholar, Fletcher argues that feminine relational practice is generally not recognized and appreciated in organizations because the dominant norm is masculine and instrumental. Fletcher names this tendency *disappearing acts*. In this sense, servant leadership is also a disappearing practice as servant leadership is not a dominant mode in the conventional organization world. Although my study participants are aware that their way of leading or serving is "against the grain," they choose to be who they are and whom they aspire to be. For them, being *the servant as leader* is a way of life; it is not a leadership methodology.

Round Dance of Servanthood, the Methodology, and My Experiences

Again, Heideggerian hermeneutical methodologies are deeply rooted in Heidegger's and Gadamer's philosophy in its interpretive approach and research assumptions. They also encourage researchers to *play* (Gadamer, 1960/2004) with pertinent philosophical accounts in their process of interpretation. "Philosophical writing brings a different language, takes us back to more primordial experience, and gets us thinking beyond our own horizon of knowing" (Smythe, Ironside, Sims, Swenson, & Spence, 2008, p. 1395). I concur with these experienced hermeneutists; philosophical accounts gave me new perspectives on the study participants' experiences. They evoked both my affective and cognitive understandings of the study participants' voices.

To my surprise, as the interpretation process deepened, I started to realize that some of the experiences of servanthood and the philosophical accounts fed and mirrored each other. In addition, my past, present, and future were also closely interwoven with them as my fore-structure was a part of the hermeneutic process, and conversely the interpretive work affected my fore-structure. All parts of my dissertation findings had an impact on me. Now, I will focus on some of the themes from the constellations, namely *eros, philia, I-Thou,* and *authenticity* to share my interpretive work and the reflection of the round dance that impacted me as a researcher, as an aspiring-servant-leader, and as a person.

Eros as Aspiration toward the Ideal

Eros is often associated with romantic or erotic love. However, its original meaning of "love as aspiration toward the ideal" (Norton & Kille, 1971, pp. 81-84) was one of the themes that emerged from the data in my study. Greenleaf (1970/2008) postulates that servant-leaders aspire to serve even before they aspire to lead. The study participants have strong aspirations toward the ideal of servanthood, and they find intrinsic satisfaction in serving. But their aspiration is two-directional, between the ideal and the insufficiency as it is evident in the following comment from one of the study participants:

> I aspire to be a good servant-leader.... I'm flattered that XXX [i.e., his ex-boss] even thought to mention me as a servant-leader, but I'm sure I have my selfish moments. I'm sure I have the things where I'm not as proud of certain choices I've made as other choices. But I do always try to come back and say, "How can I do better? How can I be a better leader? How can I be a better servant?"

In *Phaedrus,* Plato (trans. 1892; in Norton & Kille, 1971b, pp. 96-98) talks about the image of the human soul as a charioteer of a pair of winged horses. While a god's chariot has a pair of perfect winged horses that can rise to heaven easily, the chariot for humans has a pair of the mix: one with an immortal, noble white-winged horse which aims aloft, and the other with a mortal, deformed black-winged horse that plunges below. With two horses that pull the chariot in the opposite direction, the ride for humans is turbulent and challenging. David Norton and Mary Kille (1971a) write that this two-directional image is at the very core of *eros,* the dilemma between desire and insufficiency: "He [a man] is a divided being.... He is torn between impulses of self-affirmation and self-negation, self-love and self-hatred" (p. 96).

The servant-leaders in my study struggle between the ideal of servanthood and the insufficiency or selfish moments, much like the charioteer of the two winged horses. To make their experiences more complicated, they also realize that the ideal is a moving target. One study participant, who was appointed Director at a government organization, has been working on him-self in his endeavor of becoming a servant-leader. He confessed the struggle:

> Since I took the position, I have been changing and different. But I've got a long way to go; I still have things I don't do well. A lot of things. It seems like it's a never-ending growth process. Just when I feel comfortable, there's something else. And it's almost frustrating because there is no end!

The more they grow as servant-leaders, the more they become aware that their understanding of servant leadership was not deep enough and they needed to grow more. But this feeling of insufficiency makes them strive for the ideal even more and want to fly higher. It is a constant dynamic tension between the aspiration toward the ideal and the acknowledgement of the gap in the actuality, and the result is the potential growth. It is an ongoing process of learning, and it is perhaps this process of growth that contributes in large part to their aspiration.

As I proceeded with the dissertation, I realized that my purpose was no longer for a degree but to serve the community of servant leadership and the community of Heideggerian hermeneutics. I wanted to produce a study that will help servant-leaders as well as hermeneutists. As a researcher who aspires to be servant-leader and to be a profound hermeneutist, I experienced the ride of two winged horses throughout the dissertation journey, especially during the interpretive stage. The more I aspired for the ideal of producing a helpful study, the more I became aware of my insufficiency. I often became discouraged and could not move forward, being caught in the dilemma. But the image of the charioteer offered me a light in the darkness, and I could embrace the struggle, keep aspiring, and move forward.

The awareness of the charioteer as my experience also made me more mindful about accepting and appreciating others as who they are. As much as I struggle, other people, too, experience the dilemma of the charioteer. It does not mean that I had been unaware of this before, but I feel my perspective, attitude, and actions toward others deepened because of this awareness.

Philia

Philia is often translated as friendship or brotherly love, but the concept includes mutual love between family members and the civic friendship such as relationships in business, religious, or social and political settings (Cooper, 1977, p. 620). Aristotle defines philia as "wanting for someone what one thinks good, for his sake and not for one's own, and being inclined, so far as one can, to do such things for him" (as cited by Cooper, 1977, p. 621). With philia, one accepts the other person as a whole, and wishes for his or her well-being and growth for his or her sake. It is other-centered love. One of the participants expressed it this way:

> Some of the hardest feedback I ever received came from Mark. The most difficult to hear feedback. But I knew the place he was giving me the feedback from. I knew he loved me, which is, you don't hear the word love in business much. But we've loved each other in that business setting. I had enormous respect for him. And enormous trust.

This participant and "Mark," another participant, worked at the same global company as senior executives, with Mark being his boss. They had the reporting relationship in terms of the organizational hierarchy, but they were connected by philia as equal human beings and with mutual respect for who they are. I sensed that their philia is what Aristotle calls friendship of character. Aristotle (trans. 1941; in Norton

& Kille, 1971b, pp. 230-29) postulates three kinds of friendship: friendship of pleasure (loving someone because the person gives pleasure), friendship of utility (loving someone because it gives an advantage to keep the person as a friend), and friendship of character (loving someone because of who the person is). Out of the three, Aristotle explains that the friendship of character is the long lasting one since the others fade away once a friend does not provide pleasure or utility.

In the organizational world, the friendship of utility may be dominant because workers are hired for their skills and expected to perform and show results. When one does not provide a needed skill or performance, she may be replaced. However, the experiences of the study participants are closer to the friendship of character, which is to love the persons for who they are and wish for their well-being and growth. Accepting the other as a whole does not mean avoiding confrontation. Rather, because of love, they dare to confront even if confronting is not a pleasant experience. One of the participants (Chief of Police) described a time when he gave difficult feedback to his staff (Deputy Chief) because the deputy's performance was not satisfactory:

> It got tearful because he didn't see that he was doing and acting in a certain way, and he was losing respect from his own team. And I had to just tell him that, I was honest with him…"I know it hurts you to see the bad stuff in this evaluation. I wouldn't be doing you any favors if I wasn't honest with you." Well, the conversation was very uncomfortable…. I think that's why many times organizations just continue this culture of mediocrity because we're not willing to confront and have those crucial conversations with people.

> I won't talk about this a lot because it's corny, but I read a quote by great man who was a football coach in the National Football League. He said, "As the coach of this team, I don't have to like my players. But as their leader, I have to love them." And I feel exactly the same way here. I don't have to like my officers. Heck, I don't have to like my children and what they do, but I have to love them, right? Unconditionally. And I have to love my staff. I have to! Because otherwise what's the point? What's

the "why" of what I do? Why am I even here? How am I going to make a difference if I don't bring that to the table to say, "I care what you do and how you do it. And I care so much that I'm going to praise you and support you when you do it well, and I'm going to hold you accountable when you don't.

Erich Fromm (1956/2006) argues that love is not a passion but it is action: "The essence of love is to 'labor' for something and 'to make something grow'...love and labor are inseparable" (Fromm, 1956/2006, pp. 25-26). Milton Mayeroff (1971) expresses a similar idea using the term *care*: "To care for another person, in the most significant sense, is to help him grow and actualize himself" (p. 1). However, the labor of love and helping others grow is not always a rosy and uplifting experience. As the Chief of Police described, "Those two days drained me. Those conversations drain you, drain us all, and that's why we avoid them. I left here that first day, feeling like I'd just run a marathon. It was an emotional conversation." If someone was with another person only with the mode of the friendship of pleasure or the friendship of utility, he may not invest in his friend this much.

The concept of philia often challenged me. The basic characteristics of philia are quite straightforward and easy to understand—at least cognitively—but they are not easy in terms of actions in real life. I was questioning my actions and motivations in day-to-day dealings with people, and I had to question myself deeply sometimes about whether what I do for others is from the genuine other-centeredness or my hidden self-serving motives. I also found that it is a delicate balance between accepting others for who they are and confronting others for the opportunity for growth. I do not always know when or if I should or should not intervene. I also do not always have courage to give constructive feedback. My feelings are captured by a study participant who is a highly respected servant-leader.

The first time I read it [Greenleaf's essay, *The Servant as Leader*], I thought, "Oh, I believe in this." But I didn't truly understand it even though I thought I did. I think I underestimated what it meant and I thought, "I'm a servant-leader." But I was not very mature as a servant-leader. And the more I taught it, and made a personal action plan, the more I realized that I didn't have a lot of courage in holding people accountable. I didn't have a lot of skill in holding me accountable.

The awareness of philia also changed the quality of how I deal with literature as a researcher. More often than before, I tried to read other writings of philosophers and authors (or at least read about them) so that I can understand them better. With some, it was like developing a friendship with them. Engaging with literature had the element of having genuine dialogues—trying to understand the thoughts as they are, but confronting (critiquing) if there were disagreement—even with the historical philosophers whom I could have mythologized and blindly revered otherwise.

I-Thou

My study participant, the police chief, stayed with his deputy whole-heartedly during this difficult conversation. It was emotional to the degree that both of the police officers were in tears while having the conversation. The study participant (the Chief) explained, "I was just trying to be...[a moment of silence, looking for words]. *Professional* is not even the term. I was trying to be as passionate and compassionate as I could be with him." The constructive feedback made the Deputy furious, but after the Chief's endeavor of being passionate and com-passionate, their conversation got deeper and they could reach genuine understanding of each other. The connection between them transformed into *I-Thou*.

In *I and Thou*, Buber (1923/2000) contrasts two qualitatively differ-ent modes of existence or relation to others. I-Thou refers to a dialogi-cal being between self (me, I) and the other person (you, Thou), and it exists as the whole being without being subsumed by either. It is not a sum of *I* and *Thou* that exist independently; I-Thou is a dynamic and or-

196

ganic process. Contrary to I-Thou, *I-It* (or *I-He, I-She*) is a monological relation, in which each exists as an isolated entity. As *I*'s attitude toward *It* is detached, I experience It as a classifiable, predictable, usable, and manipulable object. Not like I-Thou, I-It never can be the whole being. I-It is, however, necessary for human daily interactions with others, and Buber suggests humans engage both I-Thou and I-It as a healthy alternation (Friedman, 2002, pp. xiii-xv). But only through a relation to others as I-Thou, can one become a unified whole being: "Without *It* man cannot live. But he who lives with It alone is not a man" (Buber, 1923/2000, p. 44, italics in original).

Most of my study participants are relation-oriented and good at making connections with others. One of the participants described the feeling of the connection as follows:

> When caring, you hear, you feel a human connection. You feel a spiritual connection with another person, that's just hard to explain. It's...you have empathy. At the end of the day, the greatest rewards in life really come from the connections we make with others.

However, not all servant-leaders are inherently relation oriented. Another participant confided with me that he was not naturally good at connecting with others, and he used to feel uncomfortable to share his personal sides to the people at work. He said,

> We have a couple of more locations besides the main office, but I haven't been getting to the other offices as often as I would like to. Some of that is time, but some of it is something else. You sometimes feel like you're constantly on a platform, and you're always on your game, and have to be cautious about what you say. In my mind, you have this wall up sometimes. As much as I want to be authentic and open, totally open, I still have personal things that disallow that.

But as a part of his servant leadership journey, he has started to recognize the importance of the deep human connection, and has been consciously working on it. He shared a story about visiting one of the employees, who became seriously ill.

> He became real ill recently, and I usually do what is expected of me—you send an email and whatever. But for some reason I felt I needed to go see this guy at his home. So, I went and saw him. That's something I wouldn't have done before. He told me a little bit about what was going on with him, but he made it a point to say what a nice place it is to work here. And it just set me aback. Here's this poor man, fighting this thing, and he feels strongly to tell me something like that, which is really meaningless in the big picture. But that made an impact on me about connecting with people. This is *real*. Me coming there meant something to him, and it meant something to me. It took me to another level about how important it is to connect. It's just been two weeks since that happened, and it's like... It's important to connect.

During the first two-thirds of my interview with him, I noticed that he seemed very uncomfortable to share his inner experiences with me, while he was much more talkative and animated when he was explaining the concept of servant leadership and what he has done to implement it in his organization. As the interview progressed, however, he mentioned that sharing his personal side and feelings were something he feels uncomfortable with. Therefore, when he was sharing the stories that contained intimate inner experiences towards the end of the interview, I was moved. I am very relation-oriented and appreciate connections with people, but I also have a side of being very private. Consequently, I resonated with him very much as I was learning about who he is. After the interview, he told me that he initially was nervous about doing the interview, but he felt my sincere listening made him comfortable. We were experiencing I-Thou togetherness.

Through contemplating on I-Thou, I became more aware of relationships and connections I create with others. Even if the experience does not go all the way to I-Thou, I at least started to pay more attention to how I engage with others. I recall when I caught myself depersonalizing the cashier at a store. I was in a hurry and asking her a question, and my mode of existence with her was I-It. I perceived this person as a cashier, forgetting that she is a person or human being. The realization was rather shocking to me as I had thought I treated other people well. But once I realized it, I started recognizing how one sometimes perceives and treats people as if they are job labels instead of human beings. I am not suggesting here that one needs to engage with others in I-Thou or as if they are family members or friends all the time. But I experienced that our mode of engagement with others changes the quality of relationship even if the relationship is a short encounter with strangers. The interpretive work "took me to another level about how important it is to connect" if I borrow the study participant's expression.

I-Thou became an integral part of my interpretive process because I engaged with the study participants' voices in the form of deep listening rather than treating their accounts as nothing more than data to be analyzed. Gadamerian hermeneutics "is concerned not so much with understanding more correctly...as with understanding more deeply, more truly" (Palmer, 1969, p. 215). When I first read this statement, I found it very liberating. In elementary school, I used to prepare for classes by memorizing *correct* answers. Even in literature classes I read guidebooks and memorized what these guidebooks described as the authors' intentions or the meaning of certain sentences or paragraphs. This practice influenced my way of thinking in my adult life in that I tend to be concerned whether I have right answers. Through the interpretive process of my dissertation, I realize that understanding more deeply and more truly is the act of engaging with texts in the I-Thou mode, with deep listening and dialoguing.

Authenticity as Ownedness

What I learned from the study participants' stories and actions is that they are fully aware of their values of servanthood and actively work on the values through their daily actions and reflections. They *own* the values, and it makes them who they are. One of the participants said,

I worked on my values and my life purpose for a long time.... I've been conscious about it for 40-some years. Consciously work on it. Some days better than others, but I'm always working on it. Always thinking about it.... [My mission statement] drives all my actions. I think about it every day. Not a day goes by that I don't.

Heidegger (1927/2008) argues the idea of authenticity as being in accordance with one's own, instead of following or being prescribed by social or cultural rules of what people normally do. Authenticity is "owning oneself and one's life in the sense of taking responsibility for oneself and one's life" (McManus, 2015, p. 5). For Heidegger, inauthenticity, the opposite spectrum of being authentic, is not a negative thing or thing to avoid. Heidegger does not discuss authenticity and inauthenticity in a moral sense. Inauthenticity is a part of being in a daily life. Humans are busy with coping in various roles and dealing with matters in their lives, and they often conduct these matters in the way other people normally do without being consciously aware of it. Heidegger calls such a mode the *they-self*, the un-owned self that follows the social, cultural, and average rules of other people. People are too caught up with coping, dealing with information, or living in average understanding of everydayness, and do not dwell on the significance of events (Moran, 2000, p.239).

However, all of the participants are acutely aware of their values, and they are consciously choosing to be *the servant as leader*, even though they know serving through leading is "against the grain" and "a different style from most CEOs." They follow their inner voice of "who you want to be" and "choose who you are." "It's about who you are as a person, first and foremost." They own the value of servanthood.

Charles Guignon (2015) explains Heideggerian authenticity as "becoming authentic—being disclosed to oneself as authentic—is a matter of finding out what it is to be really, fully human" (p. 16). It is the journey of becoming a whole being. To be fully human, however, is not always uplifting and delightful; it can enfold both positive and negative sides of being a human being, just like the image of the charioteer of the two winged horses. Not surprisingly, Bill George (2003), the proponent of authentic leadership, advocates that leaders be themselves, and he observes that authentic leaders use their strengths but also accept their shortcomings, which aligns with my observation of my study participants.

As I mentioned earlier in the sections on eros, philia, and I-Thou, I constantly reflected my own experiences, biases, and values as a part of the hermeneutic process. It was to interpret the data, but it was also a process of my becoming authentic—in other words, owning these values as my own. In doing so, philosophical concepts became more alive and concrete. It was the *doing* of philosophy.

Organizational theorists, Chris Argyris and Donald Schon (1974) pointed out that there is often a gap between people's *espoused theory* and *theory in use*. In other words, people's actual behaviors are sometimes different from what they think they do or value. In addition to this gap between the mind and real observable actions, I also started to question whether my espoused values were my own (authentic in Heideggerian sense) or just a result of following the they-self—and it was sometimes unclear. The participant I quoted earlier said that he has been working on his values every day for more than 40 years, but I can now understand why it is such a long process. It is a long pathway, to own oneself and be fully authentic.

The awareness of authenticity impacted me as a researcher as well. I often got stalled and could not proceed with writing or doing further interpretation because I sensed that my thinking was banal and my ideas too conventional. I also noticed that I became more uncomfortable incorporating suggestions from the committee members unless I totally agreed with their viewpoints. Even if the disagreement was because of my lack of knowledge in their fields of expertise, I preferred to contemplate long enough and stay true to my own thinking rather than correcting immediately what experts might say. My dissertation chair, a phenomenologist, was very patient and respectful about my process, letting my journey work itself out.

On Knowledge and Knowledge Creation

I have reflected upon my learning journey using the themes from my study findings. In this section, I would like to discuss my emerging thoughts from the dissertation project itself, through the lens of knowledge and knowledge creation.

The Hermeneutic Circle "Circles" – The Round Dance of Four-Fold

I completed writing my dissertation only a few weeks ago, and my hermeneutic circle is still emerging. Hermeneutical research is a never-ending process, and even writing this chapter provokes further interpretation and contemplation. I still cope with the dilemma of the charioteer about my dissertation, the dilemma between the ideal and insufficiency. But the ending of my dissertation is the beginning of the next, and I will keep the hermeneutic circle circling and the interpretive process continuing an upward (or deeper) "spiral" (Bentz & Shapiro, 1998, p. 42).

What I hope for is that I might have ignited an interpretive process so that they will find their own interpretations of what my study participants experienced. Hermeneutical researchers produce a different kind of knowledge—understanding as mode of being (ontology) instead of understanding as epistemology or cognitive information.

When a hermeneutic study is properly done, it works as Heidegger's notion of *techne*—that is, a catalyst for letting something appear, reveal, and bring-forth (Heidegger, 1954/2008; Kida, 1998). It will induce inherent knowing from the persons who read the text. Heidegger considers this process, *techne,* as a mode of knowing (Kida, 1998). Thus, it is a different kind of understanding of knowledge a scholar can provide through her research. Instead of installing a new piece of knowledge as a theory or model to readers from an expert to a non-expert (or to an-

202

other expert who lacked that piece of knowledge), hermeneutic research provokes the reader and invites her to join the journey of letting her knowing appear itself and making it her authentic knowledge.

In this knowledge creation, the relation between the researcher and the reader is equal, and the reader joins in the hermeneutic circle. This makes it the round dance of four: study participants' voices, philosophical (and non-philosophical) accounts, the researcher's voice (his or her experiences, fore-structure, and interpretation), and the reader's interpretation. Heidegger (1951/1971) poetically explores the nature of Being in his later work, "The Thing," and figuratively alludes that essential nature of a thing is unconcealed and revealed when the four-fold of earth, sky, divinities and mortals is gathered as mirroring onefold in the round dance of the four. He describes,

> Earth and sky, divinities and mortals—being at one with one another of their own accord—belong together by way of the simpleness of the united fourfold. Each of the four mirrors in its own way the presence of the others... The fouring presences as the worlding of world. The mirror-play of world is the round dance of appropriating. (pp. 177 – 178)

My experience of the dissertation has been a three-fold round dance until now, but hope I it will become the four-fold dance, including the future readers' hermeneutics. The readers' hermeneutics and their feedback will evoke new thoughts and interpretations in my hermeneutic circle, and it will make the true four-fold dance all together.

Familiarity of Researchers on Research Phenomena

I conducted the hermeneutic study on the topic I resonate and have familiarity with, but the methodology would be powerful whether or not a researcher has intimate familiarity with the phenomenon of inquiry. I recall a remark from the Director of the Institute, Pamela Ironside, during the methodology workshop I attended: "You don't have to have cancer to do a hermeneutic study on the experiences of cancer patients." I agree with her, having fully experienced the methodology myself.

During the phenomenology course at the beginning of my doctoral program, I was impressed by my classmates' phenomenological writing. A couple of them wrote deep reflections of their life challenges, such as depression. I had not personally experienced the same phenomena, but their voices and expressions evoked my inherent knowing or a feeling of familiarity in the unfamiliar. I resonated with the core of their experiences. It was the experience of feeling connected as one, or I-Thou.

As I develop a deeper relationship with phenomenology and hermeneutics, I notice that I have more genuine interests and curiosities about other people's experiences—especially the ones different from mine—not as a researcher but as a fellow human being. I want to "hear" (in the sense of deep listening) them as they experience, and I want to understand them. Even with the phenomena with which I am familiar, I am curious how others' experiences differ or what I am glossing over and assuming without noticing. I believe it is the attitude of wanting to attune to the other persons and embrace unfamiliarity and uncertainty, rather than researcher's familiarity to the subject of phenomenon, to make hermeneutical research successful.

Closing Remark: Appreciating Manifold Colors

When I was in the fifth grade, I saw Georges Seurat's painting, "A Sunday Afternoon on the Island of la Grande Jatte," for the first time in an art class textbook. I was fascinated to see a myriad of colored dots inside of what looked like one color from a distance. My experience of the Heideggerian hermeneutical study was like noticing and appreciating the manifold colors inside of shapes while delineating the figures and background.

The awareness of the colors and background goes beyond the sphere of research or being a researcher. It is a way of life for me now. My interest naturally goes to how people experience various matters. When

204

I started the dissertation project, servanthood in leaders was a topic for an inquiry, and Heideggerian hermeneutic phenomenology was just a research methodology. But both of the streams became intertwined and developed my nature and ability of deep listening, dialoging, I-Thou, authenticity, and creativity through vulnerability. In a way, my life before the dissertation journey was easier; I could get along by paying attention mainly to the outline of the figures and using the information from experts or in the manner of the they-self without questioning. Especially at the workplace which requires speed, this way of operation works well. But phenomenology and hermeneutics added more colors in my life and made my life much richer and more meaningful.

References

Argyris, C., & Schon, D. A. (1974). *Theory in practice: Increasing professional effectiveness.* San Francisco, CA: Jossey-Bass.

Benner, P. (Ed.). (1994). *Interpretive phenomenology: Embodiment, caring, and ethics in health and illness.* Thousand Oaks, CA: SAGE.

Bentz, V. M., & Shapiro, J. J. (1998). *Mindful inquiry in social research.* Thousand Oaks, CA: SAGE.

Buber, M. (2000). *I and thou* (R. G. Smith, Trans.). New York, NY: Scribner. (Original work published 1923).

_____. (2014). What is man? In *Between man and man* (R. G. Smith, Trans.; pp. 118-205). Mansfield Centre, CT: Macmillan. (Original work published 1938).

Cooper, J. M. (1977). Aristotle on the forms of friendship. *Review of Metaphysics, 30,* 619-648.

Diekelmann, N., & Diekelmann, J. (2009). *Schooling learning teaching: Toward narrative pedagogy.* Bllomington, IN: iUniverse.

Diekelmann, N., & Ironside, P. M. (1998). Preserving writing in doctoral education: Exploring the concernful practices of schooling learning teaching. *Journal of Advanced Nursing, 28,* 1347-1355. doi: 10.1046/j.1365-2648.1998.00819.x

Fletcher, J. K. (1999). *Disappearing acts: Gender, power, and relational practice at work.* Cambridge, MA: The MIT Press.

Friedman, M. S. (2002) *Martin Buber: The life of dialogue* (4th ed.). New York, NY: Routledge.

Fromm, E. (2006). *The art of loving.* New York, NY: HarperCollins. (Original work published 1956).

Gadamer, H.-G. (2004). *Truth and method.* New York, NY: Seabury. (Original work published 1960).

George, B. (2003). *Authentic leadership: Rediscovering the secrets to creating lasting value.* San Francisco, CA: Jossey-Bass.

Greenleaf, R. K. (2008). *The servant as leader.* Westfield, IN: The Greenleaf Center for Servant Leadership. (Original work published 1970).

Guignon, C. (2015). Authenticity and the question of being. In D. McManus (Ed.), *Heidegger, authenticity and the self: Themes from Division Two of Being and Time* (pp. 8-20). New York, NY: Routledge.

Heidegger, M. (1971). The thing. In *Poetry, language, thought* (A. Hofstadter, Trans; pp. 161-184). New York, NY: HarperCollins. (Original work published 1951)

_____. (2003). *What is philosophy?* (J. T. Wilde. & W. Kluback, Trans.). Lanham, MD: Rowman & Littlefield. (Original work published 1956).

_____. (2008a). *Being and time* (J. Macquarrie & E. Robinson, Trans.). New York, NY: Harper & Row. (Original work published 1927).

_____. (2008b). Building dwelling thinking. In D. F. Krell (Ed.), *Basic writings* (pp. 347-391). New York, NY: HarperCollins. (Original work published 1952).

_____. (2008c). The question concerning technology. In D. F. Krell (Ed.), *Basic writings* (pp. 311-341). New York, NY: HarperCollins. (Original work published 1954).

Inwood, M. (1999). *A Heidegger dictionary.* Oxford, England: Blackwell.

Kida, G. (1983). *Haidega* [Heidegger]. Tokyo, Japan: Iwanami.

_____. (1993). *Haidega no shiso* [Heidegger's thoughts]. Tokyo, Japan: Iwanami.

_____. (1996). *Testugaku to han-tetsugaku* [Philosophy and anti-philosophy]. Tokyo, Japan: Iwanami.

_____. (1998). *Watashi no tetsugaku nyumon* [My introduction of philosophy]. Tokyo, Japan: Shinshokan.

_____. (2000). *Haidega sonzai to jikan no kochiku* [Construction of Heidegger's Being and Time]. Tokyo: Iwanami.

May, R. (1996). *Heidegger's hidden sources: East Asian influences on his work* (G. Parkes, Trans.). London, England: Routledge.

Mayeroff, M. (1971). *On caring.* New York, NY: HarperCollins.

McManus, D. (Ed.). (2015). *Heidegger, authenticity, and the self: Themes from Division Two of Being and Time.* New York, NY: Routledge.

Moran, D. (2000). *Introduction to phenomenology.* New York, NY: Routledge.

Nishii, A. (2017). *Servanthood as love, relationships, and power: A Heideggerian hermeneutic study on the experiences of servant-leaders* (Doctoral dissertation). Fielding Graduate University, Santa Barbara, CA.

Norton, D. L., & Kille, M. F. (1971a). Eros: Love as aspiration toward the ideal. In D. L. Norton & M. F. Kille (Eds.), *Philosophies of love* (pp. 81-84). Totowa, NJ: Rowman & Allanheld.

Norton, D. L., & Kille, M. F. (Ed.). (1971b). *Philosophies of love.* Totowa, NJ: Rowman & Allanheld.

Palmer, R. E. (1969). *Hermeneutics: Interpretation theory in Schleiermacher, Dilthey, Heidegger, and Gadamer.* Evanston, IL: Northwestern University Press.

Parkes, G. (1996). Rising sun over black forest: Heidegger's Japanese connections. In R. May, *Heidegger's hidden sources: East Asian influences on his work* (G. Parkes, Trans.; pp. 79-118). London, England: Routledge.

Patterson, K. (2003). *Servant leadership: A theoretical model.* Paper presented at the Servant Leadership Research Roundtable. Regent University, School of Leadership Studies.

_____. (2010). Servant leadership and love. In D. van Direndonck & K. Patterson (Ed.), *Servant leadership: Developments in theory and research* (pp. 67-76). New York, NY: Palgrave Macmillan.

Smythe, E. (2011). From beginning to end: How to do hermeneutic interpretive phenomenology. In G. Thomson, F. Dykes, & S. Downe (Ed.), *Qualitative research in midwifery and childbirth: Phenomenological approaches* (pp. 35-54). New York, NY: Routledge.

Smythe, E. A., Ironside, P. M., Sims, S. L., Swenson, M. M., & Spence, D. G. (2008). Doing Heideggerian hermeneutic research: A discussion paper. *International Journal of Nursing Studies, 45*(9), 1389-1397.

Tomkins, L., & Simpson, P. (2015). Caring leadership: A Heideggerian perspective. *Organizational Studies, 36*(8), 1013-1031. doi: 10.1177/0170840615580008

Winston, B. E. (2002). Be a leader for God's sake. [Digital version]. Retrieved from http://www.bealeaderforgodssake.org/docs/bealea-derforgodssake05-22-2004.pdf

Wojnar, D. M., & Swanson, K. M. (2007). Phenomenology: An exploration. *Journal of Holistic Nursing, 25*(3), 172-180. doi: 10.1177/0898010106295172

Wolff, K. H. (1976). *Surrender and catch: Experience and inquiry today*. Boston, MA: D. Reidel.

About the Author

Ayumi Nishii PhD enjoys playing a role of a catalyst to *connect, collaborate, and create* with people, and has been working in the fields of organizational development, leadership training, and human resources in Japan and the United States. She was born and grew up in Japan and currently lives in the U.S. She holds a master's degree in Organization Management and Development and a doctorate in Human and Organizational Systems from Fielding Graduate University. Contact: anishii@ email.fielding.edu

CHAPTER 8
Studying Collaboration among Chamber Musicians: Phenomenological Inspirations and Insights

Dorianne Cotter-Lockard, PhD, MBA

President, DCL Associates Inc., Agoura, CA

Institute for Social Innovation, Fielding Graduate University

Abstract

This chapter provides insights into my learning journey at Fielding Graduate University and how I came to write a phenomenologically oriented dissertation. What unfolds in this chapter is the story of my affiliation with phenomenology and hermeneutics, heavily influenced by my Fielding University mentor and committee members. My dissertation is an example of "phenomenologically oriented" research because I mixed other methods into my approach, applying some aspects and not others from phenomenology. My dissertation provides insights into how the Cavani String Quartet taught advanced music students to work together in chamber music ensembles. The findings aligned with Alfred Schutz's concept of the mutual "tuning-in relationship" and the act of forming a "We-Presence." I also examined Schutz's structures of the lifeworld to better understand predecessors, successors, and relationships between the students and the legacy passed down by their chamber music coaches.

Keywords: phenomenology, Schutz, Stimulated Recall, collaboration, chamber music, We-Presence, lifeworld

Introduction

As I explored my experience with phenomenology and hermeneutics in this chapter, I re-read what I wrote almost ten years ago. I was curious about how I used hermeneutics and what I learned from my mentors about phenomenology. As I reviewed the past, I wondered why I am not using it more for my current research and writing projects. What unfolds in this chapter is the story of my affiliation with phenomenology and hermeneutics, heavily influenced by my Fielding University mentor and committee members. I use the words "affiliation with" rather than "dedication to" because my dissertation is an example of "phenomenologically oriented" research. I mixed other methods into my research approach, applying some aspects and not others from phenomenology.

Immersion in the World of Phenomenology and Hermeneutics

I met Valerie Bentz on my first day as a doctoral student at Fielding Graduate University. She remained my mentor throughout my studies and eventually become the chair of my dissertation committee. My introduction to phenomenology and hermeneutics occurred during my first course in Human Development. Valerie found a way to help us practice hermeneutic interpretive approaches for each reading assignment and essay. Embarking on the doctoral journey as a 50-year-old adult, I felt curiosity and wonder toward the world of research methods and scholarly theories. Some magic must have infused the process that matched me to her as a mentor, since I quickly came to resonate with phenomenology and hermeneutics.

The following description of my journey in this first course at Fielding illustrates how I learned about and experimented with phenomenology and hermeneutics. First, we read Valerie's book, *On Becoming Mature: Childhood Ghosts and Spirits in Adult Life* (Bentz, 1989). I used Johann Droysen's cultural/social hermeneutic interpretation (Bentz,

2007) and incorporated some of Paul Ricoeur's steps in the hermeneutic process (Bentz, 2002) to write my first paper. For the subsequent module, I sought a deeper appreciation of Ricoeur's hermeneutic approach, and applied it to my interpretation of *Theories of Human Development: Integrative Perspectives* (Goldhaber, 2000). Next, I used Droysen's four strategies of hermeneutic interpretation (Bentz, 2007) to interpret Gilligan's *In a Different Voice* (1993). I used Gadamer's hermeneutic approach (Bentz & Rehorick, 2006) to provide a critical analysis of *I am a Strange Loop* (Hofstadter, 2007), culminating with an imaginary dialog between myself and Hofstadter, in which I rode "the wild horse," applying a metaphor for Gadamer's deepest level of engagement with a text as described by Bentz and Rehorick (2006). I returned to Ricoeur's hermeneutic approach for my final reading, an interpretation of *Sri Aurobindo, or the Adventure of Consciousness* (Satprem, 1968).

I conducted a phenomenological research project for my final paper in the course. My motivation to conduct research at an early stage in my studies stemmed from my desire to master the process required by the university's Institutional Research Board. I also yearned to dive into the world of research. For this project, I asked the question: "What is the lived experience of those who have a deep and consistent meditation practice during and after meditation, and does their experience align with current Western and non-Western consciousness theories?"

In my analysis process, I applied the "Spiral of Mindful Inquiry" framework (Bentz & Shapiro, 1998, pp. 42-53). Bentz and Shapiro's framework includes four major turns in a spiral: critical social science, phenomenology, hermeneutics, and a Buddhist lens of interpretation. I explored the historical context of the year (2007) in which I conducted the research, identified potential communication distortions that might occur, and explored potential linkages between meditation practices and social change. I analyzed the narratives from my research interviews, using the phenomenological process described in *Researching Lived Experience* (van Manen, 1990) and by listening to the interview recordings as a form of meditation. I explored the lifeworlds of the people I interviewed and identified typifications of the meditation experience. Next, I used a Gadamerian approach to interpret selected consciousness theories. I explored how the lived experience of the meditators in my study aligned with the consciousness theories that I had chosen.

I presented the paper at the Society for Phenomenology and Human Sciences (SPHS) conference (Cotter-Lockard, 2008). At the conference, I had an opportunity to hear and meet some well-known phenomenologists such as Don Ihde, Lester Embree, Mary F. Rogers, Ken Liberman, Philip M. Lewin, and George Psathas. It was wonderful to connect with these people who had great passion for phenomenology—they inspired me to learn more.

In 2009, I took a seminar in Somatics with Valerie. The kickoff workshop focused on "Hermeneutic Phenomenology—Getting to the Essence of Things." We considered the idea of "The Body as Text, Embodiment as a Way of Knowing." We dug deeply into the topic of somatic experience and kept a journal of our somatic experiences. For my final Somatics paper, I wrote *The Physiology of Music, Entrainment, Resonance, and Generative Listening* (unpublished). My interest in this topic laid a foundation for later dissertation work.

The seminar concluded with a deeply moving weekend of practices designed to live fully in our bodies. These included Bartenieff fundamentals, Feldenkrais, Kundalini yoga, an OSHO humming meditation, and massage. Each of these experiences of "embodiment as a way of knowing" contributed to the foundation of my approach to research. I realized that embodiment is a critical aspect of knowing. If I were to become a researcher of experiences such as hearing or performing music, I needed to attend to the somatic experience.

My writing partner and student member of my dissertation committee, Luann Fortune, was another important influence. Luann and I critiqued each other's papers throughout our doctoral program. We jumped into the ocean of phenomenology and hermeneutics together,

212

searching, questioning, and supporting each other throughout the journey. Luann chose phenomenology as the primary methodology for her dissertation (Fortune, 2012; see also Fortune & Hymel, 2015). I served on her dissertation committee, supported her work in developing the syllabus for the Somatics seminar at Fielding, and we attended two SPHS conferences together. Luann has gone on to publish several articles on phenomenological topics, presented at and helped to organize conferences for the Interdisciplinary Coalition of North American Phenomenologists (ICNAP) and SPHS, and is currently a faculty member and Director of the Instructional Excellence and Practice and Healthcare Systems specializations at the College of Integrative Medicine and Health Sciences, Saybrook University. Phenomenology still weaves its way into our conversations as we continue to collaborate.

Music: Intersections with Phenomenology

As I worked with Valerie and David Rehorick on various projects, we learned that the three of us shared a deep love of music. While David's focus was jazz, Valerie and I shared a love for performing classical music. Both Valerie and David wrote about the phenomenology of music (Malhotra, 1981; Rehorick & Weeks, 2005a, 2005b). From an early age, classical music was the raft to which I clung, promising solace from a chaotic home life. I began piano studies at age eight and violin studies at nine. I performed my first violin solo in public at age 10. I earned scholarships to summer music programs, won competitions, and performed concerti with orchestras throughout high school. I attended prestigious music conservatories and performed as a professional musician at Lincoln Center and Carnegie Hall in New York City. However, it was difficult to earn a living doing what I loved most, which was playing chamber music. On the advice of a cellist friend, I took a three-month computer programming course at New York University, got a job programming computers, and changed my career trajectory to technology, Wall Street, and the corporate world. Though I left the world of professional musicians, I never forgot the experience of playing in ensembles, the feeling of connecting with fellow musicians, and my love of music.

Jeremy Shapiro, a colleague of Valerie's and David's, shared our passion for music. Jeremy studied with noted music sociologist Theodor Adorno, and he has written articles on music topics (1995; 2010; 2011 in press). I took an independent study seminar on the Sociology of Music with Jeremy in the fall of 2010. We dug into the works of DeNora (2000, 2003) and Adorno (1988). I used a mind-mapping process to interpret these writings. As Jeremy and I discussed the mind-maps, we shared our experiences of music by sending recordings to each other. Valerie, David, and Jeremy, along with Luann as student reader, became my dissertation committee.

At Fielding's Winter Session in 2010, I attended a symposium presented by Valerie, David, and Jeremy, called *Music, Consciousness, and Society.* In this symposium, the faculty introduced phenomenology and sociology as methods to study how people experience music. I co-presented in a continuation of the symposium during Fielding's Winter Session 2011. Based on my studies in music sociology, Jeremy and I presented a segment called "Can we be free in an un-free world? Adorno's concept of false consciousness" (2011).

Adorno (1984; Adorno & Bernstein, 2001) explored how music reflects and transforms consciousness. According to DeNora (2003), Adorno "used music to think with" (p. 3). Jeremy and I explored questions such as, "Can we have true freedom in a society that has domination, inequality, and prejudice?" and "Is it possible to stretch the limits of consciousness in musical performance within the frameworks imposed by society?" We explored these ideas within sociological contexts, playing musical excerpts to illustrate our points.

Given the influences of Valerie, David, Jeremy, and Luann, it is not surprising that I would proceed with a phenomenologically oriented dissertation.

Dissertation: Chamber Music Rehearsal Techniques and Coaching Strategies That Enable Collaboration

A string quartet is a type of team. Members of a string quartet spend years training to listen deeply to each other verbally and nonverbally. I wondered whether the deep listening experience of a string quartet could be observed and embodied by a team of non-musicians. More broadly, I desired to study how music could be used to enhance organizational learning. However, based on my committee's feedback and the invitation from the Cavani String Quartet (CSQ) to study their coaching process, I refined my research question to the following: How do members of a professional string quartet coach advanced chamber music students? Subquestion #1: What coaching strategies and rehearsal techniques help students to develop effective teamwork? Subquestion #2: How does rehearsing and studying in a string quartet enable productive collaboration within student string quartets?

This topic is important for several reasons. First, there is a desperate need for music education to be incorporated into the fabric of our educational system. Numerous studies show that early childhood music experiences increase verbal ability, logical reasoning capability, and behavioral maturity (Deasy, 2002; Stevenson & Deasy, 2005). Prior to my research, a documented approach to training classical chamber musicians did not exist. Since I posted my dissertation in 2014 on www.academia.edu, it has been accessed 2,465 times from 81 countries. I frequently receive communications from music educators, students and amateur musicians thanking me for posting this work. I received offers to translate it into Spanish and gave permission to have portions of it translated into Japanese for a blog that serves Japanese amateur musicians (Takemoto, 2016). I am currently collaborating with Annie Fullard, first violinist of CSQ, on a book tentatively titled, *The Chamber Music Effect: A Comprehensive Guide to Chamber Music Rehearsal Techniques and Coaching Strategies.*

Second, the topic of team collaboration has been in the spotlight for the past decade, with a variety of popular books and scholarly articles written on the topic, using sports or military teams as metaphors for team collaboration (Arnatt & Beyerlein, 2014; Megdal, 2016). In the past, scholars conducted studies using the metaphor of jazz groups to examine creativity and improvisation for organizational teams (Bastien & Hostager, 1995; Jeddeloh, 2003; Seddon, 2005). However, few looked deeply into the phenomenon of how musicians learn to collaborate.

Finally, I secretly hoped that I would discover insights into the phenomenon of deep listening. This discovery came to pass in a wonderful way. A group of rehearsal techniques that I categorized in my dissertation as helping with "group dynamics" are now being categorized in our forthcoming book as "techniques for deep listening." These techniques help musicians transform their awareness so they can listen more deeply and collaborate more effectively.

Methodology Choices

I did not explicitly choose phenomenology as my dissertation research methodology. In fact, I resisted the idea of conducting a pure phenomenological study. Instead, I decided to take a general interpretive social science research approach, using interpretive inquiry techniques that were informed by phenomenological strategies.

My exploration centered on the teaching and learning processes that took place *within* and *between* participants in the context of a music conservatory's chamber music coaching program. With permission from Cleveland Institute of Music (CIM), I conducted my research during two site visits to CIM in 2011. The coaches who formed the central focus of my study included four members of CSQ, along with the chair of the Chamber Music Department, Peter Salaff.

I consciously adopted a social constructionist perspective. Social constructionist researchers focus on the process of meaning-making

216

within the context of social interactions (Creswell, 2003). A social constructionist view assumes that humans create their own meaning for a world they experience through interactions with others.

Data gathering was organized by using a case study approach (Stake, 1995, 2006; Yin, 2009). Each coaching session represented one case, which consisted of the video recording of the coaching session, interviews with each member of the student string quartet, and an interview with their coach. Since the researcher is part of the system under study, I incorporated observations of my experience of the coaching sessions into the case studies in my field notes. The process of taking field notes provided a rich description of the coaching environment and participant interactions (Warren & Karner, 2010). This process aligned with the phenomenological technique of writing protocols (Dowling, 2007; van Manen, 1990). I included my observations in the field, inferences based on my observations, and personal reflections, distinguishing between these three perspectives during the note-taking process. I also captured candid photos and short videos during my site visits.

Research Techniques

In my dissertation, I acknowledged that my perceptions, history, context, and biases contributed to my interpretation of the data (Maxwell, 2005). I noted that I studied at a music conservatory and had ties to the same legacy of teachers who influenced CSQ's coaching processes and techniques. My initial walk through the hallways of the conservatory brought back memories and emotions as I listened to the sounds emanating from practice rooms. In addition, memories of my life as a serious classical music student arose as I observed the master classes and coaching sessions. I documented these self-observations in the field notes.

How does a researcher come to understand how classical musicians collaborate when much of the collaboration takes place through body gestures and musical sound vibrations? I decided to use a combination of video recording and Stimulated Recall techniques during the post-session interviews. The Stimulated Recall (SR) process has been used extensively for more than 30 years to reveal the thought processes of teachers and students (O'Brien, 1993). I chose this method because video recordings capture nonverbal gestures and human interactions that cannot be observed through audio recordings or field notes.

I observed and video-recorded coaching sessions with four selected student chamber ensembles, each with a different coach. During the coaching sessions, I placed the video camera on a tripod at the back of the room behind the students as I sat in the far corner of the room. With minor exceptions, the students said they forgot that the camera and researcher were present.

John O'Brien (1993) recommended that the entire video recording be played during the SR process, allowing participants to push the pause button when they desired to explain their internal thought process. Because the musical performances took large amounts of video time, I selected shorter video clips to focus on the coaching process at the post-coaching interviews. I defined selection criteria for choosing the video clips prior to the data gathering process to mitigate researcher bias: (a) include examples of CSQ's coaching strategies and rehearsal techniques, and (b) exclude long portions of musical performance to examine conversations that occurred during the session.

Using NVivo analysis software, I annotated the video recording and included the video as primary data for analysis (Rich & Hannafin, 2009). During the interviews, I asked participants to stop the video as needed to make comments. I queried the coaches regarding their choices to introduce ideas, techniques, and strategies. I asked students open-ended questions about what they noticed while they tried out different techniques, which techniques were most helpful, and what they learned during the session. I avoided asking leading questions that might influence participants' answers. The video and Stimulated Recall techniques helped participants re-live the experiences of the coaching sessions. I delved into transcriptions of the interviews to understand shared perspectives of each learning moment. For example, one student shared her perspective with me of a learning moment as it related to her performance anxiety:

> Honestly, I felt really nervous...I like being in the background....
> I still felt like, you know, I was at the top of the pyramid. And they're supporting me but I'm still up there and visible.... I was so happy though, like my quartet members, they are really, really sensitive.... I felt really supported by them because they really *crescendoed* [increased the sound volume] with me and then they helped me grow in this and really bring me out and feature me (Lindsey, a pseudonym).

During the post-coaching session interviews, I asked the coaches if my presence influenced their use of certain techniques during the coaching sessions. They said my presence did not influence their use of specific techniques. However, the process of video recording and conducting interviews initiated a reflective process within each coach. After my pilot study, the coaches mentioned that they thought of ways to improve their coaching process after our interviews. Members of the CSQ told me at different times that the interviews inspired them to formalize their thinking about the techniques, which resulted in the creation of a "Rehearsal Techniques Seminar" which did not exist when I began the research, and CSQ now presents at the beginning of every school year.

Phenomenological Influences

Alfred Schutz (1962) said that "the social scientist replaces the thought objects of common-sense thought relating to unique events and occurrences" to create a model of a portion of the social world that is "relevant to the scientist's particular problem under scrutiny" (p. 36). I transcribed the coaches' implicit process into an explicit model for coaching chamber music. This model, which contains 38 rehearsal techniques and a foundation for creating a positive coaching environment, has proven valuable and useful to the world-wide chamber music community.

Rehorick's (2011) data analysis process guidelines helped me organize the interview transcription data. Next, I created case descriptions and elicited themes. From side-by-side case comparisons, I created diagrams and wrote research memos to encapsulate my findings. I looked at the findings through a phenomenological lens, considering the coaches' and students' perspectives and my own experience. I analyzed the structures of the lifeworld within the coaching session as related to predecessor and successor relationships (Schutz & Luckmann, 1973). Finally, I compared the evidence to my research questions and developed models to reflect the findings.

Qualitative social science knowledge is based on evidence that is "embedded in the context of fluid social interactions" and is valid if the evidence "resonates or feels right to those who are being studied" (Neuman, 2006, p. 105). I sent drafts of my findings to the coaches for review, requesting confirmation that I accurately captured their experiences and intentions regarding the coaching strategies and rehearsal techniques. The coaches affirmed the accuracy of my observations and explication of their coaching process with a few minor corrections to the model: "I really like the organization of your writing. What you wrote is very affirming and does make us seem like real people. I hear our voices in your quotes" (Coach A).

Though not directly associated with phenomenology, I used Kenneth Burke's (1945) dramatism technique, the *pentad,* to imagine how my case study findings might apply in different contexts. The pentad process includes identifying the act, scene, agent, agency (how the agents behave), and purpose (the agents' motives). This process resembles the phenomenological technique of *imaginative variations.* The pentad process helped me explore external validity, referred to as *generalizability* or *transferability*, of my study results to other contexts such as organizational teams.

Schutz: Mutual Tuning-In and Forming a We-Presence

I have been most influenced by Schutz's writings about phenomenology, such as the concept of temporality. Temporality is a differentiator between how we experience visual art or literature, and how we experience live performances of music, theatre, or dance (Hamilton, 2007). Valerie Malhotra (1981) referenced Schutz's notion of *dureé* in her examination of how symphony musicians live in two temporal worlds simultaneously during a performance. Malhotra defined *dureé* in her article as "the internally perceived pattern of rhythmic sound as felt by the musicians" (p. 110).

Most important to my research analysis was Schutz's (1964) concept of the "mutual tuning-in relationship" (p. 161). Schutz examined the social interactions between participants in the music-making process, including composer, performers, and the audience. The mutual tuning-in relationship occurs resulting from the relationship between "I" and "Thou" to form a "We" presence. Schutz described the structure of this relationship, which he wrote "originates in the possibility of living together simultaneously in specific dimensions of time" (pp. 161-162).

Schutz (1964) contended that musicians and audience members enter into the stream of the composer's consciousness as they share temporal dimensions during a musical performance. Performers and audience members experience *simultaneity* through the mutual tuning-in relationship. The listener's experience is internal, whereas the musician's experience is both internal and external. The musician plays her part, reacts to colleagues' interpretations, and attends to others' responses to her performance. Consequently, members of a music ensemble merge multiple streams of consciousness to form one We-Presence.

Another phenomenological concept from Schutz (1973) is the notion of structures of the lifeworld, which I used to explore relationships in the coaching sessions, especially predecessors, contemporaries, and successors. For example, the coaches and students experienced a face-to-face We-relation in the moment. At the same time, coaches mentioned contemporaries such as famous cellist Yo-Yo Ma, who represent a They-relation to students. On several occasions during the coaching sessions, the coaches told stories about their mentors or attributed certain techniques to their teachers. In one case, a coach attributed a rehearsal technique to Don Weilerstein, who taught and mentored the CSQ. This example illustrates both a predecessor and a current We-relationship because Weilerstein still coaches chamber music and he had coached some of the students.

Schutz (Brodersen, 1964) also said that we cannot imagine the future lifeworld of our successors. Members of the CSQ made intentional choices to pass on coaching strategies and rehearsal techniques from prior generations. However, they were not able to predict how these lessons might be carried forward.

Chamber Music Techniques that Enable Collaboration

In addition to a model that organized rehearsal techniques into categories, I represented my findings in an experiential view (see Figure 1). The coaches created an environment of love, inspiration, and relationship. Within this environment, coaches empowered students to create a shared interpretation of the music and to express their collective interpretation more fully. I compared my participants' descriptive accounts of their experiences in coaching sessions and rehearsals with a set of intended outcomes as stated by the coaches. These outcomes included (a) awareness, (b) rhythmic connection, (c) shared interpretation, (d) shifting perspective, (e) listening deeply, and (f) becoming one with the other. An additional outcome emerged that the coaches did not explicitly describe prior to my observations: (g) embodying expression.

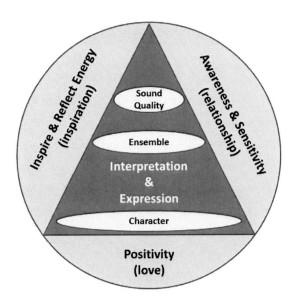

Figure 1. An Experiential View of the Chamber Music Coaching Model

Next, I explored how the unique coaching environment and process at CIM affected students' learning about collaboration. From these two analyses, I developed the *Generative Team* model. I define *team* as: "A group of people that form an intact social system within a larger social system, with boundaries and an identity, a common purpose, mutual accountability, interdependence, and a commitment to group performance goals" (Cotter-Lockard, 2012a, p. 26). Furthermore, "a team is generative when it has the capability to originate and evolve ideas, relationships, and processes" (p. 193). My definition of *collaboration* is "a relational process in which people communicate diverse perspectives with honesty and care, share a common mission, and contribute passion, ideas, and energy to create a shared outcome" (p. 30). A generative team has the capacity to express what I call *collective virtuosity*, a magical connection within which, per Mark Marotto and colleagues (Marotto, Roos, & Victor, 2007), "individual virtuosity becomes collective in groups through a reflexive process in which group members are transformed by their own peak performance" (p. 395).

The original elements of the Generative Team model included (a) positivity, (b) caring communication, (c) empowerment, (d) commitment, (e) shifting perspective, (f) becoming the other, (g) leaving a legacy, and (h) expressing energy and love. I have since revised the model to place greater focus on collective virtuosity. The enablers of collective virtuosity include perspective, positivity, and resonance. Perspective includes "seeing through another's eyes" and emotional intelligence. Positivity includes caring communication, commitment, and empowerment. Resonance includes the ability to *mirror* and *inspire, forming a We-Presence,* and acting with *energy* and *love.*

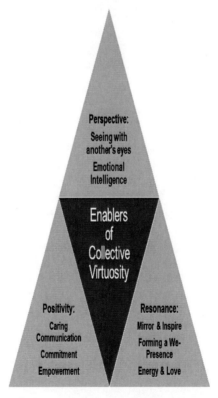

Figure 2. Enablers of Collective Virtuosity

The concept of collective virtuosity, along with elements of the generative team, align with Schutz's (1964) concept of mutual tuning-in and forming a We-Presence. The next section contains descriptions of selected chamber music rehearsal techniques which illustrate alignment with Schutz's phenomenological concepts.

Techniques for Mirroring and Reflecting Energy

The human development process includes mirroring facial expressions, arm movements, and breathing (Iacoboni, 2009; Mainieri, Heim, Straube, Binkofski, & Kircher, 2013). The coaches employed a *Theatre Exercise* of mirroring in dyads (2 partners) as a process to learn how to cue beginnings and endings of music without the use of instruments. The coaches intended "to focus the students on relating to one another's leadership and to trust it" (Coach C). Coach C introduced the concepts of *initiating, inspiring,* and *reflecting* and asked the students to inspire each other to reflect their energy. During a post-coaching interview, one student noted that the exercise was surprisingly relevant and wondered if it would change the group's chemistry.

In a more advanced technique, called *Live, Breathe, and Die* (LBAD), each member in turn, initiated playing a musical passage with instruments while other members mirrored the initiator's movements, musical interpretation, and gestures. The LBAD technique included matching the bow speed, *vibrato*, breath, and body movement, essentially mirroring all musical and physical nuances. LBAD followed from the mirroring exercises as each member of the group had an opportunity to be the initiator-inspirer (leader) as well as a reflector (follower).

During the Stimulated Recall process, the coaches said they intended to help students shift their frame of reference to broaden awareness and engage differently with group members. The coaches aimed to help students develop trust and understanding within their group. During the Stimulated Recall process, students revealed that they experienced dramatic shifts in their awareness while practicing the LBAD technique,

which encouraged complete commitment to the *other*. They expanded their awareness of each other, committed to each other's ideas, and
merged their consciousness.

LBAD opens the door to an emerging group consciousness, as
defined in Keith Sawyer's (2006) concept of *group flow*. Sawyer contended that the phenomenon of group flow has emergent characteristics
based on concepts of systems and complexity theory (Stacey, 2003).
The phenomenon arises when musicians simultaneously listen to themselves and listen to each other while playing their instruments. LBAD is
the most well-suited technique to help groups embody Schutz's (1964)
mutual tuning-in relationship. One student eloquently expressed the
lived experience of practicing LBAD:

> And it's really interesting to see how each person goes, the pre-
> vious person before them has inspired them in some way, and so
> the way they feel about the music as we go along is changing,
> because everyone's adding in something to the mix.... It's like
> unfired clay or something. And so, each person that plays, the
> next person is a little influenced by what they just heard, what
> they liked, what they didn't like, and by their own ideas. And by
> the time you get to the first violinist, it's really something that's
> collective.... And then...everyone initiates. And that's for me, I
> think it's like the kiln (Jonathan, pseudonym).

Somatic Techniques for Shifting Perspectives

The coaches utilized several techniques that included spatial and somatic changes to force perceptual shifts in the consciousness of the musicians. For example, in the technique of *Switching Seats*, students sat in
different positions from the usual string quartet configuration. The vio-
list sat in the first violinist's seat. The cellist sat in the second violinist's
seat, and so on. This exercise helped students to adopt different perspectives and to hear anew. In addition, students enhanced somatic awareness through the technique of standing or sitting with their *Backs to
Each Other*, which removed students' visual dependencies and obliged
them to use other senses while playing. *Standing and Walking* helped

students to sense, trust, and reach out to each other across the room.

The coaches said they used these techniques to help students connect with each other; the use of the spatial dimension impacted interrelationships in subtle ways. Furthermore, the ability to shift perceptions and view a context from multiple perspectives enabled better teamwork. These techniques helped students to expand their conscious awareness and to strengthen relationships with each other.

Techniques for Expressing Energy and Love

In some techniques, students learned how to *send and receive energy*. In a technique called *Play to the Center*, Coach E asked students to remove their music stands, sit close to each other, and play the music from memory to experience the vibrations of sound through their bodies. This technique enhanced listening and nonverbal communication between group members.

In a technique called *Sphere of Energy,* coaches invited students to imagine a magical sphere of energy suspended above the center of the group. Next, coaches asked the students to project the sphere of energy around the room and toward the audience. Although the exercise was a thought-experiment, the imagination process induced the musicians to produce and project different sound vibrations from their instruments.

Phenomenology in My Work and Life

The learning continued after I completed my dissertation. Soon after graduation, I presented some of my dissertation findings at the SPHS conference (Cotter-Lockhard, 2012b): I examined the somatic aspect of rehearsing in a string quartet, using a phenomenological analysis approach, exploring the essence of somatic awareness within my study data.

I found additional ways to connect my dissertation findings to my other research interests, especially spirituality at work. For example, I presented a paper (Cotter-Lockard, 2013) in which I discussed how

227

the elements of a Generative Team align with the literature related to spirituality at work, and how they might be applied to non-musical organization settings. Subsequently, I presented a professional development workshop at the IAMSR Fourth World Congress, *Spirituality and Creativity in Management,* titled "Spiritual Intelligence Development: Techniques Leaders Can Learn from Musicians." I introduced workshop participants to the *SQ21: Spiritual Intelligence* model developed by Wigglesworth (2012), and illustrated how selected SQ21 skills mapped to the enablers of collective virtuosity. I then facilitated several exercises to allow participants to practice musicians' rehearsal techniques which help to develop and deepen SQ skills.

In 2014, I submitted a proposal for a chapter in the book *Leadership for a Healthy World: Creative Social Change,* which was rejected. My proposed chapter focused on how musicians deepen mindful awareness to a level in which collaboration becomes a process of forming Schutz's We-Presence. I aimed to incorporate relevant concepts presented in *On Dialogue* (Bohm & Nichol, 1996), Otto Scharmer's *Theory U* (Scharmer & Senge, 2007), and the concept of *Presencing* (Senge, Scharmer, Jaworski, & Flowers, 2005). Also in 2014, I submitted a proposal for a chapter in the book *Performance Phenomenology: The Thing Itself.* My proposal, "The Mutual Tuning-In Relationship: Forming a We-Presence in Music Performance," was not accepted for the book, but the editors found merit enough to forward my proposal to the journal *About Performance.*

In 2015, I presented a professional development workshop at the IAMSR Fourth World Congress, *Spirituality and Creativity in Management.* My workshop was called "Spiritual Intelligence Development: Techniques Leaders Can Learn from Musicians." I introduced workshop participants to the *SQ21: Spiritual Intelligence* model developed by Cindy Wigglesworth (2012), and illustrated how selected SQ21 skills mapped to the enablers of collective virtuosity. I then facilitated several exercises to allow participants to practice musicians' rehearsal techniques which help to develop and deepen SQ skills.

I am currently writing two books based on my dissertation research, and I publish posts to a blog called *Collective Virtuosity: Music Lessons for Leaders* (2014). The phenomenon resulting from this research that most interests me is deep listening. In my writing, I continue to explore Schutz's (1964) concepts of mutual tuning-in and forming a We-Presence in support of learning more about deep listening. I intend to include a chapter in my forthcoming book, focusing on how musicians deepen mindful awareness to a level in which collaboration becomes a process of forming Schutz's We-Presence. I will incorporate relevant concepts presented in *On Dialogue* (Bohm & Nichol, 1996), Otto Sccharmer's *Theory U* (Scharmer, 2007), and the concept of *Presencing* (Senge, Scharmer, Jaworski & Flowers, 2005).

I am in the process of developing and testing out experiential workshops for leaders and teams to learn deep listening skills. At Fielding's Winter Session 2016, Valerie Bentz chaired a seminar, "Performance as Knowing." I prepared an experiential segment, *Collective Virtuosity: Music Lessons for Leaders,* in which I facilitated a group experience of several techniques that chamber musicians use to arrive at a We-Presence. I included references to Schutz's work, mirror neuron research, emotional and social intelligence, and introduced the Generative Team model. I paired the concepts with exercises, such as the Theater Mirroring exercise, *Chamber Music Aerobics* (body movement to music with participants taking turns leading movements in small groups), speaking rhythmic patterns together, and the final exercise, *Live, Breath, and Die.*

Most recently, I have begun to incorporate live music at workshops by playing my violin. Since Valerie was a keynote speaker at the European Sociological Association *Qualitative Methods Conference* in Cracow, Poland, she invited several of her former students to submit papers. In addition to presenting my paper (Cotter-Lockard, 2016), I joined Fielding participants at the conference to facilitate a two-hour workshop called *Trauma Recovery: Insights from Contemplative In-*

quiry, Somatics, Phenomenology, and Communicative Management of Meaning (CMM), in which I played violin to enhance the connection between participants and increase somatic awareness.

A Closing Thought

When David Rehorick and Valerie Bentz invited me to contribute a chapter to this book, I wondered if I had a sufficiently interesting story to tell about my learning journey and how I integrated phenomenology and hermeneutics into my life as a scholar. Upon reflection, I now realize that their work, and the community of scholars at Fielding, had a profound influence on my approach to research and writing on scholarly topics. It is clear to me now that phenomenology and somatic studies form a foundation for my current and future work.

References

Adorno, T. W. (1984). *Philosophy of modern music.* New York, NY: Continuum.

Adorno, T. W. (1988). *Introduction to the sociology of music* (E. B. Ashton, Trans.). New York, NY: Continuum.

Adorno, T. W., & Bernstein, J. M. (2001). *The culture industry: Selected essays on mass culture.* London, England: Routledge.

Arnatt, M. J., & Beyerlein, M. M. (2014). An empirical examination of special operations team leaders' and members' leadership characteristics. *Policing, 37*(2), 438-453.

Bastien, D. T., & Hostager, T. J. (1995). On cooperation: A replication of an experiment in jazz and cooperation. *Comportamento Organizacional e Gestão, 2*(1), 33-45.

Bentz, V. M. (1989). *Becoming mature: Childhood ghosts and spirits in adult life.* New York, NY: de Gruyter.

Bentz, V. M. (2002). *Paul Ricoeur's hermeneutics.* Unpublished manuscript, School of Human and Organizational Development, Fielding Graduate University, Santa Barbara, CA.

Bentz, V. M. (2007). *Hermeneutics and Droysen.* Unpublished manuscript, School of Human and Organizational Development, Fielding Graduate University, Santa Barbara, CA.

Bentz, V. M., & Rehorick, D. (2006). *Gadamer's three levels of hermeneutics*. Bentz and Rehorick: Transformative Phenomenology online research forum. Fielding Graduate University. Santa Barbara, CA.

Bentz, V. M., & Shapiro, J. J. (1998). *Mindful inquiry in social research* Thousand Oaks, CA: SAGE.

Bohm, D., & Nichol, L. (1996). *On dialogue*. London, England: Routledge.

Brodersen, A. (Ed.) (1964). *Studies in social theory* (vol. II). The Hague, Netherlands: Martinus Nijhoff.

Burke, K. (1945). *A grammar of motives*. New York, NY: Prentice-Hall.

Cotter-Lockard, D. (2008). *Higher consciousness states through meditation: A phenomenological study*. Paper presented at the Society for Phenomenology and Human Sciences, Fall 2008, Duquesne University, Pittsburgh, PA.

Cotter-Lockard, D. (2012a). *Chamber music coaching strategies and rehearsal techniques that enable collaboration*. (Doctoral Dissertation). Retrieved from ProQuest Dissertations & Theses database. (Order No. 3542521).

_____. (2012b). *Playing in a string quartet: Somatic awareness and embodied expression*. Paper presented at the Annual Meeting, Society for Phenomenology and Human Sciences, Fall 2012, Rochester, NY.

_____. (2013). *The generative team: How chamber music coaches use love and energy to enable student musicians to collaborate effectively*. Paper presented at the Third Conference of the International Association of Management, Spirituality, and Religion, Lourdes, France.

_____. (2014). Collective virtuosity: Music lessons for leaders. Retrieved from https://collectivevirtuosity.com/.

_____. (2016). *Exploring the work of classical musicians: Use of video and stimulated recall*. Paper presented at the Qualitative Methods Conference, September 1-3, 2016, Cracow, Poland.

Cotter-Lockard, D., & Shapiro, J. J. (2011). *Can we be free in an un-free world? Adorno's concept of false consciousness*. Paper presented at the Fielding Graduate University Winter Session 2011, Santa Barbara, CA.

Creswell, J. W. (2003). *Research design: Qualitative, quantitative, and mixed method approaches* (2nd ed.). London, England: SAGE.

Deasy, R. J. (Ed.) (2002). *Critical links: Learning in the arts and student academic and social development.* Washington, DC: Arts Education Partnership.

DeNora, T. (2000). *Music in everyday life.* Cambridge, England: Cambridge University Press.

_____. (2003). *After Adorno: rethinking music sociology.* Cambridge, England: Cambridge University Press.

Dowling, M. (2007). From Husserl to van Manen: A review of different phenomenological approaches. *International Journal of Nursing Studies,* 44(1), 131-142.

Fortune, L. D. (2012). *How do seasoned massage therapists accomplish a whole session with established clients?* (Doctoral dissertation). Retrieved from ProQuest Dissertations & Theses database. (Order No. 3498722).

Fortune, L. D., & Hymel, G. M. (2015). Creating integrative work: A qualitative study of how massage therapists work with existing clients. *Journal of Bodywork & Movement Therapies,* 19(1), 25-34. doi:10.1016/j.jbmt.2014.01.005.

Gilligan, C. (1993). *In a different voice: Psychological theory and women's development.* Cambridge, MA: Harvard University Press.

Goldhaber, D. (2000). *Theories of human development: Integrative perspectives.* Mountain View, CA: Mayfield Pub.

Hamilton, A. (2007). *Aesthetics and music.* London, England: Continuum.

Hofstadter, D. R. (2007). *I am a strange loop.* New York, NY: Basic Books.

Iacoboni, M. (2009). Imitation, empathy, and mirror neurons. *Annual Review of Psychology, 60*(1), 653-670. doi:doi:10.1146/annurev.psych.60.110707.163604.

Jeddeloh, S.C. (2003). *Chasing transcendence: Experiencing & "magic moments" in jazz improvisation.* (Doctoral dissertation). Retrieved from ProQuest Dissertations & Theses database. (Order No. 3103587).

Mainieri, A. G., Heim, S., Straube, B., Binkofski, F., & Kircher, T. (2013). Differential role of the mentalizing and the mirror neuron system in the imitation of communicative gestures. *Neuroimage, 81,* 294-305. doi:http://dx.doi.org/10.1016/j.neuroimage.2013.05.021.

Malhotra, V. (1981). (Now Bentz, V.M.). The social accomplishment of music in a symphony orchestra: A phenomenological analysis. *Qualitative Sociology, 4*(2), 102-124.

Marotto, M., Roos, J., & Victor, B. (2007). Collective virtuosity in organizations: A study of peak performance in an orchestra. *Journal of Management Studies, 44*(3), 388-413.

Maxwell, J. A. (2005). *Qualitative research design: An interactive approach* (2nd ed.). Thousand Oaks, CA: SAGE.

Megdal, H. (2016). *The Cardinals way: How one team embraced tradition and Moneyball at the same time* (1st ed.). New York, NY: Thomas Dunne Books/St. Martin's Press.

Neuman, W. L. (2006). *Social research methods: Qualitative and quantitative approaches* (6th ed.). Boston, MA: Pearson.

O'Brien, J. (1993). Action research through stimulated recall. *Research in Science Education, 23*, 214-221.

Rehorick, D. (2011). *Preparing transcribed data for analysis: Some visual hints.* Knowledge areas seminar document. Human and Organizational Development. Fielding Graduate University. Santa Barbara, CA.

Rehorick, D., & Weeks, P. (2005a). *Performance phenomenology: Jazz variations in rehearsal conference opening address.* Paper presented at the Annual Meetings of the Society for Phenomenology and the Human Sciences, Fall 2005, Salt Lake City, UT.

_____. (Ed.). (2005b). *Sociology of music: Selected readings* (2nd ed.). Fredericton, New Brunswick: University of New Brunswick Imaging Services.

Rich, P., & Hannafin, M. (2009). Video annotation tools: Technologies to scaffold, structure, and transform teacher reflection. *Journal of Teacher Education, 60*(1), 52.

Satprem. (1968). *Sri Aurobindo: Or, the adventure of consciousness* (1st U.S. ed.). New York, NY: Harper & Row.

Sawyer, R. K. (2006). Group creativity: Musical performance and collaboration. *Psychology of Music, 34*(2), 148-165. doi:10.1177/0305735606061850.

Scharmer, C. O. (2007). *Theory U: Leading from the emerging future* (1st ed.). Cambridge, MA: Society for Organizational Learning.

Schutz, A. (1962). On the methodology of the social sciences. In M. A. Natanson (Ed.), *Collected papers volume I: The problem of social reality* (pp. 3-98). The Hague, The Netherlands: Martinus Nijhoff.

_____. (1964). Making music together: A study in social relationship. In A. Brodersen (Ed.), *Collected papers: Studies in social theory* (vol. II). The Hague, The Netherlands: Martinus Nijhoff.

Schutz, A., & Luckmann, T. (1973). *The structures of the life-world*. Evanston, IL: Northwestern University Press.

Seddon, F. (2005). Modes of communication during jazz improvisation. *British Journal of Music Education, 22*(1), 47-61.

Senge, P. M., Scharmer, C. O., Jaworski, J., & Flowers, B. S. (2005). *Presence: An exploration of profound change in people, organizations, and society* (1st ed.). New York, NY: Doubleday.

Shapiro, J. J. (1995). My funeral music. In C. B. Kenny (Ed.), *Listening, playing, creating: Essays on the power of sound*. Albany, NY: SUNY.

Shapiro, J. J. (2010). Adorno's praxis of individuation through music listening. *Música em Perspectiva, III*(2). doi:http://dx.doi.org/10.5380/mp.v3i2.21980

_____. (2011). Adorno's praxis of individuation through music listening. *Zeitschrift für kritische Theorie, XVII*, 32-33.

_____. (in press). Musical theory of society, communication theory of society, and the social situation of music today. *Zeitschrift für kritische Theorie, XXII*, 44-45.

Stacey, R. D. (2003). *Complexity and group processes: A radically social understanding of individuals*. Hove, England: Brunner-Routledge.

Stake, R. E. (1995). *The art of case study research*. Thousand Oaks, CA: SAGE.

_____. (2006). *Multiple case study analysis*. New York, NY: The Guilford Press.

Stevenson, L. M., & Deasy, R. J. (Ed.). (2005). *Third space: When learning matters*. Washington, DC: Arts Education Partnership.

Takemoto, M. (2016). Labyrinth of the string quartet. Retrieved from http://string-quartet-labyrinth.blog.jp/.

Van Manen, M. (1990). *Researching lived experience: Human science for an action sensitive pedagogy*. Albany, NY: SUNY.

Warren, C. A. B., & Karner, T. X. (2010). *Discovering qualitative methods: Field research, interviews, and analysis* (2nd ed.). New York, NY: Oxford University Press.

Wigglesworth, C. G. (2012). *SQ21: The twenty-one skills of spiritual intelligence* (1st ed.). New York, NY: SelectBooks, Inc.

Yin, R. K. (2009). *Case study research: Design and methods* (4th ed.). Los Angeles, CA: SAGE.

About the Author

Dorianne Cotter-Lockard, PhD served as an executive of a Fortune 100 company, where she was a key member of the C-level leadership team, making divisional decisions for a billion-dollar subsidiary with 9,000 employees. In her prior career, she was a professional violinist, performing at Carnegie Hall, Lincoln Center, and the Aspen Music Festival. Dorianne left the corporate world in 2007 to earn a PhD in Human and Organizational Systems from Fielding Graduate University. In her current work, she uses classical chamber music as a metaphor for deep listening to inspire and guide young entrepreneurs to master communication, collaboration, and organizational dynamics. Contact: dcotter-lockard@email.fielding.edu

CHAPTER 9
Rising Sun: Actioning Hermeneutic Phenomenological Inquiry for Community Based Social Innovation

Michael Wilson, PhD
Director, Phoenix Society & Fielding Graduate University Alumnus
Ann Wilson, EdD
Simon Fraser University & Director, Phoenix Society

Abstract

The authors demonstrate how hermeneutic phenomenological inquiry influenced their development of a socially innovative project to improve the lives of marginalized citizens. They show its influence in the practical actions of coordination and collaboration with multiple stakeholders to bring into being places and spaces in the community that provided material pathways to formal education, employment, affordable housing, and home ownership for citizens who had been left behind due to homelessness, addiction, declining mental health, and unemployment. This unique project design demonstrated that such citizens can recover, achieve employment that provides a sustainable livelihood, and own their own homes in less than two years. Hermeneutic phenomenological inquiry also informed the design of inclusive interactive civic spaces to promote broader inclusive participatory inquiry: what had been perceived as individual troubles (for example, homelessness, addiction) could now be transformed into community issues for public deliberation towards more socially just public policy.

Keywords: inquiry, phenomenology; hermeneutics; social innovation; social justice

Introduction

In this chapter, Michael and I have worked together to describe how we engaged with hermeneutic phenomenological inquiry and how this has influenced our work as community-based practitioners committed to social innovation that improves the lives of marginalized citizens in our community. First, we locate ourselves within the context of our work and the questions we were living. Secondly, we describe how these questions led us in our learning pathways toward Alfred Schutz's social phenomenology and Hans-Georg Gadamer's self-reflective hermeneutics through learning opportunities with Valerie Bentz and David Rehorick at the Fielding Graduate University. We show how hermeneutic phenomenological inquiry shaped the Rising Sun Project that exists today in the community as a $12-million, 34,000-square-foot, comprehensive urban development project combining three kinds of affordable housing and interactive civic elements. Finally, we also address how we came to identify what we call a living practice of hermeneutic phenomenological inquiry, or a practice of living that displays its continuing relevance in our lives and work together as scholar-practitioners.

Context of Our Work and Our Location

In order for a person to grasp the nature of our living hermeneutic phenomenological inquiry for social innovation, it is important for us to address the context of our work and our location. We have worked together for 25 years toward social justice goals in a community-based nonprofit organization called the Phoenix Society (www.phoenixsociety.com). Social justice efforts in our work means working toward a community, and a world, in which resources are distributed more equitably; in which race, gender, and other social categories do not lead to various forms of oppression and structural inequality; and in which hierarchical power is countered by a resurgence of democracy, on both the local and global levels, as the power of the private sector is balanced by that of government and civil society.

It is also important to say that our work in the organization has profoundly shaped us as scholar-practitioners. Our particular story is rooted in the rich humus of our everyday lived interactions in our practice setting, in which we have been immersed with citizens whose lives are marginalized by homelessness, trauma, declining mental health, addiction, criminal justice involvement, and poverty. Our research and action for social innovation has been directed toward creating spaces and opportunities for these citizens to flourish and find their way to full participation in the social, economic, political, and cultural life of the community (Wilson, 2013).

We describe the process of inquiry, learning, and transformational change that was inspired by hermeneutic phenomenological thinking as it occurred across the domains of business, education, finance, civil society, governance and the law, and the arts in the Rising Sun Project. Infusing hermeneutic phenomenological inquiry in action for change was a process of developing creative capacities of inquiry and learning across individual, group, organizational, and institutional levels of praxis. These levels of learning, theorizing, and praxis are also associated with particular kinds of action for transformational change together known as social innovation. In our work, social innovation refers to the mobilization of social and institutional resources to respond to deprivations of all kinds: material (poverty, lack of housing), social (lack of access to education, health resources), political (no citizenship, lack of access to participate), economic (lack of access to stable employment and income supporting a sustainable livelihood), and existential (lack of connection to purpose, meaning, contribution). Processes characterized by these social change efforts are directed at four scales of change (Westley, 2008):

- individual level: changes of heart and habits of mind;
- group level: changes in conversations, routines, and resources;
- organizational level: changes in procedures and strategies; and

- institutional level: changes in social and power relations.

Change at an individual level demanded attention to citizens' lived experience of profound social, economic, cultural, spiritual, and political deprivation. This required a shift of consciousness prompting phenomenological inquiry. We describe shifts in consciousness that occurred through hermeneutic phenomenological inquiry. Change also demanded critical hermeneutic work—a deepening of awareness and analysis of how one perceives one's relationship with and makes sense of the social world, and how one's subsequent interpretations inform one's own actions and affect others. At a group level, it demanded changes in methods of formerly learned thinking and relating. At an organizational level, change efforts involved examining and changing language, conversations, and familiar routines, policies, and procedures. At an institutional level, it demanded critical analytical efforts to understand and engage with the deep complexity of the conditions in which we worked. Actions for social justice demanded transdisciplinary efforts: the shift to expanding the capacity to build collaborative relationships and partnerships across disciplines as well as across private and public sectors, and civil society.

The Rising Sun Project brings knowledge generation into accountable relations with social justice aims in delivering a comprehensive urban development project. Rising Sun combines three kinds of affordable housing and features a new design prototype to increase access to home ownership for excluded groups. Important interactive civic elements were key parts of the design. These include a social innovation centre, all nations' gallery, and large community gardens surrounding the project.

Both of us have had a lifelong curiosity about learning and knowledge generation, and we have both pursued scholarly work to inform our practice. We were first introduced to phenomenology in our training as Gestalt therapists, where our lives and learning pathways initially converged. Our wayfinding in practice and action in these early days was guided by phenomenology's view of human beings as creative agents in constructing their social worlds; its focus on awareness of our present experiencing and processing; and its prizing of the relationship with self and other guided by empathy, curiosity, thoughtfulness, and embodied consciousness. Gestalt approaches also drew on Kurt Lewin's (1951) field theory to appreciate the coherent whole (*gestalt*) of the person in the field or life space in which they are situated. The limitation we soon encountered, however, was that the stories of the citizens we served were also enmeshed in the larger fields of sociopolitical life, which were unsupportive and often hostile to their attempts at restoring the gestalt of person-world connectedness. Gestalt approaches pointed to these larger fields but did not suggest pathways toward action for social change in broader social arenas.

What we noted in these larger fields of sociopolitical life was a significant disconnection in the "theory-research-policy relationship" (Kovach, 2015, p. 373), in which policy knowledge seemed to erase the local lived experiences of citizens and individualized responsibility for social inequality. One dominant story in Canada that emerged from this disconnection is that fiscal responsibility must trump a compassionate response to Canadians living in poverty (Gaetz, 2012). This kind of thinking viewed complex community issues such as citizens becoming homeless as largely private or singularly personal matters to be treated by remedial or therapeutic intervention rather than as a critical loss of citizenship capability resulting from multi-scalar socio-economic-political shifts. We take our reference point on citizenship capability from Daniel Schugurensky (2006), who are argues that citizens who become marginalized lose their social, economic, and political citizenship status. We take Schugurensky to mean that becoming marginalized means citizens lose their capacity to participate in social, economic, cultural, and political life. In *Development as Freedom*, Amartya Sen also noted that poverty is a deprivation of capabilities (2000). We learned that homelessness and poverty formed a phenomenon converging on cities in post-industrial states across the globe. We also observed this disturbing phenomenon of disconnection and separation in more generalized understandings of the human experiences of homelessness, addiction, and poverty. The citizens and the deprivations they endured were viewed in terms of such a radical otherness that they suggested non-humanness. And further, these citizens and their dire circumstances were spoken of as if they existed outside of any relationship to the larger social, historical, and political world.

The dilemma for us as scholar-practitioners lay in how to create a research story big enough to draw the disconnectedness and separation evident in the whole of individual, group, organizational, and institutional life into a coherent whole (*gestalt*) with a view to actualizing social innovation to restore capabilities to the lives of the citizens we served. This kind of inquiry demanded broader, more critical, and complex perspectives than those bounded by particular disciplines, theories, or particular policy sectors.

An inspiring discovery in our research—as we looked for social movements globally where voluntary sectors were at the forefront of actions for social justice—were the efforts of a research collaboration that produced the Alternative Models of Local Social Innovation or AL-MOLIN model of social innovation (Gonzalez, Moulaert, & Martinelli, 2010; Moulaert, Swygedouw, Martinelli, & Gonzalez, 2010). We were interested in ALMOLIN'S critical analytical model for three reasons. First, like our inquiry process, ALMOLIN emerged from a collaboration of researchers across disciplines (Moulaert, Martinelli, Gonzalez, & Swygedouw, 2007; Moulaert, Swygedouw, Martinelli, & Gonzalez, 2010; Miciukiewicz, Moulaert, Novy, Musterd, & Hillier, 2012; Novy, Swiatek, & Moulaert, 2012; MacCallum, Moulaert, Hillier, & Vicari Haddock, 2009). Second, the working definition of alternative local social innovation began from an ethical position of social justice. Third, the various researchers wanted to make knowledge generation directly accountable to the lives of marginalized citizens. Their concern with the connection between inquiry and action for social justice led them to identify three dimensions of social innovation as a tangible set of measures about knowledge generation (epistemology) that contributed to actual change towards social justice: (a) whether a social innovation responded to human deprivation; (b) whether it empowered previously silent or excluded social groups by creating new capabilities; and (c) whether it changed social and power relations towards a more inclusive and democratic governance system (Gonzalez, Moulaert, & Martinelli, 2010, p. 56). Frank Moulaert and his colleagues (Moulaert, Martinelli, Swygedouw, & Gonzalez, 2005) viewed these three dimensions as axiological: that is, as interconnected features of individual and collective well-being.

In addition, the entry point to their research on social innovation was located as we were at the local level, where the multiple deprivations of social exclusion were evident. Further, the research collaborators studied the complex multilayered realities of selected European cities marked by social disintegration resulting from market failure, the erosion of welfare state policy, and the failure of the labor market. To this end, their studies included a diversity of actors, citizens, agencies, sectors, social relations, and governance processes that demonstrated a dialectical process between exclusion conditions and the collective processes and practices deployed to overcome them in the work of alternative local social innovation. These researchers articulated a process for practitioners like us, acting at a local scale, to analyze both the dynamics of social exclusion in the local and particular context in which we were located (individual, group, organization), and how these were connected with broader structural levels (institutional).

The researchers sought to develop theoretical orientations for social innovation efforts and seemed to point to the necessity of critical analysis as well as a metatheoretical approach to the construct of social innovation that served social justice aims. Moulaert's (2009) research

242

suggested that for local social innovation efforts involving multiple stakeholders, like our inquiry, knowledge generation required the development of an epistemology characterized as an "activity of inquiry leading to a negotiated consensus on the way to develop knowledge" (p. 2). Knowledge, for Moulaert, was relationally conceived; criteria for truth of the knowledge should be concerned with the relevance of scientific answers in responding to human needs, the transformation of social relations, and the empowerment of populations and communities. In this view, consensus should be reached on what knowledge is relevant to overcome social exclusion across a wide range of stakeholders, including marginalized citizens. This was the case in our inquiry. Similarly, Moulaert advocated for an open ontology to validate the multiple realities in play across a range of stakeholders in an inquiry like ours to inform a future vision of more socially just communities.

Learning Pathways

Embodying the tensions evident in the need to integrate research and action for change led Michael to pursue doctoral research in the Human and Organization Development Program at Fielding Graduate University and Ann to pursue a doctoral degree in a transformational change program in the Faculty of Education at Simon Fraser University. Locating ourselves in the deep immersion of our lived relations with the citizens we were striving to help rather than in a specific disciplinary space had significant implications for undertaking knowledge generation for social innovation that would improve the lives of the citizens we served.

Ann's attention in her scholarly research was drawn to actively questioning research methodology itself (Wilson, 2017). She was concerned that an inquirers' disengagement or separation from the lifeworlds they study could occur through their selection of methods and methodology (Kajner & Schultz, 2013). In addition, we had both been influenced by Edgar Morin's *Seven Complex Lessons in Education for the Future* (1999b), where Morin had acknowledged the need for alternatives in knowledge generation in light of an emergent global context of complexity and uncertainty. Morin argued that the dominating instrumental-rationalist pattern of thinking had decontextualized knowledge generation from the human, lifeworldly realm. This had not only created conditions where "we can no longer learn what human being means" (Morin, 1999b, p. 10); it had also resulted in the complex interconnected crises, or "polycrisis," that we now face on a global level—in the economy, climate, war, loss of species, environmental degradation, and an unprecedented scale of social polarization, poverty, marginalization, human deprivation, and suffering.

Morin (1999a) also forcefully argued that these global crises were the result of human thinking and action. He proposed that we must learn to "think the complex" (p. 130) in order to engage effectively with the complexity of the conditions we were facing. He proposed that "thinking the complex" was a kind of thinking that "relinks that which is disjointed and compartmentalized" (Morin, 1999a, pp. 130-132). He advocated for the notion of a "connective tissue" that existed between knowledge, its context, and human beings rather than the disciplinary separation of knowledge and the decontextualization of knowledge generation from the human, lifeworldly realm. The need for research-informed strategies that improved the lives of marginalized citizens placed our inquiry in the context of complexity that Morin described. We needed to develop our capacity for thinking the complex in order to engage effectively with the conditions in which we found ourselves as scholar-practitioners.

What kind of knowledge paradigms and methodologies could assist community-based practitioners like us to generate knowledge that prioritized accountability to individual and social well-being? Questions like this multiplied as we progressed with our inquiry. The messy, complex nature of the conditions we lived and worked with as practitioners did not fit neatly within disciplinary boundaries of conventional scholarly inquiry. At the start of Michael's learning journey at Fielding, important orienting ideas in situating himself as a scholar-practitioner came from Valerie Bentz and Jeremy Shapiro in their book *Mindful Inquiry in Social Research* (1998). Mindful inquiry advocated for locating oneself as a researcher at the center of the research process rather than in research techniques or methods. This model of the scholar-practitioner felt congruent for Michael since he felt he was learning to become a researcher in a variety of practice settings. He wanted to keep individual and community well-being at the forefront while he was engaged in problem-solving with others with a wide range of diverse interests. Bentz and Shapiro's (1998) proposal for *embodying* the process of inquiry in such a way that inquiry is part of the way one engages with the world also felt deeply intuitive and validating for Michael and Ann. They posed a startling question that resonated strongly with both of us: "Through the practice of compassion and right conduct, pay attention to the suffering of sentient beings in the world, and ask yourself what kind of inquiry and action would diminish that suffering" (Bentz & Shapiro, 1998, p. 52). This incisive question made inquiry and action directly accountable to the citizens with whom we worked, who experienced the suffering of multiple forms of deprivation: lack of access to a safe, affordable home, food, clothing, access to health care, education, sanctuary, and existential solidarity with a community of supportive others.

A further important step in our research trajectory for social innovation lay in our learning about the approach of transformative phenomenology where David Rehorick & Valerie Bentz (2008) integrated Husserl's (1970/1936) phenomenological thinking and the social phenomenology of Schutz (1970; 1967/1932). They encouraged, validated, and demonstrated an appreciation of one's living process of being in the world. Being as a source of knowing, they argued, comes of inner spaciousness, embodied awareness, the co-construction of the social intersubjective structures of the lifeworld (typifications) and consciousness of typifications as they are applied in the lifeworld. In their teaching, David and Valerie encouraged cultivating a genuine curiosity about one's experience and noticing one's ongoing process of experiencing including how one is presently framing, conceptualizing, and evaluating it. This idea of an embodied inquiry also accounted for the idea of researching ourselves, exploring the processes of our own self-formation-construction as well as our formulation of ideas about the world. This kind of living practice strengthened a focus on our development as scholar-practitioners and the process of becoming embodied in our research and in the lifeworlds to which we were accountable (Bentz & Shapiro, 1998).

Hermeneutic inquiry invites inquirers to undertake a reflexive process to uncover what modes of consciousness, assumptions, and biases we are using in the process of interpretation that informs action. Like Buddhist mindfulness practices, its purpose is to help inquirers to move beyond surface interpretations and habituated seeing and thinking. Because Gadamer playfully extended self-reflective hermeneutic inquiry to social relationships and interactions, our hermeneutic inquiry highlighted how our interpretations as practitioners have profound implications for the lives and lifeworlds of the disenfranchised citizens with whom we work. Hermeneutics was helpful in a very practical way for contextualizing our work as practitioners and clarifying our relational responsibility to the citizens with whom we worked more fully. Gadamer (1975, 1976) proposed that in our everyday human attempts to understand our world, we always bring our foremeanings or what he calls "prejudices" to bear in our work of hermeneutic understanding. Rather than seeing prejudices as an obstacle to understanding, Gadamer saw them as an integral part of our human meaning-making process, presenting important opportunities for deepening our understanding of self and other. Gadamer's playful and inclusive approach helped us to move beyond binary structures of thinking when working within and against prevailing rational-instrumentalist systems in the development of the Rising Sun Project. Gadamer's three levels of self-reflective hermeneutics served as an important guide in our living practice of focusing on the moral, ethical nature of our relationships with others having different horizons of understanding.

Influence of Transformative Phenomenology

In the section that follows, we will illustrate the affordances of hermeneutic phenomenological thinking at individual, group, organizational, and institutional levels of change in our process of developing a socially innovative project. Phenomenology's focus on the complexity and wholeness of human experience held promise as an essential foundational component of social innovation research that we had not encountered in the literature. In view of the disconnection and disjointedness we located in the "theory-research-policy relationship" (Kovach, 2015, p. 373) related to the lives of citizens we served, Husserl's (1970/1936) radical proposal was that what we recognize as features of the world are actually constituted by our consciousness. This we saw as a relevant inquiry guide to restore wholeness to an inquiry process informed by social justice. Further, we saw Schutz's notion of the intersubjectivity of our human consciousness as relevant to our active, agentic exploration of the deeper meanings of a phenomenon through a more democratic process of sharing these understandings of a phenomenon constituted by our consciousness shaped by the social world.

We experimented with hermeneutic phenomenological inquiry by taking our everyday lived reality in our practice setting as an object of curiosity using the practice of bracketing (the phenomenological practice of setting aside the usual preconceptions that structure our everyday perceptions and experiences). The object was not to fully remove our preconceptions but to become more deeply conscious of how they structured a particular reality we encountered (Rehorick & Bentz, 2008, p.11). These experiments presented us with opportunities to inquire into and appreciate our location and positionality, to critically engage with and challenge our views about ourselves, to consider how we were actively making sense of the citizens we were attempting to help, and

247

to articulate what we thought we knew about society, how it worked, and our place in it (Wilson, 2013; Wilson, 2017). A dynamic process, both iterative and reflexive, our inquiry became richer as we shared our learning with staff and colleagues. It uncovered the high stakes in knowledge generation and how it structured our relations with the citizens we were trying to help. Hermeneutic phenomenological inquiry served as a deconstructing process. It illuminated how the walls of safety provided by our own frameworks, concepts, and assumptions could keep us from authentic contact with the citizens we were trying to assist. While such critical deconstructing work can generate disturbing existential questions as we are brought face to face with human lived experiences of innocent suffering and helplessness, it may also build existential solidarity in our discovery of human lived experiences that we held in common. Such life-changing experiences compel one to act.

An example using Schutz's social phenomenology serves to illustrate how practitioners can bring focus, intention, and awareness to contextualizing texts such as the case management document below, as well as to its related institutionalized products and practices. Schutz's (1932/1967) unique contribution in social phenomenology was his proposal that we take for granted the intersubjective world that is given to us as an organized world, one that has a quality of coherence and unity such that we take its thereness for granted. We are not usually mindful of our everyday experience. We tend to view our experiences as unfolding automatically. We are usually not mindful of how our lived experience is influenced by broader social, economic, or historical structures. Schutz (1970, p. 253) referred to this as "the world of common sense and daily life" and called this wide-awake quality of our consciousness our *natural attitude*. This field note is a brief excerpt of instructions from a typical, standard case management document we examined that organizes our work in practice settings such as the Phoenix Centre:

> Describe the client's personal appearance, including whether or not the client was appropriately dressed for the weather on the day of the interview, the client's personal hygiene, abili-

ty to maintain eye contact and the client's mental orientation (awareness of person, place, time and event). Reports are often written in a narrative form that tells the story of the client's current problem or problems and how and when those problems initially appeared.

In our experiment with hermeneutic phenomenological thinking, we explored the case management document as an interpretive work, an institutional discourse, a socially constructed practice providing direction on how to produce a technical rendering of a particular social reality. We viewed it as an "active text" (Smith, 1992) that serves to organize us and our work as practitioners, and prescribes our ways of being with the citizens we work with in our practice setting. We observed the relations of power that structured a one-way directional flow of conversation, how it instructs practitioners like us on how to interpret persons we encounter in an interview using socially constructed norms that the interviewer deploys to tell the story of the interviewee. It encourages the practitioner to view the person instrumentally as someone and/or something to be regulated. Without awareness, practitioners can easily become persuaded to view themselves as experts legitimately positioned to do the regulating. The storyline is prescriptive. What often emerges is a narrative of individualized problems authored by a proxy expert.

Schutz theorized that typifications provide interpretive schemes—formulas or recipes that provide the structures of our lifeworld—that help us make sense of our everyday reality, influence our understanding, and guide our actions. Through our lived experiences and primarily through language, we learn the already existing socially constructed and shared objectifications or typifications of the lifeworld from our parents, teachers, and other authorities (Schutz, 1970). Layers of typifications accumulate over time through our ongoing experience, becoming the stocks of knowledge that help us find our way through the complexity of our everyday experience in the lifeworld we share with others (Schutz,

1970, p. 72). Our stocks of knowledge inform the way we speak to each other individually, as a group of practitioners, or with others at organizational and institutional levels. Stocks of knowledge are operationalized as systems of typifications that shape consciousness and the ways practitioners communicate with each other. Stocks of knowledge then are organized by systems of relevance shaping the constitution of what useful knowledge is, how we interpret events in the lifeworld, and what actions we take. Rehorick and Bentz helpfully explained the interplay between typifications and relevances:

> What we see as relevant is shaped by our personal stock of knowledge, an accumulation of our typifications. In turn, our typifications are formed by what is relevant to us, and relevancy is shaped by our tacit awareness of what we think we should be doing with our lives, moment to moment and situation to situation. (2008, p. 18)

Schutz's theorizing that lifeworlds are co-created through networks of relationships (Rehorick & Bentz, 2008, p. 19) guided an exploration of the implications of an assessment form prescribed for use in our practice setting. The assessment form below represents a world view that locates and defines an individual according to common psychological, behavioral, or personal problems rather than as a citizen located within a complex web of structural, political, and economic conditions.

Table 1

Assessment Form: Excerpt from Global Appraisal of Individual Needs–Short Screener

The following questions are about common psychological, behavioural or personal problems. These problems are considered significant when you have them for two or more weeks, when they keep coming back, when they keep you from meeting your responsibilities, or when they make you feel like you can't go on.		3	2	1	0
		In the past month	Two to 12 months ago	One or more years ago	Never
IDScr	When was the last time you had significant problems?				
	With feeling very trapped, lonely, sad, blue, depressed, or hopeless about the future?				
	With sleeping such as bad dreams, sleeping restlessly, or falling asleep during the day?				
	With feeling very anxious, nervous, tense, fearful, scared, panicked, or like something bad was going to happen?				
	When something reminded you of the past and you became very distressed and upset?				
	With thinking about ending your life or committing suicide?				

The citizens with whom we work are in contact with the health, mental health or addiction treatment, social services, or the criminal justice system. For these citizens, the disclosure of personal histories through such assessment processes is accepted practice for identifying individual disorders and deficits. The assessment will determine eligibility for or disqualification from shelter, housing, medical treatment, or income assistance—or to provide the basis of evidentiary claims that support the enactment of public policy that may contribute to deepening their marginalization. As part of our inquiry into the assessment form, we wondered what kind of assessment form could be designed based on an ontology of individual and community well-being? What would emerge if we enumerated strengths and trajectories of resilience in the face of the enormous challenges that citizens who live in poverty endure? What problems would we find that we shared in common, rather than consigning problems solely to individuals? In this hermeneutic phenomenological inquiry, we recognized that we were engaged in a considerably more spacious process of uncovering a complex process of thinking, remembering, experiencing, deconstructing, and constructing than was typically outside our awareness in our everyday lived activities and interactions. By bringing our attention to our lived experience in everyday interactions, we got a sense that we were uncovering how our processes of knowing were based on our lived experience and through our interactive engagement with the social worlds we inhabited.

As we explored our everyday lived reality in our practice setting as an object of curiosity, our analysis identified our work as practitioners as structured predominantly by a clinical paradigm aligned with the prevailing hegemony of managerialism and so-called evidence-based approaches that measure effectiveness in restricted economic terms. In our everyday interactions structured by the systemic routines, rules, expectations, and norms of managerial paradigms, hermeneutic phenomenological thinking deepened our awareness that citizens we were striving to assist who experienced homelessness, addiction, and criminal justice involvement (among other poverty-related issues) were increasingly objectified and typified as *clients, patients,* or *persons in care.* The natural attitude was characterized by prevailing typifications that privilege a medical and increasingly psychiatric and criminogenic analysis that highlighted individual deficits in social skills, thinking, and behavior problems.

We analyzed the implications of dominant typifications, systems of relevance, and stocks of knowledge for the life chances of disenfranchised citizens. Cultural stereotypes of citizens such as *addicts* or *homeless people* or *the mentally ill* were homogeneous typifications. Such typifications were reproduced and distributed in wider cultural venues as commonplace understandings, and they were internalized in the interactive engagement characterizing the lifeworld of our practice setting. As practitioners, we also heard typifications recited in citizens' self-appraisals, such as "I am..." *an addict, sick, a worthless person, morally defective, a deviant, a piece of shit.* These typifications and systems of relevance reinforce a naïve, uninformed perception of the experience of homelessness as an isolated, exceptional, singularly individual plight. Until critically examined, these typifications can powerfully shape the everyday reality of citizens with whom we work. If they remain uncritically accepted, they can also powerfully shape our own everyday reality as practitioners and our natural attitude: our everyday understanding about the citizens the organization served and who we were as practitioners.

At an organization level, we wondered how we could create lifeworldly spaces in the Rising Sun Project that counteracted negative typifications; that could produce alternative active texts of empowerment and emancipation, and encourage the construction of new broader typifications and stocks of knowledge according to relevances that prioritized individual and collective well-being. Below we show how an alternative set of understandings emerged against the constraints of professional norms and economic efficiency through hermeneutic phenomenological inquiry.

Phenomenological inquiry is a deconstructing and reconstructing process (Bentz and Shapiro, 1998). This involved exploring the practice of bracketing our preexisting structures of thinking and acting to explore alternative ways of being and knowing, guided by *empathic immersion*, described as "a slowing down and dwelling, magnification and amplification of the situation, suspension of belief, employment of intense interest, turning from objects to their lived meaning" (Bentz & Shapiro, 1998, p. 99). We agreed that creating inclusive learning spaces meant that these would be spaces that could come to be organized for individual and collective well-being. We used the term *well-being* as a critical ontological mainstay in the Rising Sun Project and as a future-oriented vision of how citizens might be placed first in considering how we could imagine a web of life-giving relationships among places, communities, and cities that were socially, economically, and environmentally sustainable into the future.

Coming to use the language of *creating spaces* also importantly acknowledged that, as the ALMOLIN analysis revealed, marginalization had spatial implications, that increasingly fewer spaces exist in the city to provide access to education and other resources that empower dispossessed citizens to exit poverty, to achieve a sustainable livelihood, and to participate actively in the social, economic, political, and cultural life of the community. We agreed that we would actively use the term *citizens* to refer to the persons with whom we worked rather than such distancing objectifications as *the homeless*, *the mentally ill*, or *addicts*. This purposefully disruptive act directed attention to the recognition that citizens who become marginalized lose their access to social, economic, and political participation (Schugurensky, 2006). Designing the Rising Sun Project in terms of socially inclusive spaces in the city solidified its integral connection to the restoration of and enactment of active citizenship (Wilson & Wilson, 2014).

We envisioned the Rising Sun Project in phenomenological terms of the lifeworld. Place, home, and individual and collective well-being are systems of relevance that hold citizens and the world together in relationship. We envisioned how we could create lifeworldly spaces that counteracted negative typifications that infused citizens' experiences. We also envisioned how we could create alternative active texts of empowerment and emancipation, and new typifications and stocks of knowledge according to relevances that promoted individual and collective well-being. These relevances were noted in expressions of participants who were grasping new possibilities of person-world connectedness. For one citizen, it was a vision of *what it is possible for me to achieve*; for another it was a vision of *ever learning*. Another citizen's vision was of connection to a lifeworld where *I have something to contribute*. We envisioned the Rising Sun Project as not only identifying the process of consciousness construction but finding alternative ways of "thinking *and being* the complex" that expanded possibilities for creating new social contexts, relational processes, and experiences, and new patterns of interconnectedness that would provide platforms for the reconstruction of self, other, and world.

Rising Sun Villa

Hermeneutic phenomenological thinking also infused the design process of Rising Sun as a philosophical, political, and practical exercise. It involved creating opportunities for a deep attunement to how embodied citizens and their environment interrelate experientially, and the complexes of pattern and meaning that create a sense of "dwelling"

(Heidegger, 1971). This was an essential consideration in designing the project in view of the lack of safety; the compounding losses of employment, home and emotional ties; and the experiences of violence, displacement, isolation, discrimination, deprivation, alienation, and abiding loneliness that characterize citizens' endurance of prolonged homelessness. We created spaces and processes where citizens shared the lived meanings of these experiences with the architect. The architect infused the building design process with these hermeneutic architectural meanings. The result was a relational flow in the design between a sense of home (safety, my personal world) in relation to place (relations with the history of the city, roads, parks, schools and neighbourhoods, urban planning, on the border of the new city centre, and how place might be invented or reinvented). This relational flow also informed outer spaces (social innovation centre, gallery, and community gardens) that communicated a sense of interconnectedness, hopefulness, and vision of the future beyond the Rising Sun Project's immediate and familiar spatial boundaries.

We strove to guide these hermeneutic architectural meanings into action within and against prevailing traditions and assumptions about building designs of social housing projects that typically leave out connections with social, epistemological, and civic webs of participation. Hallways, for instance, are traditionally regarded as devoid of meaning, impersonal passageways to the more highly valued personal and private spaces of residents' homes. An example of opening to hermeneutic architectural meanings occurred when residents identified hallways as significant intermediary spaces between their homes. Hallways emerged as a specific design feature and built form—as purposeful places of residents' connection with their neighbors, and as civic spaces where they could give and receive support, and exchange views, valuable information, and resources. They were designed in ten-foot widths, with large windows at either end to allow in natural light, and open onto views of the community outside the property's boundaries. As an interesting aside, during the building appraisal, no additional value was detected by professional appraisers, who were unused to imagining hallways as significant civic spaces connecting residents with increasing socio-political-epistemological capability.

An important historical precedent for this kind of community-based work is found in the example of Hull House, the social settlement community developed by Jane Addams in Chicago in 1889. Hull House was a refuge that responded to the multiple deprivations of social exclusion experienced by new immigrants. Addams incorporated sanctuary with music, art, and theater offerings to prototype an inclusive community where citizens could experience companionship and solidarity with others coping with the challenges of urbanization and industrialization in the modern city. Hull House also evolved to meet needs for employment and educational assistance, and practical and technical training as well as civic education to empower citizens to participate more fully in the social, economic, cultural, and political life of the city. The significant role of the arts in community life emphasized by Addams at Hull House also found expression in the inclusive interactive space of the social innovation centre we describe below.

Hermeneutic Phenomenological Influences on Spatializing Citizenship: Making Public Space into Sites for Knowledge Exchange

A significant design strategy that emerged from hermeneutic phenomenological thinking directly addressed knowledge generation and ownership of knowledge by marginalized citizens. A Social Innovation Centre was designed as a vibrant, interactive incubation space for a broader, more inclusive kind of social convening that promoted participatory research approaches to encourage a diverse exchange of ideas to take action on creating just, sustainable communities. The Social Innovation Centre included an All Nations' Art Gallery, which was designed to provide inclusive, interactive space for local and global indigenous artisans to work, teach, share knowledge, and exchange ideas about the role of the arts in community life. Its operation was structured by fair trade agreements.

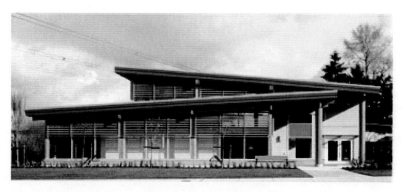

Rising Sun Social Innovation Centre, Gallery, and Cafe

Community gardens included in the design of the Rising Sun Project were also an example of reinventing public spaces for inclusive dialogue and exchange. Jointly imagined and designed by and with marginalized citizens, the gardens were developed by the Phoenix Society in partnership with the city on lands adjacent to existing common walking trails in an urban greenway. The gardens were strategically designed as a widely welcoming community engagement space promoting social inclusion. They brought together "the civic web of the political domain, the biotic web of the natural world, the social web of human life, and the epistemological web of knowledge production" (Kincheloe, 2003, p. 49). The gardens were envisioned as means of creating significant opportunities for co-constructing meanings in a space that embodied a relational view of social, economic, and environmental sustainability, posing disruptive challenges to the dominant interpretations of so-called urban development. While they proposed possibilities for connecting culture and nature, they were also an unapologetically political project, congruent with the purposes of the Rising Sun Project. Their colocation on city property adjacent to but part of the Rising Sun project reinvented civic spaces for diverse, inclusive, social, and cultural encounters and knowledge exchange on critical issues such as food security, social inclusion, affordable housing, community safety, sustainability, and urban development. Curating this convergence of spaces in the Rising Sun Project meant that the gardens existed as a negotiated space of meaning construction, calling into awareness the need for more harmonious relationships between humans and between humans and nature. They also provided an example of building urban landscapes that could heal and empower communities.

The Influence of Hermeneutic Phenomenological Thinking at Institutional Levels of Change in Social Innovation Efforts in the Rising Sun Project

An important indicator of social innovation, according to the AL-MOLIN model, is whether an initiative changes social relations—that is, whether it "determines durable changes in social-power relations between social groups, among scales of government, and among civil society, the state and the market sectors" (Gonzalez, Moulaert, & Martinelli, 2010, p. 55). Exploring the conventional problematization through policy concepts of insufficient affordable housing in the city, we began our appreciation of the issue with an acknowledgement that the complexity of this problem was located both inside and outside the boundaries of our local community, and it would therefore need to be addressed in a systemic way. Secondly, we recognized that we needed to adopt an experimental approach while working with actual realities on the ground in the community. Thirdly, we acknowledged that it would be most important to demonstrate a different way of thinking of the problem of insufficient affordable housing in the city. We acknowledged that not only was *home* a need for all citizens, but our collective thinking across systems and sectors about the social risks of homelessness was fundamentally unsustainable into the future and needed to change.

Changes in rules, resources, and authority flows and a redistribution of knowledge and resources occurred in dialogue with city management, urban planners, housing authorities, and with a financial cooperative about how the Phoenix Society might respond differently to interpretations of social risks in our city. For example, in complex discussions with the planning department at the city management level, we recognized that, thinking through and with Gadamer's first level of hermeneutics, the city had its historical consciousness, traditions, precedents, and prejudices in the form of laws and procedures. Gadamer might say that its horizon of understanding about creating affordable housing for marginalized citizens was based on a set of interpretive acts about what a city is. These take the form of structures like planning and zoning templates. Similarly, the historical consciousness of the housing authority informed its horizon of understanding about what social housing looked like. It had produced a set of structures—design templates—for architects and constructors to set out what buildings should look like, where they would be located, the size of units, and the materials used.

In thinking through and with Gadamer's I and Thou relationship at this first level, we experimented with thinking of "the I" as representing the institutional arrangements and "the Thou" as our organization. In our conversations about the potential of the Rising Sun Project, we brought from our historical consciousness different horizons of understanding about city governance, inclusive spaces in the city, and what a home would look like and feel like, based on the values of social justice and the lived realities, dreams, and aspirations of the citizens we served. These conversations progressed through to Gadamer's third level of hermeneutics, where the city entered fully into the conversation, taking in and acting on a different horizon of understanding about the potential of the Rising Sun Project to create a new prototype for inclusive spaces in the city.

Actions indicative of Gadamer's third level of hermeneutics were reflected in how city management collaboratively worked with the Phoenix Society on changes in city governance (a social innovation in itself) to accommodate the multifaceted comprehensive development of the Rising Sun Project that combined three different kinds of afford-able housing: an innovation centre, a gallery, and a community garden, in collaboration with the city and on city land. This collaboration also produced other social innovations such as the modification of zoning templates, and the development of unique strata documents that were approved and filed to enable the creation of a new prototype for in-clusive and affordable housing developments in the city. Evidence of the positive progression through Gadamer's three levels of interpretive understanding in the ongoing encounters in the relationship between city management and the Phoenix Society was a significant contribu-tion made by the city toward the construction of the social innovation centre and community gardens as essential components of an affordable housing project.

Similarly, our dialogue and evolving cross-sector collaboration with a financial cooperative was influenced by thinking through and with Ga-damer's self-reflective hermeneutics. In the progress of our encounters in our continuing relationship with the financial cooperative, we kept in mindful awareness the deep expertise that financial institutions had de-veloped over time. They had already systematized their interpretations of the financial risk of lending to applicants for mortgages or other kinds of financing. These were the technical-rational horizons of understand-ing, as Gadamer would say, that had developed about how social risk was treated in our society.

Our organization proposed to the financial institution the consider-ation of lending to the Phoenix Society's constituents, those who might have poor credit histories, experiences of addiction, criminal justice in-volvement, short or sporadic employment histories, and other barriers to accessing traditional financing. In our organization's dialogue with the financial cooperative, we considered interpretations of risk within and against social, economic, and historical consciousness and traditions. We introduced our reflections on conventional interpretations of what risk was to them. We also acknowledged their deep financial expertise—the development of systems of algorithms that quantified risk—while also introducing axiological questions about how relations of trust could also be considered in developing a new model of inclusive access to home ownership. In these ongoing discussions, we noted that they used their historical traditions or precedents to make sense of our alternative ideas about how inclusive spaces could be created in the city. As an organization with social justice values, we had demonstrated our credibility and trustworthiness over many years in our work with disenfranchised citizens to show that citizens who become homeless should not be left behind, but assisted in developing their capability for social, economic, and political participation. Our organization and the financial institution shared a common commitment to become more deeply connected with and supportive of citizens in the community. Out of these relations of trust we were able to create a collaborative arrangement with the financial cooperative that was based on a different horizon of understanding of social risk, in order to create opportunities for excluded groups to ladder into the housing market through the prototype of shared equity home ownership.

Out of this cross-sector collaboration, customized financial products and processes were developed for applicants whose poor credit histories would typically have disqualified them from home ownership. The financial cooperative developed a financing protocol that accepted a letter from our organization as part of the prospective homeowner's application process, based on our relationships of trust with homeowner applicants, and our relations of trust with the financial cooperative. These in turn were based on a period of treatment, where critical destabilizing features of prolonged homelessness such as addiction and declining mental health were addressed, and where the applicant demonstrated stability in employment and income. The financial institution contributed the legal fees and appraisal for homeowner applicants, and provided financial literacy education sessions and assistance to prospective buyers to prepare for home purchase. Through our ongoing self-reflective encounters in our relations with the financial cooperative, this cross-sector collaboration has made home ownership accessible to previously disenfranchised citizens based on a wage rate of $15 per hour.

This is a clear example of knowledge generation for social justice that meets ALMOLIN's criteria of changing social and power relationships: the relationships among citizens, the market and institutions to improve the lives of marginalized citizens. The bank's technical procedures for calculating financial risk comprised one horizon of understanding. From our organization's work with disenfranchised citizens, we brought our horizon of understanding informed by social justice. A fusion of horizons of understandings occurred that has allowed institutions and community organizations to build relationships of trust in order to create new horizons of understanding about how a society or a city can respond to citizens whose lives are marginalized by unemployment, homelessness, and poverty.

Through financial investment and construction financing from the financial cooperative, the Phoenix Society was empowered to develop a design prototype of the project that expands the continuum of housing supports and provides an increasing stock of affordable home ownership options, in perpetuity, for low and moderate income home buyers. To ensure a perpetual supply of affordable housing (in the context of an inflated real estate market), the shared equity model design prototype determines that homeowner participation in equity gains over time is defined by a covenant in place that guides future resale of the unit. To ensure long-term affordability for future purchasers of these units, a specific resale framework is in place which limits the maximum allowable selling price. Through this mechanism, equity in the unit is "shared" between the seller and the homeowner community. By retaining a portion of the equity value in the housing unit, the Phoenix Society created the platform for subsequent purchasers to also access home ownership at a price below future market price—thus ensuring continuing accessibility for future home purchasers. Home buyers are not only attracted to the opportunity for home ownership, the interactive elements of the project such as the community gardens, social innovation centre and gallery, but also by the opportunity through their contribution of shared equity to leave a legacy in the form of opportunities for others to own their own home.

Prevailing neoliberalist policy rationalities in the province prioritize economic development and argue that only jobs can end poverty. However, this single policy plan has failed to meaningfully reduce poverty. Thirteen percent of British Columbians continue to live in poverty despite being employed. The last province to formulate a poverty reduction plan, poverty costs the BC provincial government $8 to $9 billion annually in higher public health care and criminal justice costs and lost productivity. It is estimated that a comprehensive poverty reduction plan would cost a third to half that amount (BC Poverty Reduction Coalition Committee, 2013). Rising Sun deconstructs the neoliberalist narrative that poverty is too great a challenge to address. Not only does Rising Sun clearly demonstrate that creative, cross-sector collaborations produce clear economic benefits, its hermeneutic phenomenological design drawing on the lived experience of citizens shows how it is possible for urban development projects to address the broader social determinants of health to enhance individual and community well-being.

A relational appreciation of our process of working collaboratively across sectors and systems to create the Rising Sun Project deepened our awareness that a system's or sector's current position can be viewed as a horizon of understanding. This relational appreciation helped us to unseat what we had often experienced as a binary conflict of positions. This deepening awareness encouraged a hermeneutic phenomenological focus on paying attention to the nuances in the progress of the relationship with the other. This had an unmistakable influence on the emergent process of dialectical reciprocity in the relationship and on the process of practical accomplishment of meaning and the making of the Rising Sun Project based on the social justice values of improving the lives of disenfranchised citizens.

Reflecting on the influence of hermeneutic phenomenological thinking, our critical analysis at institutional levels showed that the alignment of research-knowledge generation and policy with neoliberal policy logics and rationalities was highly problematic in light of the consequences for the already marginalized citizens we wanted to assist. The neoliberalization process focuses on promoting a free-market economy, economic development, and trade liberalization. It withdraws investment in human and social development and restructures social policy investments according to economic efficiencies and market logics to address social issues for the least cost (Wilson & Wilson, 2013). Hermeneutic phenomenology, combined with critical analysis, showed the path dependency of the construction of identities of marginalized citizens through scientific classification, categorization, and subjectification processes according to regimes of truth (criminology, law, economics, education, medicine, psychiatry, and social policy). A hermeneutic approach helped us as practitioners to understand the historical consciousness, traditions, and trajectories of these institutional dynamics. It allowed us to explore and uncover what modes of consciousness, assumptions, and horizons of understanding informed the changing rationalities in multilevel layers of public policy that acted to rename and reshape the meanings of social welfare, citizen, citizenship, risk, and the responsibilities of communities, governments, and citizens. Rising Sun demonstrates how new broader typifications and stocks of knowledge according to relevances that prioritized individual and community well-being prizes citizen participation to mobilize many different kinds of knowledge in the service of making our city more inclusive, democratic, and socially just.

Conclusion

In this chapter, we have shared some key moments showing the influence of hermeneutic phenomenological inquiry in a process of social innovation occurring at individual, group, organizational, and institutional levels of change in the development of the Rising Sun Project. The living practices encouraged by hermeneutic phenomenological inquiry sustained necessary spaces and clearings for contemplating questions concerning what kind of inquiry and action would diminish the suffering of the citizens with whom we worked (Bentz & Shapiro, 1998). These mindful spaces also sustained focus on intention for action for social justice. Hermeneutic phenomenological inquiry guided our wayfinding through complex and emergent conditions of uncertainty and offered significant openings for making the shift in consciousness required for thinking and being the complex. van Breda (2007) captures the spirit of our experience of Morin's (1999a) notion of thinking the complex when he proposed that we must imagine "our coming into consciousness as a process in which we become aware of our 'otherness' in the world in a self-affirming and inclusive way" (van Breda, 2007, p. 3). Our experience of hermeneutic phenomenological inquiry is consistent with Bentz's (2013) proposal that in a mindful inquiry there is the spiraling movement of the interpreter outward to the world, to observe, obtain data, communicate, analyze, comprehend, intervene, and act; this is followed by the return to the self/interpreter who is changed and grows through and by the new understandings. Our inquiry shows how hermeneutic phenomenological inquiry significantly influenced knowledge generation and how in particular it influenced applied design and prototyping work for more socially just and sustainable alternatives in urban development. Working in a context where powerful policy makers increasingly set the terms of debate about what is useful knowledge, hermeneutic phenomenological inquiry allowed us to view much broader horizons of potentialities in our work as community-based practitioners, which had not been visible to us or to the community previously.

References

BC Poverty Reduction Coalition. (2013). Five things you should know about poverty in BC. Retrieved from http://bcpovertyreduction.ca/learn-more/poverty-reduction-in-canada/

Bentz, V. M. (2013). The mindful scholar-practitioner MS-P. [Blog entry October 26, 2013]. Retrieved from http://valeriebentz.com/the-mindful-scholar-practitioner-ms-p/

Bentz, V. M. & Shapiro, J. J. (1998). *Mindful inquiry in social research.* Thousand Oaks, CA: SAGE.

Gadamer, H. (1975). *Truth and method* (2nd rev. ed.). (J. Weinsheimer & D. Marhsall, Trans.). New York, NY: Continuum.

Gadamer, H. (1976). *Philosophical hermeneutics.* Berkeley, CA: University of California Press.

Gaetz, S. (2012). *The real cost of homelessness: Can we save money by doing the right thing?* Toronto, ON: Canadian Homelessness Research Network Press.

Gonzalez, S., Moulaert, F., & Martinelli, F. (2010). How to analyze social innovation at the local level? In F. Moulaert, E. Swyngedouw, F. Martinelli, & S. Gonzalez, (Ed.), *Can neighbourhoods save the city? Community development and social innovation* (pp. 49–67). London, England: Routledge.

Heidegger, M. (1971). Building dwelling thinking. In *Poetry, language, and thought* (A. Hofstadter, Trans.). New York, NY: Harper and Row.

Husserl, E. (1970). *The crisis of European sciences* (D. Carr, Trans.). Evanston, IL: Northwestern University Press. (Original work published 1936).

Kincheloe, J. L. (2003). Critical ontology: Visions of selfhood and curriculum. *Journal of curricular theorizing, 19*(1), 47–64.

Kajner, L., & Schultz, T. (Ed.). (2013). *Engaged scholarship: The politics of engagement and disengagement.* Rotterdam, the Netherlands: Sense.

Kovach, M. (2015). Thinking through theory: Contemplating Indigenous situated research and policy. In N. Denzin & M. Giardina (Ed.), *Qualitative inquiry, past, present, and future: A critical reader* (pp. 372–386). Walnut Creek, CA: Left Coast Press.

Lewin, K., (1951). *Field theory in social science: Selected theoretical papers.* (D. Cartwright, Ed.). New York: Harper and Brothers.

MacCallum, D., Moulaert, F. Hillier, J., & Vicari Haddock, S. (Ed.).

(2009). *Social innovation and territorial development*. Farnham, England: Ashgate.

Mehmood, M., & Moulaert, F. (2010). Analysing regional development and policy: A structural-realist approach. *Regional Studies*, *44*(1), 103-118.

Morin, E. (1999a). *Homeland earth: A manifesto for the new millennium* (S. E. Kelly & R. LaPointe, Trans.). Cresskill, NJ: Hampton Press.

Moulaert, F. (1999b). Seven complex lessons on education for the future. Retrieved from http://unesdoc.unesco.org/images/0011/001177/117740eo.pdf.

_____. (2009). Workpackage 4: Social innovation (Integration exercise). Retrieved from http://katarsis.ncl.ac.uk/wp/wp4/documents/D4DISSEM.pdf.

_____. (Ed.). (2013). *International handbook on social innovation: Collective action, social learning, and transdisciplinary research*. Cheltenham, England: Edward Elgar.

Moulaert, F., & Hillier, J. (2009). *What is social innovation? And why is it politically relevant?* Paper presented at a policy dissemination workshop entitled Social Innovation: An Opportunity for Europe, October 7, 2009. Brussels, Belgium. Retrieved from http://katarsis.ncl.ac.uk/ws/documents/Katarsispolicybrief1-5Oct2009.pdf.

Moulaert, F., Hillier, J., Miciukiewicz, K., MacCallum, D., & Cassinari, D. (Ed). (2011). European agenda for research on cities and social cohesion. Retrieved from http://www.socialpolis.eu.

Moulaert, F., MacCallum, D., Mehmood, A., & Hamdouch, A. (2013). General introduction: The return of social innovation as a scientific concept and a social practice. In *The international handbook on social innovations* (pp. 1-8). Cheltenham, England: Edward Elgar.

Moulaert, F., Martinelli, F., Gonzalez, S., & Swyngedouw, E. (2007). Introduction: Social innovation and governance in European cities urban development between path dependency and radical innovation. *European Urban and Regional Studies*, *14*(3), 195–209.

Moulaert, F., Martinelli, E., Swyngedouw, & Gonzalez, S. (2005). Towards alternative model(s) of local innovation. *Urban Studies*, *42*(11), 1969-1990.

Moulaert, F., & Mehmood, A. (2010). Analysing regional development and policy: A structural-realist approach. *Regional Studies*, *44*(1).

Moulaert, F., Swyngedouw, E., Martinelli F., & Gonzalez, S. (Ed.). (2010). *Can neighbourhoods save the city? Community development and social innovation.* London, England: Routledge.

Novy, A., Swiatek, D. C., & Moulaert, F. (2012). Social cohesion: A conceptual and political elucidation. *Urban Studies, 49*(9), 1873-1889.

Rehorick, D. A., & Bentz, V. M. (Ed.). (2008). *Transformative phenomenology: Changing ourselves, lifeworlds, and professional practice.* Plymouth, England: Lexington.

Schugurensky, D. (2006). Adult citizenship education: An overview of the field. In T. Fenwick, T. Nesbit, & B. Spencer (Ed.), *Contexts of adult education* (pp. 68-80). Toronto, ON: Thompson Educational.

Schutz, A. (1970). *On phenomenology and social relations.* (H. Wagner, Ed.). Chicago, IL: University of Chicago Press.

Schutz, A. (1967). *The phenomenology of the social world* (G. Walsh & F. Lehnert, Trans.). Evanston, IL: Northwest University Press. (Original work published 1932).

Sen, A. (2000). *Development as freedom.* New York, NY: Anchor Books.

Smith, D. E. (1992). Sociology from women's experience: A reaffirmation. *Sociological Theory, 10*(1), 88-98.

van Breda, J. (2007). *Towards a transdisciplinary hermeneutics.* Paper presented at the Building the Scientific Mind Conference at Emily Carr University of Art + Design, Vancouver, BC. May 28-31, 2007. Retrieved from http://www.learndev.org/dl/BtSM2007/JohnVan-Breda.pdf.

Westley, F. (2008). Introduction to scaling. Retrieved from http://sig-knowledgehub.com/2012/05/01/introductio-to-scaling/.

Wilson, A. (2017). *Joining learning and making: A practitioner's retrospective auto/biographical account of how inquiry can contribute to social justice efforts in a community.* (Unpublished doctoral dissertation). Simon Fraser University. Burnaby, British Columbia, Canada.

Wilson, A. & Wilson, M. (2013). *Creating Spaces for Community Change.* Presentation at Kanankil Institute, March 15-16, 2013, Merida, Mexico.

Wilson, A. & Wilson, M. (2013). *Creating learning spaces for margin-alized citizens in the complex tensions of emerging governance in-teractions*. Proceedings: Cities Learning Together Conference: Lo-cal communities in the healthy and sustainable learning city. Hong Kong, China. http://pure.pascalobservatory.org/sites/default/files/ cities_learning_together_conference_-_final_precedings.pdf.

Wilson, M. (2014) Presentation: *Homeless in paradise: From innova-tion to transformation.* Keynote address at symposium conducted at Fielding Graduate University, Santa Barbara, CA.

Wilson, M. (2013). *When systems and lifeworlds collide: A schol-ar-practitioner's inquiry into an analytical foundation for social innovation using transformative phenomenology, transdisciplinar-ity, and critical social theory.* (Unpublished doctoral dissertation). Fielding Graduate University: Santa Barbara, California.

About the Authors

Michael Wilson, PhD, and Ann Wilson, EdD, are scholar-practi-tioners in action for 25 years in the community-based, non-profit sector. They have set about disrupting traditional boundaries between theory and practice, between academic scholarship and practical scholarship in community settings, between the academy and the community and siloed government departments. They have demonstrated the potential of qualitative research and practitioner inquiry to address some of our most intransigent problems of social injustice. They believe that the key to social innovation is in staying close to the lived experience, insight, and wisdom of the citizens they serve whose lives are most impacted by inequality. Together, the Wilsons have built a multi-service organization with four facilities actively engaged in countering the complex prob-lems of homelessness, addiction, crime, unemployment, and poverty in their city. Michael Wilson is founding and executive director of the Phoenix Society. Recognized for his vision and leadership in many task forces and committees on health, affordable housing and social innova-tion, Michael was named Surrey's Citizen of the Year in 2015. Michael completed a doctoral degree in Human and Organizational Systems at Fielding Graduate University. Ann Wilson has been the Phoenix Society's Director of Program Development since 1992. Specializing in creating a diverse portfolio of program development activities that lead their constituents to full participation in the social, economic and cultural life of the community has involved combining adult education, asset development approaches, sustainable livelihoods frameworks, behavioral health, community-based justice re-integration programs and workforce development strategies. Ann completed a doctoral degree in Transformational Change in the Faculty of Education at Simon Fraser University. Michael and Ann were awarded honorary doctoral degrees by Kwantlen Polytechnic University in May 2017 for their humanitarian work in the community.

EPILOGUE
New Horizons for Phenomenology

Valerie Malhotra Bentz and David Rehorick

In 2016, The Fielding Graduate University School of Human and Organization Development merged with the School of Education to become the School of Leadership Studies. The contributions of Fielding alumni such as those in this book demonstrate the importance of phenomenology to leadership development. Each of them illustrate that phenomenologically based research is directly relevant and applicable to particular human problems and concerns as actually lived. What, then, is the continuing place of phenomenology and hermeneutics in a curriculum/ concentration with an expanded substantive scope?

Under the leadership of Provost Gerald Porter, Fielding reinvigorated its historical emphasis on the "competencies" which our adult learners achieve through obtaining the doctoral degree. We highlight below some of the competencies which our phenomenology alumni demonstrate. They are aspects of phenomenologically based research and practice.

In 2016, the faculty approved a new doctoral concentration called "Somatics, Phenomenology and Communicative Leadership" (SPCL). The new concentration includes: a course called "Writing Phenomenology," which includes a unit of hermeneutic theories, and the basic readings from the Advanced Research Module (see Appendix A). Students begin writing protocols at the start of the course, generating eight of them using a range of essential Husserlian and Schutzian lifeworld techniques. We also include a somatics course taken from a phenomenological perspective to highlight the "embodied" nature of conscious-ness and knowledge. A somatic face-to-face retreat enhances students' ability to bring their bodies into the process of inquiry. Finally, we in-clude a course on social construction of reality and communications. To be an effective phenomenologist scholar-leader requires the ability to facilitate the co-construction of meaning in group situations. These components of the SPCL concentration do not divide neatly into cours-es, just as an actual experience is at once embodied, full of structures of meaning, and exists in communications, past, present and future. Simi-larly, the competencies of the phenomenologically based scholar-leader are achieved throughout the concentration. Below we highlight some of the competencies which phenomenologists from Fielding exhibit in their work and practice as scholar-leaders.

Ten Competencies of Phenomenologically Based Scholar/Leaders

In this section, we highlight ten "competencies" that our Fielding phe-nomenological students have demonstrated in their work. We include examples not only from contributors to this book, but others from among the seventy-six dissertations rooted in phenomenology.

"Finding the Whatness" of Experience

Getting the "what" wrong may lead to dangerous unintended conse-quences, like mistaking a rope for a poisonous snake causing undue fear and anxiety (Bentz, 2016a, 2016b). The Husserlian based phenomenol-ogy of essences helps us discover the actual "what" of our experiences. Schutz's lifeworld phenomenology guides us to realize the structures of everyday life as shared experiences, determined by our "relevances" and "typifications." "Stocks of knowledge" exist in all lifeworlds that provide the way we interpret meanings.

Each of the Fielding phenomenological researchers/leaders con-tributing to our edited collection bring forward significant insights into actual situations. For example, Michael Wilson's and Ann Wilson's refusal to accept diagnostic labels of those in need of housing and employment services, redefining them as "citizens" was a component in the success of their Rising Sun project (see Chapter 9). Similarly, Jim Marlatt's phenomenology of the coaching relationship results in a deepened form of practice (see Chapter 1).

Phenomenologists as "Authentic" Leaders

Our phenomenologist researcher/leaders also exemplify that phenomenology is not just a "methodology" but is a way of being. One becomes a phenomenologist and therefore her own life and practice sparkle with the sense of wonderment as she engages with lifeworld challenges (for example, see Simpson, 2008). Susan Skjei's (2014) phenomenological dissertation on authentic leadership exemplifies this. She is an originator of authentic leadership training. Likewise, Carol Laberge's work as a leader of Provincial health care systems rests clearly upon the bedrock of her phenomenological research about patients' experience of heart attack (see Chapter 5). Dorianne Cotter-Lockard's consulting practice is based upon her research into communication between musicians in string quartets. She demonstrates this integration by playing violin as part of her work in organizations (see chapter 8). Ayumi Nishi makes it clear that she herself aspires to be a "servant leader" as exemplified by those she studied in her Heideggian phenomenological analysis (see Chapter 7).

Somatics and the "Flesh"

For phenomenology, consciousness must be understood as embodied. In our phenomenology Advanced Research Module, we discussed the importance of Maurice Merleau-Ponty's focus on the phenomenology of the body. Merleau-Ponty's (1968) late work expands the notion of "flesh" to include the "entire world, past, present, and future, in which our bodies and minds are entangled."

Given our scholar-practitioner orientation, we integrate the research and practice called "somatics" into a regular course. This course reviews research on the embodiment of knowledge from neuroscience through social and cultural sciences based on a phenomenological focus. It is now a part of the SPCL doctoral concentration. The dramatic structure of everyday life (Burke, 1969) and the interconnection of autobiographical selves is fully elucidated from somatic phenomenological perspectives.

The passion Valerie developed for phenomenology and its thinkers broke the bounds of scholarly writing. To express the complexities of her relationship with Alfred Schutz, Martin Heidegger, Helmut Wagner, and other scholars, they appear as fictionalized characters in her book *Flesh and Mind: The time travels of Dr. Victoria Von Dietz* (Bentz, 2013). Michael Barber's comments on Bentz' novel gets to the core of phenomenology as applied at Fielding: "It is as though the visions of Merleau-Ponty and Levinas resist and complement each other, and, at the same time, it is as though Levinas's thought reveals the secret dimensions of ethics and justice at the heart of the flesh" (Barber, 2016). From the perspective of phenomenology as method, a novel may be seen as an example of the technique of "imaginative variation," to achieve deeper understanding of experience. Students in the writing phenomenology course have similarly used fictional writing to help clarify a phenomenon.

Phenomenology as Writing and Collaborative Interpretation of Meaning

"Writing Phenomenology," a required course in the new concentration, is built upon the Advanced Research Module in phenomenology taught by Valerie, and David who continued to co-teach this course for several years after his official retirement. The new version of the course incorporated three basic readings from the advanced module then expanded the writing component. Students practice eight aspects of exploring their chosen phenomenon using techniques from Edmund Husserl, Schutz, and Kenneth Burke. Writing and rewriting to get at the nuances and meanings of an experience is basic to phenomenological work. Interpreting the meaning of a phenomenon is best done through a deeply collaborative process, which we accomplish through sharing the protocols in an on-line forum and discussing them in on-line conference calls.

Creativity and "Wonder"

The work of our Fielding researchers illustrates that, within the powerful frameworks of Husserlian and Schutzian phenomenology, each phenomenologist's work requires a flexible, creative process. Each instance is unique, while bearing some essential aspects of consciousness (Husserl) and similar structures (Schutz). In order to be true to the "things themselves," phenomenologists bear an open frame of mind and thereby discover new aspects of phenomena which will bring surprise and wonder. As in the case of Novokowsky (2008), the phenomenologist may change course, even his research question, as he uncovers the nature of what he is investigating. Knobel (Chapter 3) shifted her sources of data to the Mandela archives based on her pilot interviews with persons who worked with Mandela, a turn she did not originally anticipate.

Contribution to Method

Phenomenological studies contribute to the method of phenomenology as well as the substance of the phenomena. Shirley Knobel invented a technique of an imagined dialogue with Nelson Mandela, based on his letters from prison, to develop a sense his unique leadership style. She based this creative process on Schutz's notion of "fully intended meaning" (see Chapter 3). This is meaning that the person stands behind, not simply what one may say at a given time. Aman Gohal (2016) discovered an additional structure of the lifeworld, not mentioned by Schutz. The women "green" farmers in the D.C. area she studied all had "rituals of renewal" that they used to restore their energy from the extreme challenges of sustainable farming.

Lifeworlds as Constructed in Communication

We have added a communication course to the SPCL concentration, in acknowledgement of the philosophical connection between social constructionism and phenomenology (Berger & Luckman, 1967). As scholar-leaders, alumni of Fielding had been practicing the CMM "communicative management of meaning" (Pearce, 2007). We bring contemplative awareness and understanding of the lifeworld to the forefront of our communicative practices in groups and communities. For example, a group of Fielding phenomenologists and members of the SPCL concentration group facilitated a session at the European Sociological Association conference in Cracow, Poland (September, 2016) using CMM techniques for trauma recovery.

Phenomenologists are Deeply Immersed in the Work of Our Founders and Colleagues

The work of founding thinkers and seasoned phenomenologists is studied deeply and reflected upon by Fielding phenomenologists. Often this takes the form of "falling in love" with the work of one of them, which can become a life-long intellectual passion. Ann Alexander, current Fielding phenomenology student, has become a dedicated scholar of the work of Schutz. Lori Schneider became so immersed in Heidegger while writing her dissertation that she devoted an entire chapter on his work to his thought (see Chapter 6). Chris Mare (2016) became a scholar of Husserl, bringing his work on the use of "reduction" in phenomenology into connection with deep meditation practice.

Phenomenologists Work from the "Epoche"

Phenomenologists learn to "bracket" or set aside their understandings and preconceptions of what a phenomenon is in order to allow the overlooked aspects to appear. In lifeworld analysis, they learn to make apparent the assumed, ordinarily unacknowledged aspects of a situation. Jo-Anne Clark felt that being a phenomenologist was like stripping down to "naked" in the way she approached the experiences of women entrepreneurs (see Chapter 4).

The Transcendent in Lived Experience: Phenomenology and the Contemplative Movement

Several Fielding phenomenologists have delved into areas of experience which transcend the everyday reality but are increasingly recognized as part of human experience of living and dying (Porath, 2016; Haines, 1999). For example, Ellena Gillespie (2014) worked with dying patients and found a pattern to their experiences of a transition to what is beyond the "life"world.

Bentz (2016a, 2016b) demonstrates that somatics and phenomenology are inherently contemplative practices. Scholars across disciplines have found that contemplative practices, such as meditation and yoga, bring to them a sense of interconnection with all beings (Bentz & Giorgino, 2016). Several Fielding scholars (Nelson, 2016; Fortune, 2016; Mare, 2016) contributed to this worldwide effort that brings together the work of scholars across disciplines from Europe and North America who have realized the transformative value of contemplative practice. These scholars seek to unify and direct economies and technologies toward the good of communities of life on earth.

The transcendental aspects and common understandings reached via somatic phenomenology are congruent with a renewed interconnection with the divine essence or if you will "god." Kris Konecki (2015) connects the popularization of yoga in the West with a way of connecting the body to the soul. Doug Porpora (2016), through the philosophy of "critical realism," asks social scientists to stop shying away from using the "god" term despite its despoliation by religious orthodoxies. A phenomenology and contemplative approach to the great ineffable is needed to unify humanity. As Swami Vivekananda (1953) said, "All gods are one."

Transformative Phenomenology and the Future

David Rehorick and Valerie Bentz have centered their life work on phenomenology and hermeneutics because they have seen again and again with wonderment the impact this legacy has on students and colleagues, and the transformative outcomes for them and their scholarship and practice. We hope to see this continue in the work of future generations of Fielding colleagues, with the development of a Center for Transformative Phenomenology. This center would provide learning and support to scholars and practitioners inside Fielding and beyond. Contact Information: Valerie Bentz, vbentz@fielding.edu or President Katrina Rogers, krogers@fielding.edu.

Figure 1: The Logo of the Somatics, Phenomenology, and Communicative Leadership

Concentration

End Notes

In 2016, the faculty approved a new doctoral concentration called "Somatics, Phenomenology and Communicative Leadership" (SPCL).

A group of HOD alumni and students met regularly over several years developing this concentration. They are too numerous to mention; however, special appreciation goes to Barton Buechner, PhD, who consistently supports this effort, including supporting the student learners on-line and face-to-face. He is truly the "angel" of SPCL.

She demonstrates this integration by playing violin as part of her work in organizations (see chapter 8).

Dorianne Cotter-Lockhard played her violin to enhance a session on trauma recovery sponsored by Fielding Graduate University European cluster at the European Sociological Association Conference in Cracow, Poland September 1-3, 2016.

Given our scholar-practitioner orientation, we integrate the research and practice called "somatics" into a regular course.

Luann Fortune came to Fielding to work with Valerie because of her interest in somatics and phenomenology. Fortune assisted Valerie in developing a course on somatics at Fielding.

References

Barber, M. (2016) *Flesh and ethics*. Presented in session on Valerie Bentz's Contributions as a Scholar, Society for Phenomenology and Human Sciences Conference, October , 2016 Salt Lake City, UT.

Berger, P. and Luckmann, T. (1967). *The social construction of reality: A treatise in the sociology of knowledge*. Garden City, NY: Doubleday Press.

Bentz, V. M. (2016a). Knowing as being: Somatic phenomenology as contemplative practice. In V. M. Bentz & V. M. B. Giorgino (Ed.), *Contemplative social research: Caring for self, being, and lifeworld* (pp. 50-79). Santa Barbara, CA: Fielding University Press.

_____. (2016b). *Who is the researcher? Soma, contemplation, and lifeworld in 'Digitneyland.'* Keynote presentation at European Sociological Association: Qualitative Methods and Research Technologies. Cracow, Poland, September 2, 2016.

_____. (2013). *Flesh and mind: The time travels of Dr. Victoria Von Dietz*. New York, NY: Amazon.

Bentz, V. M. & Giogino, V. M. B. (Ed). (2016). Contemplative social research: Caring for self, being, and lifeworld. Santa Barbara, CA: Fielding University Press.

Bentz, V. M. & Shapiro, J. J. (1998). *Mindful inquiry in social research*. Thousand Oaks, CA: SAGE.

Burke, K. (1969). *A grammar of motives*. Berkeley, CA: University of California Press.

Fay, D. (2008). *Integral consciousness and intercultural competency: Gebser, Husserl, and the task of our time*. (Unpublished Doctoral dissertation). Fielding Graduate University. Santa Barbara, CA. Proquest.

Fortune, L. (2016). Retracing the labyrinth: Applying phenomenology for embodied interpretation. In V. M. Bentz and V. M. B. Giogino, (Ed.), *Contemplative social research: Caring for self, being, and lifeworld* (pp. 261-275). Santa Barbara, CA: Fielding University Press.

Gadamer, H. (1975). *Truth and method*. New York, NY: Seabury Press.

Gebser J. (1986). *The ever-present origin*. (N. Barstad & A. Mikunas, Trans.) Athens, OH: Ohio University Press.

Gillespie, E. (2014). *Assisting with dying: A phenomenological analysis of six case studies*. (Unpublished Doctoral dissertation). Santa Barbara, CA: Fielding Graduate University.

Gohal, A. (2016). *The life-worlds of urban women farmers in sustainable agriculture.* (Unpublished Doctoral dissertation). Santa Barbara, CA: Fielding Graduate University.

Haines, M. (1999). *Interior spaciousness: The hidden openness of some who walk a mystical path with practical feet.* (Doctoral dissertation). Santa Barbara, CA: Fielding Graduate University. Proquest.

Husserl, E. (1970). *The crisis of European sciences and transcendental phenomenology: An introduction to phenomenological philosophy.* (D. Carr, Trans). Evanston, IL: Northwestern University Press.

Konecki, K. (2015). *Is the body the temple of the soul? Modern yoga practice as a psychosocial phenomenon.* Lodz, Poland: University of Lodz Press.

Mare, E. C. (2016). Designing for consciousness: Outline of a neurophenomenological research program. In V. M. Bentz and V. M. B. Giorgino. (Eds.), *Contemplative social research: Caring for self, being, and lifeworld* (pp. 300-334). Santa Barbara, CA: Fielding University Press.

Maxwell, D. (2013). *Classical horsemanship: A phenomenological and dramatist study.* (Unpublished Doctoral dissertation). Santa Barbara, CA: Fielding Graduate University.

McCown, D. (2016). Inside out: Mindfulness-based interventions as a model for community building. In V. M. Bentz and V. M. B. Giorgino. (Ed.), *Contemplative social research: Caring for self, being, and lifeworld* (pp. 98-128). Santa Barbara, CA: Fielding University Press.

Melville, K. (2016). *A passion for adult learning.* Santa Barbara, CA: Fielding University Press.

Merleau-Ponty, M. (1968). *The visible and the invisible.* (A. Lingis, Trans.) Evanston, IL: Northwestern University Press.

Nelson, A. (2016). Contemplative psychology and imagery. In V. M. Bentz and V. M. B. Giorgino (Ed.), *Contemplative social research: Caring for self, being, and lifeworld* (pp. 239-260). Santa Barbara, CA: Fielding University Press.

Novokowsky, Bernie. (2008). Personal power: Realizing self in doing and being. In D. Rehorick & V. M. Bentz, (Eds.), *Transformative phenomenology: Changing ourselves, lifeworlds, and professional practice.* Lanham, MD: Lexington Press.

Oliver, K. (2004). *The colonization of psychic space: A psychoanalytic theory of oppression.* Minneapolis, MN. University of Minnesota Press.

Pearce, B. (2007). *Making social worlds: A communication perspective.* Malden, MA: Blackwell Publishing.

Polkinghorne, D. (1983). *A Methodology for the human sciences: Systems of inquiry.* Albany, NY: SUNY.

Porpora, D. (2016). Critical realism and spirituality. In V. M. Bentz and V. M. B. Giorgino, (Ed.), *Contemplative social research: Caring for self, being, and lifeworld* (pp. 80-97). Santa Barbara, CA: Fielding University Press.

Porath, P. (2006). *The lived experience of an unexpected, unintentional mystical experience.* (Unpublished Doctoral dissertation). Santa Barbara,CA: Fielding Graduate University.

Rehorick, D. & Bentz, V. M. (Eds). (2008). *Transformative phenomenology: Changing ourselves, lifeworlds, and professional practice.* Lanham MD: Lexington Press.

Simpson, S. K. (2008). Experiencing phenomenology as mindful transformation. In D. Rehorick, & V. M. Bentz, (Ed.), *Transformative phenomenology: Changing ourselves, lifeworlds, and professional practice* (pp. 51-64). Lanham, MD: Lexington Press.

Skjei, S. (2014). *Authentic leadership moments: A mindful inquiry.* (Unpublished Doctoral dissertation). Santa Barbara, CA: Fielding Graduate University.

Tesch, R. (1980). *Phenomenological and transformative research: What they are and how to do them.* Santa Barbara, CA: Fielding Institute.

Tesch, R. (1990). *Qualitative research analysis types and software tools.* London, UK: RoutledgeFalmer.

Vivekananda, S. (1953). *The Yogas and other works.* (Nikhilananda, Ed.) New York, NY: Vivekananda Center Press.

Wagner, H. (1983). *Phenomenology of consciousness and sociology of the lifeworld.* Edmonton, Alberta, Canada: University of Alberta Press.

Walsh, Z. (2016). *Critical theory and the mindfulness industry.* (Unpublished document).

APPENDIX A
(Chapter 1)

Advanced Research Module: Phenomenological Inquiry
HOD-764PH

An Online Intensive
February 22–March 29, 2015

Valerie Bentz, Ph.D.
HOD Faculty

David Rehorick, Ph.D.
Professor Emeritus, HOD

Revised 6 February 2015

Bentz and Rehorick have developed what they call "Transformative Phenomenology" based on their work over the past thirty years. Phenomenological inquiry and practice go hand-in-hand with personal transformation and growth. Phenomenology is an embodied way of exploring the full range of human experience: mental, physical, emotional and spiritual. Hermeneutic strategies are employed to enhance the explication of meaning.

In a five-week intensive, we will work through three readings that Bentz and Rehorick have used as core texts in past Phenomenology seminars and workshops. You should obtain these books now, and begin reading on your own, using the general guide prompts for each reading below. We will not be responding to questions or queries on the material until we launch the course with an opening Go-To-Meeting conference call on Sunday, February 22 at 2 p.m. Pacific time. The online seminar will be delivered using Moodle.

About Contracting and Course Requirements

To contract for this course, please contact Valerie Bentz (vbentz@fielding.edu)

To receive credit for the course, all registered participants must contribute to online postings for all three readings. We would anticipate at least an opening offering by each person, and at least two responses to the offerings by others for each of the three readings. In addition, it is expected that you will participate in each of the three scheduled conference calls, and share your phenomenological protocol commentary on the closing event on Sunday, March 29.

Schedule

February 22 (Sunday):	2 p.m. Pacific time (60-minute confer ence call)
February 23–March 4:	Postings on Reading #1
March 5–14:	Postings on Reading #2
March 15 (Sunday):	2 p.m. Pacific time (60-minute confer ence call)
March 16–24:	Postings on Reading #3
March 25–28:	Preparation of Individual Phenomeno logical Protocol Commentaries
March 29 (Sunday):	2 p.m. Pacific time (90-minute confer ence call)

Reading #1

Rehorick, D. A. & Bentz, V. M. (Eds.). (2008). *Transformative phenomenology: Changing ourselves, lifeworlds, and professional practice.* Lanham, MD: Lexington Books. [paperback edition 2009]

While the chapters by Rehorick and/or Bentz offer wider insights into phenomenology, the chapters generated by many of the HOD alums are, in effect, a step beyond the fullness of their individual dissertation work. We asked them to address the influence of phenomenology on their lives and work in a way that transcended the dissertation production phase. Nonetheless, the contributions in this collection display the efficacy of using phenomenological and hermeneutics approaches and strategies to generate one's central research question, and to apply these approaches to guide the overall research thrust.

Some Discussion Prompts:

1. The three chapters in Part I explicate some of the central concepts, foundational ideas, and key thinkers that inform what Rehorick and Bentz have called "Transformative Phenomenology." Here are some general prompts to kick-start your thinking and reflections on these chapters:

(a) Whether you are coming to phenomenology for the first time, or already into your explorations, consider what might constitute push-pull and attraction-repulsion experiences in entering this new domain of inquiry? (Chapter 1 in particular).

(b) Edmund Husserl stated clearly that phenomenology aims to end where the empirical human sciences begin. Despite this, many scholars contend that phenomenology and empirical science are in opposition, thus shaping how phenomenology is cast in some methodology and methods textbooks. How does Chapter 2 inform your understanding of this issue?

(c) Philosophical phenomenological scholars maintain that reading the original sources and tomes is the only way to understand what phenomenology is about and how to go about "doing it." Yet over the past three decades, an increasing number of so-called secondary sources have been generated to explicate the "what and how" of phenomenological inquiry. It was 1985 before something akin to a "phenomenological cookbook" was created, giving way to an outburst of criticism from philosophical phenomenologists. In Chapter 3, Sandy Simpson has articulated how she moved from an intuitive sense that she "was a phenomenologist" to becoming an explicit phenomenological practitioner. How might her story inform your own search for the meaning and relevance of phenomenological inquiry?

2. From Parts II, III, and IV of *Transformative Phenomenology*, skim through and select one chapter from each part that catches your attention and curiosity (only ONE chapter from each part). Comment on how each of your selected chapters inform your understanding of the research process, and how this might help shape your research/dissertation topic?

3. Consider generating and responding to your own self-generated Discussion Prompts from ideas and thoughts emerging as you work through *Transformative Phenomenology*.

Reading #2

van Manen, M. (1997). *Researching lived experience: Human science for an action sensitive pedagogy* (2nd ed.). London, Ontario, Canada: The Althouse Press. [Some booksellers only carry the 1st edition, 1990. This is fine too since the only change was to the Preface.]

We have chosen to examine the full text of van Manen since it is a lucid examination of the relevance and place of phenomenology and hermeneutics in the human sciences. It bridges the gulf between the need to read original phenomenological tomes and the call for something to help one find one's way into the work. Many of our students who have embraced phenomenology for their dissertation research have found van Manen to be a solid and helpful source. As well, there are explicit discussions about the meaning and relevance of generating phenomenological protocol statements and commentaries.

van Manen, M. (2014). *Phenomenology of practice: Meaning-giving methods in phenomenological research and writing.* Walnut Creek, CA: Left Coast Press Inc.

NOTE: More recently, van Manen has published a new book that pulls together many of the strands of his thought in past published papers and other texts. You may find it helpful to read selected chapters in particular (Ch. 1, 2, 8, 10, 11, 13, 14). A limitation is that van Manen has barely touched on the social phenomenology of Alfred Schutz, and he does not address the rich tradition of phenomenological sociology that emerged in the 1960s, along with ethnomethodology and conversational analysis.

If you are a beginner to phenomenological inquiry, we recommend that you focus on van Manen (1997), and dip into van Manen (2014) very selectively. Even van Manen says that the 1997 book is a "workable outline of human science pointers, principles, and practices to conduct a phenomenological research project" (2014, p.16).

The discussion prompts below are intended to help you enter into and engaged with the readings in each unit. In preparing your individual postings to the forum, it is not expected that you will answer each of the prompts as though they are a series of questions to be answered. We encourage you to organize your thoughts in whatever way makes sense to you.

Some Discussion Prompts:

1. Characterize what is meant by a hermeneutic phenomenological human science (1997 text, chapters 1 & 4 in particular). In the 2014 book, van Manen refers to phenomenology as "hermeneutic or interpretive-descriptive phenomenology" (chapters 2, 10 & 11 in particular).
2. The ideas of "wonderment" and "lived experience" are central to phenomenological inquiry. What is meant by these concepts, and can you generate some examples from any phenomena of interest to you that

elicits the meaning? (1997 book, chapters 2 & 3; 2014 book, chapter 1).
3. What is meant by phenomenological writing? (and hermeneutic, phenomenological writing). (1997 book, chapter 5; 2014 book, chapters 13 &14).

NOTE: this discussion is especially relevant to the final seminar task of writing your own phenomenological protocol commentary.

Reading #3

Wagner, H. (1983). *Phenomenology of consciousness and sociology of the life-world.* Edmonton, Alberta, Canada: The University of Alberta Press.

NOTE: This is a great, comprehensive overview of Alfred Schutz with an excellent annotated bibliography. Wagner's book has been out of print for many years, and the second-hand market for copies has dried up (any now circulating are priced out of reach). As a consequence of David Rehorick's correspondence with the publisher, The University of Alberta Press, one can now download a free copy of the book by following these links: (1) direct link to the book at http://www.uap.ualberta.ca/ UAP.asp?lid=42&bookid=191 or (2) by starting at the University's web page, and following the internal links to their publications page: http:// www.uap.ualberta.ca/.

The work of Schutz emerges, in particular, from his critical and creative blending of the thought of Edmund Husserl and Max Weber. Schutz adopted only selective features of Husserl's phenomenological approach and methodology. He integrates this with Weber's vision for interpretive studies. Schutz's fresh integration of ideas from Husserl and Weber created the groundwork for the introduction of phenomenological inquiry into the social and human sciences, and later into many more domains of inquiry, including nursing and education. We have selected the book by Helmut Wagner reading since it still stands as one of the best and more accessible ways to entering into Schutz's thinking.

Some Discussion Prompts:

1. What were some of the reasons for the development of the phenomenological movement, starting with Edmund Husserl?

2. How does the phenomenology of consciousness depart from one's usual, typical ways of thinking?

3. In what ways did Schutz depart from Husserl's thinking, and why did he do so?

4. What are some of the concepts and ideas from Schutz that catch your attention in particular? Can you provide examples from your own personal and professional experiences?

Supporting Reference List

This list contains additional references and sources related to phenomenology, hermeneutics, interpretive studies, and ethnomethodology. For anyone wishing to explore beyond the three texts required for our seminar, the references below offer solid places to begin.

Bentz, V. M. (1993). Creating images in dance: The works of Hanstein and Ziaks. In P. Mayes & V. M. Bentz, (Eds.), *Visual images of women in the arts and mass media*. Lewiston, NY: Edwin Mellen Press.

Bentz, V. M. & Shapiro, J. J. (1998). *Mindful inquiry in social research*. Thousand Oaks: SAGE.

Bentz, V. M. (1989) *Becoming mature: Childhood ghosts and spirits in adult life*. New York, NY: Aldine de Gruyter. (Uses Schutz as one basis for a research project in the area of interpretive phenomenology, also includes use of sensory memory bracketing exercise.)

Bentz, V. M. (1995). Husserl, Schutz, Paul, and me: Reflections on writing phenomenology. *Human Studies*, *18*, 41-62. (A discussion of scholarly writing and the meaning of phenomenology.)

Bentz, V. M. (2002). From playing child to aging mentor: The role of *Human Studies* in my development as a scholar. *Human Studies, 25*,

441-448. (Discusses becoming a phenomenologist and the importance of relationship to the journal and a professional association
such as the Society for Phenomenology and the Human Sciences
(SPHS).)

Braud, W. & Anderson, R. (1998). *Transpersonal research methods for
the social sciences: Honoring human experience.* Thousand Oaks:
SAGE.

Dinwiddie, L. (2008). The lifeworld of high-performance teams: An
experiential account. In D. A. Rehorick & V. M. Bentz, (Ed.),
*Transformative phenomenology: Changing ourselves, lifeworlds,
and professional practice*, (pp. 113-127). Lanham, MD: Lexington
Books.

Emerson, Joan P. (1970). Behavior in public places: Sustaining defini-
tions of reality in gynecological examinations. *Recent Sociology*,
8, 74-97. (This is a landmark study in early "ethnomethdological
breeching experimentation." Although now deemed mostly uneth-
ical, some of these early works were most interesting and elucidat-
ing.)

Gadamer, H.-G. (1975). *Truth and method.* New York, NY: Seabury.

_____. (1992). The diversity of Europe: Inheritance and future. In
D. Misgeld & G. Nicholson (Ed.), *Hans-George Gadamer on ed-
ucation, poetry, and history: Applied hermeneutics*, (pp. 221-236).
Albany, NY: SUNY.

Garfinkel, H. (1967). *Studies in ethnomethodology.* Englewood Cliffs,
NJ: Prentice-Hall. (Original articles from which the domain of EM
began.)

Giorgi, A. (2009). *The descriptive phenomenological method in psychology: A modified Husserlian approach.* Pittsburgh, PA: Duquesne
University Press. (A culmination of his long-term commitment to
phenomenological inquiry.)

Haddad, D. (2008). Intentionality in action: Teaching artists phenomenology. In D.A. Rehorick & V. M. Bentz (Ed.), *Transformative
phenomenology: Changing ourselves, lifeworlds, and professional
practice*, (pp. 193-206). Lanham, MD: Lexington Books.

Hammond, M. I., Howarth, J., & Keat, R. (1991). *Understanding phenomenology.* Oxford, England: Basil Blackwell.

Heidegger, M. (1971). "The Thing." In *Poetry, language, thought*, (pp.
165-186). (A. Hofstadter, Trans). New York, NY: Harper.

Heap, J. L. (1982) Practical reasoning in depression: A practice. *Human
Studies*, *5*(4), 345-356. (Using accounts of his experiences of de-

pression, Heap discovers steps in his thinking that leads to depression and how to avoid them.)

Jeddeloh, S. C. (2008). Chasing transcendence: Experiencing magic moments in jazz improvisation. In D. A. Rehorick & V. M. Bentz, (Ed.), *Transformative phenomenology: Changing ourselves, lifeworlds, and professional practice*, (pp. 207-223). Lanham, MD: Lexington Books.

LaFountain, M. J. (2008). A breath of fresh air: Phenomenological sociology and Tai Chi. In D. A. Rehorick & V. M. Bentz, (Ed.), *Transformative phenomenology: Changing ourselves, lifeworlds, and professional practice*, (pp. 175-191). Lanham, MD: Lexington Books.

Leiter, K. (1980). *A primer on ethnomethodoloogy*. New York, NY. Oxford University Press. (Still one of the most accessible introductions written. Copies still available through Amazon.com. Used and out of print markets may also have copies available.)

Levesque-Lopman, L. (1983). Decision and experience: A phenomenological analysis of pregnancy and childbirth. *Human Studies, 6*, 247-277. (Displays how a Schutzian framework and concepts can be applied to explore a woman's experience.)

_____. (1988). *Claiming reality: Phenomenology and women's experience*. Totowa, New Jersey: Rowman & Littlefield. (Builds upon her creative application of Schutz's framework and concepts to study her own experience of pregnancy, childbirth, and labor.)

Malhotra, V. (1981). The social accomplishment of music in a symphony orchestra: A phenomenological analysis. *Qualitative Sociology, 4*(2), 102-125.

Mehan, H., and Wood, H. (1975). *The reality of ethnomethodology*. New York, NY: John Wiley & Sons.

Merleau-Ponty, M. (1962). *Phenomenology of perception*. (C. Smith, Trans.). London, England: Routledge & Kegan Paul. (Central work in development of phenomenology of the body and of embodiment.)

Moustakas, C. (1996) *Phenomenological research methods*. Thousand Oaks, CA: SAGE. (A method of phenomenological research based on Husserl's eidetic method.)

Nakkula, M. J., & Ravitch, S. M. (Ed). (1998). *Matters of interpretation: Reciprocal transformation in therapeutic and developmental relationships with youth*. San Francisco, CA: Jossey-Bass.

Natanson, M. (1973). *Edmund Husserl: Philosopher of infinite tasks*. Evanston, IL: Northwestern University Press. (An accessible overview of the development of Husserl's thought.)

Novokowsky, B. (2008). Personal power: Realizing self in doing and being. In D. A. Rehorick & V. M. Bentz, (Ed.), *Transformative phenomenology: Changing ourselves, lifeworlds, and professional practice*, (pp. 129-140). Lanham, MD: Lexington Books.

Paget, M. A. (1988). *The unity of mistakes: A phenomenological interpretation of medical work*. Philadelphia, PA: Temple University Press. (Exemplar study of applying interpretive and phenomenological approaches; read the entire book. Reissued 2004 with new forward by Joan Cassell.)

_____. (1990). Unlearning to not speak. *Human Studies*, *13*, 147-161. (Displays an array of discourse and conversational analytical excerpts of women's voice.)

Palmer, R. E. (1969). *Hermeneutics: Interpretation theory in Schleiermacher, Dilthey, Heidegger, and Gadamer*. Evanston, IL: Northwestern University Press. (Still one of the best classic sources.)

Psathas, G. (1989). *Phenomenology and sociology: Theory and research*. Washington, D.C.: Center for Advanced Research in Phenomenology & University Press of America. (Solid secondary source presentation of Schutz in theoretical and applied terms.)

Rehorick, D. A. (1980). Schutz and Parsons: Debate or Dialogue? *Human Studies*, *3*(4), 347-355. Reprinted in K. H. Wolff (Ed.), *Alfred Schutz: Appraisals and developments*. The Hague, The Netherlands: Martinus Nijhoff (1984). (Contributes to the wider discussions about the theoretical interchange between Parsons and Schutz.)

_____. (1986). Shaking the foundations of lifeworld: A phenomenological account of an earthquake experience. *Human Studies*, *9*, 379-391. (Applied social phenomenology; helpful to see how data excerpts are used to illustrate and exemplify thematic ideas.)

Rehorick, D. A., & Bentz, V. M. (Ed). (2008). *Transformative phenomenology: Changing ourselves, lifeworlds, and professional practice*. Lanham, MD: Lexington Books. [Paperback edition 2009]

Rehorick, D. A., & Buxton, W. (1988). Recasting the Schutz-Parsons dialogue: The hidden participation of Eric Voegelin. In L. Embree (Ed.), *Worldly phenomenology: The continuing influence of Alfred Schutz on North American human science*, (pp. 151-169). Washington, D.C.: The Center for Advanced Research in Phenomenology and University Press of America. (Challenges all previous interpretations of the intellectual dialogue and debate between Parsons and Schutz; uses archival data sources to critique other work.)

Rehorick, D. A. & Taylor, G. (1995). Thoughtful incoherence: First encounters with the phenomenological-hermeneutical domain. *Human Studies, 18*(4), 389-414. (Individual expressions of first experiencing the phenomenological domain and collaborative work to expand our understandings.)

Ricoeur, P. (1991). *From text to action: Essays in hermeneutics, II.* (K. Blamey & J. Thompson, Trans.). Evanston, IL: Northwestern University Press.

_____. (1974). *The conflict of interpretations.* Evanston, IL: Northwestern University Press.

Schutz, A. (1970). Phenomenological baseline. In H. Wagner (Ed.), *Alfred Schutz on phenomenology and social relations*, (pp. 53-71). Chicago, IL: University of Chicago Press.

_____. (1970). Transcendences and Multiple Realities. In H. Wagner (Ed.), Alfred *Schutz on phenomenology and social relations*, (pp. 245-262). Chicago, IL: University of Chicago Press.

_____. (1971). The Stranger. In A. Brodersen, (Ed.), *Collected Papers Vol. II: Studies in social theory*, (pp. 91-105). The Hague, The Netherlands: Martinus Nijhoff. (Schutz uses lifeworld phenomenology to describe the essential form of the experience of being a stranger.)

Simpson, S. K. (2008). Experiencing phenomenology as mindful transformation: An autobiographical account. In D. A. Rehorick & V. M. Bentz, (Ed.), *Transformative phenomenology: Changing ourselves, lifeworlds, and professional practice*, (pp. 51-64). Lanham, MD: Lexington Books.

Tower, D. O. (2008). Trial by fire: The transformational journey of an adult male cancer survivor. In D. A. Rehorick & V. M. Bentz, (Eds.), *Transformative phenomenology: Changing ourselves, lifeworlds, and professional practice*, (pp. 67-92). Lanham, MD: Lexington Books.

Turner, d. S. (2003). Horizons revealed: From methodology to method. *International Journal of Qualitative Methods,* 2 (1) Winter 2003. (retrived on-line__http://www.ualberta.ca/~iiqm/backissues/2_1/html1/turner.html. (Detailed account of what it is like to apply Gadamer's hermeneutic phenomenology to study the phenomenon of hope.)

van Manen, M. (1997a). *Researching lived experience: Human science for an action sensitive pedagogy* (2nd ed.). London, Ontario,

Canada: The Althouse Press. (Broad-based coverage of phenomenological and hermeneutic research. *Note*: We recommend that you purchase van Manen's book since it has almost turned into a "methodological bible" around Fielding. Be attentive to getting the 2nd edition, 1997. Some booksellers, including Amazon.com, have been pushing the 1st edition, 1990 as the latest).

van Manen, M. (1997b). From meaning to method. *Qualitative Health Research, 7*(3), 345-369. (Addresses the shift from thematic meaning to expressive meaning, enriching and expanding analysis beyond thematic level.)

_____. (Ed.). (2002). *Writing in the dark: Phenomenological studies in interpretive inquiry.* London, Ontario, Canada: The Althouse Press. (Offers descriptive accounts of phenomena explored phenomenologically.)

Varela, F. & Shear, J. (Ed.). (1999). *The view from within: First-person approaches to the study of consciousness.* Thorverton, England: Imprint Academic.

Wagner, H. R. (Ed.). (1970) *Alfred Schutz: On phenomenology and social relations.* Chicago, IL: University of Chicago Press.

_____. (1983). *Phenomenology of consciousness and sociology of the life-world.* Edmonton, Alberta, Canada: The University of Alberta Press. (Great, comprehensive overview of Schutz. Search out of print and used booksellers.)

Waksler, F. (1986.) Studying children: Phenomenological insights. *Human Studies, 9,* 71-82. (Uses phenomenological techniques to uncover bias about children inherent in developmental research and theories of socialization.)

_____. (Ed.) (1991). *Studying the social world of children: Sociological readings.* London, UK: The Falmer Press. (Expands beyond her 1986 insights.)

Welton, D. (Ed.). (1999). *The essential Husserl: Basic writings in transcendental phenomenology.* Bloomington, IN: Indiana University Press.

Wolff, K. H. (1978). Phenomenology and sociology. In T. Bottomore & R. Nisbct, (Eds.), *A history of sociological analysis,* (pp. 499-556). New York, NY: Basic Books. (Excellent theoretical and conceptual overview of the rise of phenomenological sociology through thought of Weber and Schutz.)

Young, I. M. (1990). Is male gender identity the cause of male domination? In *Throwing like a girl and other essays in feminist philosophy and social theory*, (pp. 36-59). Bloomington, IN: Indiana University Press. (Offers a critique of Chodorow and other feminist theories of gender identity by a phenomenological analysis of the meaning of gender in their work.)

Fielding HOD Dissertations: Selected Applications

This is only a partial list. Other fine dissertations have been completed in HOD.

Clark, A. (1997). *Hidden textures: Memories of unanticipated mortal danger*. Santa Barbara, CA: Fielding Graduate Institute. [Captures an authentic sense of phenomenological wonderment and the ways in which data and interpreter become one.]

Córdova, G. L. (2004). *The lived experience of Norteñas de Nuevo Méjico: Finding voice and reclaiming identity.* Santa Barbara, CA: The Fielding Graduate Institute. [Gives voice to the participant Latinas who live between cultures and reveals the essence of their lived experience.]

Dinwiddie, L. (2000). *A mindful inquiry into understanding how the individual constructs the experience of high performance within a team context.* Santa Barbara, CA: The Fielding Graduate Institute. [Uses Schutz's concept of "puppets" to construct typical roles of persons in high performance teams.]

Fay, D. H. (2008). *Jean Gebser's structures of consciousness, Husserlian phenomenological method and cultural competency: The essential interconnections.* Santa Barbara, CAQ: Fielding Graduate University. [Elucidates the structures of integral consciousness in Gebser and explores how Husserl's phenomenological method and cross-cultural competency training evoke integral consciousness. This work reveals processes for evoking a new consciousness which is necessary for building a sense of one world in the face of global crises.]

Fortune, L. D. (2012). *How do seasoned massage therapists accomplish a whole session with established clients?* Santa Barbara, CA: Fielding Graduate University.

Grossman, V. (2004). *Preventing Mautam: Participatory action research and phenomenology at work to avoid rat-induced famine in Mizoram, India.* Santa Barbara, CA: Fielding Graduate Institute. [Includes a discussion of the way phenomenological practice allowed for effecting collaboration between persons from vastly different cultural backgrounds.]

Haines, M. B. (1999). *Interior spaciousness: The hidden openness of some who walk a mystical path with practical feet.* Santa Barbara, CA: The Fielding Graduate Institute. [Displays an application of van Manen's and Moustakas' phenomenological approaches.]

Jeddeloh, S. (2003). *Chasing transcendence: Experiencing "Magic Moments" in jazz improvisation.* Santa Barbara, CA: The Fielding Graduate Institute. [Explores transcendent states of improvising jazz musicians using phenomenological methods informed by Husserl and Schutz.]

Jonas, R. (1996). *Footprints on the soul: The journey from trauma to resilience.* Santa Barbara, CA: The Fielding Graduate Institute. [A phenomenological study of individuals who had experienced extreme traumas, revealing how meaning-making is lived rather than told.]

Jones, H. M. (2002). *From conflict to collaboration: Experiences of multiparty policy-level stakeholder situations.* Santa Barbara, CA: The Fielding Graduate Institute. [Demonstrates the value of applied social phenomenological and reflexive research perspectives. Adds to understanding of stakeholder processes by exploring experiential accounts.]

Kitchel, A. S. (2012). *Eliciting open-mindedness: A phenomenological study of acceptance of same-gender marriage by Vermont residents.* Santa Barbara, CA: Fielding Graduate University. [Explored the lived experience of changing one's mind about civil unions and/or same-gender marriage in Vermont.]

Laberge, C. G. (2012). *The lived experience of heart attack: Individual accounts of primary percutaneous coronary intervention survivors.* Santa Barbara, CA: Fielding Graduate University. [Explores the meaning people from rural areas make of their experience of heart attack and treatment in a Canadian urban hospital, with attention to how healthcare systems can provide better support and resources to post-heart attack survivors.]

Marlatt, J. (2012). *When executive coaching connects: A phenomenological study of relationship and transformative learning.* Santa Barbara, CAQ: Fielding Graduate University. [Seeks to understand the nature of human relationships and how they can contribute to transformative learning, focusing on the context of executive coaching relationships.]

Nagata, A. L. (2002). *Somatic mindfulness and energetic presence in intercultural communication: A phenomenological/hermeneutic exploration of bodymindset and emotional resonance.* Santa Barbara, CA: The Fielding Graduate Institute. [Explores the power of phenomenology at work interculturally, with particular attention to practice in Japan.]

Nahai, A. E. (2012). *Trauma to Dharma: The journey home a phenomenological study of the practice of Kundalini yoga as taught by Yogi Bhajan.* Santa Barbara, CA: Fielding Graduate University.

Novokosky, B. (1998). *Personal power: The realization of doing and being.* Santa Barbara, CA: The Fielding Graduate Institute. [An exploration using phenomenological protocols of the experience of empowerment in the context of organizational consulting.]

Piraino, J. L. (2001). *The lived experience of personal and spiritual integration through a process of transpersonal psychoanalysis.* Santa Barbara, CA: The Fielding Graduate Institute. [Uses a recursive hermeneutic-phenomenological approach to study the lived experience of personal and spiritual integration.]

Robin, C. S. (1998). *Existential perspectives on meaningful work: Explorations with executive men.* Santa Barbara, CA: The Fielding Graduate Institute. [Uses phenomenologically grounded interviews to explore "meaningful work," an often-used term but rarely described phenomenon.]

Schmidt, J. B. (2013). *Accessing the transcendent in therapy: A phenomenological inquiry into how therapists do healing.* Santa Barbara, CA: Fielding Graduate University. [Examines the enaction of the transcendent in dyadic therapeutic encounters by analyzing therapists' descriptions of what they identified as transcendent aspects of therapy.]

Simpson, S. K., (2003). *Mindful transformation: A phenomenological study.* Santa Barbara, CA: The Fielding Graduate Institute. [An excellent review of major phenomenological thinkers along with a rich description of how emersion in phenomenological reading and writing can be transformative.]

Smith, P. (1998). *Centeredness and the lived experience of family/divorce mediators as facilitators of dispute resolution and as leader-advocates within an emerging profession.* Santa Barbara, CA: The Fielding Graduate Institute. A fine example of how concepts and ideas from phenomenological sociology, especially the work of

Schutz, can be applied and connected to data on the topic of mediation.]

Tower, D. O. (2000). *Trans-Survivorship: The cancer survivor's journey from trauma to transformation.* Santa Barbara, CA: The Fielding Graduate Institute. [An account of the developmental effects of men who survived life-threatening cancer. Includes a first person phenomenological exploration along with interviews of other survivors.]

Turnbull, H. A. (2005) *The experience of internalized oppression among female diversity workers of different social identity groups.* Santa Barbara, CA. Fielding Graduate University. [A mixed methods study combining phenomenological protocols with personal construct psychology.]

Vittitoe, B. J. (2005) *Becoming and being an animal communicator: A phenomenological study.* Santa Barbara, CA: Fielding Graduate University. [Studies of how expert animal communicators understand their experiences with animals and their owners.]

Wing, L. (1999). *Transforming doctoral candidates: An exploration of faculty-student relations through dissertation creation.* Santa Barbara, CA: The Fielding Graduate Institute. [A clear expression of Gadamer's hermeneutic approach followed by a systematic application of each interpretive order to the data collected.]

Websites and Other Professional Resources

The Encyclopedia of Phenomenology. (1997). Lester Embree, series Editor. New York, NY: Springer. Excellent source to trace phenomenological movement and development of phenomenological thinking.

Phenomenology Online: Hosted by Max van Manen, Professor Emeritus of Education, The University of Alberta, Edmonton, Canada http://www.phenomenologyonline.com

Society for Phenomenology and the Human Sciences (SPHS)
SPHS encourages the application of phenomenological methodology to specific investigations within the human sciences. You are invited to join SPHS in its effort to achieve a deeper understanding of and engagement with the Life-World. SPHS holds its meetings in conjunction with SPEP (Society for Phenomenology and Existen-

tial Philosophy). http://sphs.info

International Human Science Research Conference & Newsletter (Seattle University)
http://www.seattleu.edu/artsci/map/Inner.aspx?id=3492

International Human Science Research Network
A relatively new website set up by Linda Finlay and Darren Langdridge from the Open University after the 2011 conference at Oxford University, England. It has links to phenomenology related journals and copies of recent newsletters. Over time, it will provide a wide array of material, related to the Human Science Research Community.
http://www.open.ac.uk/socialsciences/ihsrc/

Archives of SPHS
http://listserv.utk.edu/archives/sphs.html
The Alfred Schutz Archive—Waseda University, Tokyo, Japan
http://www.waseda.jp/Schutz/

Study Project in Phenomenology of the Body (SPPB), Elizabeth (Betsy) Behnke, PhD
www.ipp-net.org

Simon Silverman Phenomenology Center, Duquesne University
This web site has almost all of the abstracts of the psychology dissertations done at Duquesne University, University of Dallas, and a number from Georgia State University and the Saybrook Institute. The dissertations cover a vast spectrum of topics including hopelessness, forgiveness, depression, infidelity, magic and science, psychotherapy, eating disorders, and many more. http://www.library.duq.edu/silverman/index.htm

Center for Interpretive and Qualitative Research
Located at Duquesne University, this center has as its purpose the exploration and development of interpretive and qualitative methods.
http://www.duq.edu/academics/schools/liberal-arts/centers/interpretive-and-qualitative-research

Environmental and Architectural Phenomenology (EAP)
This newsletter has been in existence for twenty years. Edited by David Seamon, the newsletter is published three times a year. EAP is a forum and clearing house for research and design that incorporates a qualitative approach to environmental and architectural experience. Back issues are now available on the website.
http://www.arch.ksu.edu/seamon/EAP.html

Lester Embree's Homepage (links to other phenomenology sites)
http://www.lesterembree.net/

Center for Advanced Research in Phenomenology (CARP)
http://www.ipp-net.org

Human Studies: A Journal for Phenomenology and the Social Sciences (Springer publisher)

Journal of the British Society for Phenomenology
Research in Phenomenology

Gendlin Online Library
In mid-October the Focusing Institute launched a powerful new web-based resource containing over 100 of Eugene Gendlin's works from 1950 to present. Gendlin is distinguished among philosophers and psychologists for his articulation of the link between logic and felt understanding, which he calls the *Philosophy of Implicit Entry*. Included in the library are published articles, chapters, monographs, and many unpublished articles and conference presentations, all available for free downloading. In some instances, several chapters from his books or a special introduction to them are available. Gendlin's books are also listed in the library and can be purchased from the Focusing Institute or elsewhere. The library is a great resource for the Human Sciences.
http://www.focusing.org/gendlin/

Newsletter of Phenomenology
This free weekly newsletter provides information about what is going on in the world of phenomenology, including information about conferences and workshops, lectures, new books.
http://www.phenomenology.ro/newsletter/

International Coalition of North American Phenomenologists
www.icnap.org

Schutzian Research: A Yearbook of Worldly Phenomenology and Qualitative Social Science
This is an on-line journal edited by Michael Barber, Washington University. St. Louis, MO.

Center for Applied Phenomenological Research at the University of Tennessee
The Center represents scholars from a variety of disciplines including psychology, philosophy, nursing, and literature. The focus is on utilizing phenomenological and other qualitative methods to gain a better understanding of human experience.
http://phenomenology.utk.edu

YouTube humorous commentary on phenomenology, performed by Ivor Pritchard at PRIM&RS, 35th Anniversary Party.
http://www.youtube.com/watch?v=rBvljZN4TJ4&feature=youtu.be

APPENDIX B
(Chapter 1)
Completed HOD Dissertations (1996-2016):
Phenomenological and/or Hermeneutic Inquiry
Compiled by David Rehorick, PhD
August 13, 2016

All dissertations were completed at the Fielding Graduate University (formerly The Fielding Institute March 1974–June 2001, and Fielding Graduate Institute July 2001–December 2004) in Santa Barbara, California. Therefore, place and institutional details are omitted for each item.

This bibliography is a representation of work that utilizes phenomenology and hermeneutic research to varying degrees. With the assistance of Abby Rae, Fielding Librarian, the list below is the best expression that we could capture through electronic review of dissertation files.

Seventy-six (76) dissertations were identified, and assigned one of three classification designations:

PB – phenomenologically-based (count is 30)

PO – phenomenologically-oriented (count is 24)

PI – phenomenologically-inspired (count is 22)

The conceptual distinctions above are discussed in detail in Chapter 1. This is an empirical, criteria-based classification stemming from a review of all dissertations abstracts and Tables of Contents. In addition, the choices are supplemented by the long-standing background knowledge of Valerie Bentz and David Rehorick. Collectively, we have served on most doctoral dissertations in the domains of phenomenology and hermeneutics.

NOTE: David and Valerie have supervised or served on relevant MA theses and PhD dissertations as faculty at other universities. In addition, they have been invited as External Examiners on relevant dissertations at other universities. These are not included in the list below since our focus is on the Fielding experience.

Acker, K. (2000). Developmental processes and structures requisite to the integration of spirituality and work. **[PI]**

Bailey, T. R. (2007). The experience of the storyteller: Moving from the personal to the collective. **[PI]**

Behal, A. (2014). Negative capability: A phenomenological study of lived experience at the edge of certitude and incertitude. **[PI]** *IPA methodology*

Berg, M. (2010). What are the lived experiences of women over 50 who report a dramatic shift from a negative to positive self-image? **[PO]**

Buechner, Barton. (2014). Contextual mentoring of student veterans: A communication perspective. **[PO]**

Byrnes, R. T. (2010). Transition at the top: CEOs' sense of self when separating from their company. **[PI]**

Callos, C. T. (2012). The transformative nature of Greek dancing: A qualitative inquiry of adolescent experience. **[PO]**

Carville, A. (1999). Experiences of faith and rationality in leadership selection: Election processes. **[PO]**

Cavalli, C. (2014). Synchronicity and the emergence of meaning. **[PO]**

Chetty, Morgan (Yagambaram). (2016). Social justice transition of privileged persons: A phenomenological study. **[PB]**

Chudleigh, D. S. (2014). The lived experience of empowerment: Varied senses of personal empowerment from the act of interpersonal negotiation. **[PI]**

Clancy, A. L. (1996). Toward a holistic concept of time: Exploring the link between internal and external temporal experiences. **[PB]**

Clarke, J.-A. M. (2015). The integrative entrepreneur: A lifeworld study of women sustainability entrepreneurs. **[PB]**

Clark, V. A. (1997). Hidden textures: Memories of unanticipated mortal danger. **[PB]**

Conti, B. P. (1998). Surviving the fall: Making meaning of involuntary job loss. **[PO]**

Cordova, G. L. (2005). The lived experience of norteñas de nuevo méjico : Finding voice and reclaiming identity. **[PB]**

Cotter-Lockard, D. (2012). Chamber music coaching strategies and rehearsal techniques that enable collaboration. **[PO]**

DeSanti, L. (2014). Workplace bullying, cognitive dissonance, and dissonance reduction: Exploring the alleged perpetrator's experience and coping. **[PI]**

Dinwiddie, L. A. (2000). A mindful inquiry into understanding how the individual constructs the experience of high performance within a team context. **[PB]**

Donahue, D. M. (1999). Toward a contextual understanding of the leadership process of Lillian D. Wald and her associates. **[PO]**

Fay, D. (2008). Integral consciousness and intercultural competency: Gebser, Husserl, and the task of our time. **[PB]**

Fortune, L. D. (2012). How do seasoned massage therapists accomplish a whole session with established clients? **[PB]**

Foster, B. A. (2000). Barriers to servant leadership: Perceived organizational elements that impede servant leader effectiveness. **[PI]**

Gillespie, E. E. (2014). Assisting with dying: A phenomenological analysis of six case studies. **[PB]**

Gohal, Amanpreet K. (2016). The life-worlds of urban women farmers in sustainable agriculture. **[PB]**

Grossman, V. (2004). Preventing Mautam: Participatory action research and phenomenology at work to avoid rat-induced famine in Mizoram, India. **[PI]**

Hackett, W. L. (2000). Exploring the sense of self in the workplace. **[PI]**

Haddad, D. B. (2002). Intentionality as an instrument in action research. **[PB]**

Haines, M. B. (1999). Interior spaciousness: The hidden openness of some who walk a mystical path with practical feet. **[PO]**

Haynes, C. J. (2012). A hermeneutic reappraisal of Thomas Merton's approach to spiritual development. **[PO]**

Hochberg, J. E. (2007). The experience of severe self-criticism: A phenomenological, psychological, linguistic, and cultural exploration. **[PB]**

Jeddeloh, S. C. (2003). Chasing transcendence: Experiencing "magic moments" in jazz improvisation. **[PB]**

John-Baptiste, A. (2014). Intersecting identities of individuals in the workplace: A phenomenological study of the lived experiences. **[PI]**

Johnson, G. W. (2007). In the moment: Identity shift by multiple language users. **[PI]**

Jones, H. M. (2003). From conflict to collaboration: Experiences of multiparty policy-level stakeholder situations. **[PO]**

Kitchel, A. S. (2012). Eliciting open-mindedness: A phenomenological study of acceptance of same-gender marriage by Vermont residents. **[PB]**

Knobel, S. G. (2014). Becoming a leader: A hermeneutic phenomenological study of the lifeworld of Nelson Mandela. **[PB]**

Laberge, C. G. (2012). The lived experience of heart attack: Individual accounts of primary percutaneous coronary intervention survivors. **[PB]**

Lau-Kwong, K. (2012). Triggering transformative possibilities: A case study of Leaders' Quest in China. **[PI]**

Legault, M. (2010). Becoming an ethical leader: An exploratory study of the developmental process. **[PI]**

Lennox, S. L. (2005). Contemplating the self: Integrative approaches to transformative learning in higher education. **[PO]**

Lustgarten, R. S. (2007). Women's wisdom in leadership. **[PI]**

Marlatt, J. L. (2012). When executive coaching connects: A phenomenological study of relationship and transformative learning. **[PB]**

Maxwell, D. (2013). Classical horsemanship: A phenomenological and dramatist study. **[PB]**

Meier, M. D. (2014). Safety culture in high reliability organizations: A phenomenological inquiry of senior leaders in the United States commercial nuclear industry. **[PI]**

Meyer, P. S. (2006). Learning space and space for learning: Adults' intersubjective experience of improvisation. **[PI]**

Nagata, A. L. (2002). Somatic mindfulness and energetic presence in intercultural communication: A phenomenological/hermeneutic exploration of bodymindset and emotional resonance. **[PB]**

Nahai, A. E. (2012). Trauma to dharma: The journey home A phenomenological study of the practice of kundalini yoga as taught by Yogi Bhajan. **[PB]**

Nathanson, C. (2013). The experience of vocational alignment in midlife. **[PO]** *IPA methodology*

Nonemaker, J. L. (2001). Cardboard hero/tin saint: A look behind, a look within. **[PI]**

Novokowsky, B. (1999). Personal power: The realization of doing and being. **[PB]**

Ostroff, S. A. (2001). Body, soul, and role: Toward a holistic approach to well-being in organizations. **[PI]**

Piraino, J. L. (2002). The lived experience of personal and spiritual integration through a process of transpersonal psychoanalysis. **[PO]**

Porath, P. (2006). The lived experience of an unexpected, unintentional mystical experience. **[PB]**

Reilly, M. A. (1998). A phenomenology of place: The journal of an itinerant learner. **[PO]**

Robin, C. S. (1998). Existential perspectives on meaningful work: Explorations with executive men. **[PI]**

Schmidt, J. B. (2013). Accessing the transcendent in therapy: A phenomenological inquiry into how therapists do healing. **[PB]**

Schneider, L. K. (2009). At home in the global work place: Remote workers' experience of local place in global corporations. **[PB]**

Scott, V. A. (2006). Direct-support staff workers—their lives: A phenomenological interpretation. **[PO]**

Simpson, S. K. (2003). Mindful transformation: A phenomenological study. **[PB]**

Skjei, S. (2014). Authentic leadership moments: A mindful inquiry. **[PB]**

Smith, P. R. (1998). Centeredness and the lived experience of family/divorce mediators as facilitators of dispute resolution and as leader/advocates. **[PB]**

Spector, M. (2000). Moments of awakening in the presence of impending danger: A phenomenological study of police officers in critical situations. **[PO]**

Turnbull, H. A. (2005). The experience of internalized oppression among female diversity workers of different social identity groups. **[PI]**

Tower, D. O. (2000). Trans-survivorship: The cancer survivor's journey from trauma to transformation. **[PB]**

Turner, C. (2014). The rebound experience of managers: An inquiry into the experience of managers who recovered from involuntary job loss. **[PO]**

Vincenti, M. (2013). Emotions and innovative leadership: An interpretative phenomenological analysis. **[PO]** *IPA methodology*

Vittitoe, B. J. (2005). Becoming and being an animal communicator: A phenomenological study. **[PB]**

Volger, B. J. (2009). The power of shame in Jewish women: A phenomenological exploration of cultural messages. **[PO]**

Wilson, M. (2013). When systems and lifeworlds collide: A scholar-practitioner's inquiry into an analytical foundation for social innovation using transformative phenomenology, transdisciplinarity, and critical social theory. **[PB]**

Wing, L. S. (2000). Transforming doctoral candidates: An exploration of faculty-student relations through dissertation creation. **[PO]**

Winslow, E. (2010). Parents with physical and other disabilities: A study of the adult developmental stage of generativity. **[PI]**

Wocher, D. M. (2010). Making the invisible visible: Organization development practitioners' interactive drama in forming a sense of professional identity. **[PI]**

Wyatt, S. J. (2003). Inquiry and the medial woman: An intuitive hermeneutic of encounters with archetypal images. **[PO]**

Yu, A. E. (2013). Cocreating a shared reality: Exploring intersubjectivity in intercultural interaction through executive coaching relationships. **[PO]**

About the Editors

David Allan Rehorick, PhD (Senior Editor) is *Professor Emeritus* at the University of New Brunswick (UNB), Canada where he taught from 1974 to 2007. He is also *Professor Emeritus* at the Fielding Graduate University, serving as Research Consulting Faculty (1995–2006), then full-time faculty (2007–2012). His research, publications, and editorial contributions encompass the domains of phenomenology and interpretive studies, educational praxis and theory, sociological theory, population studies, the healthcare sciences, and the creative arts. He has served on six editorial boards of academic journals, including Review Editor of *Human Studies: A Journal for Philosophy and the Social Sciences*. As a developer in higher education, David was appointed Founding Faculty and Fellow in Comparative Culture at The Miyazaki International College in Japan (1994-97). He was also founder of Renaissance College, the first undergraduate leadership studies program in Canada, and became the first Director of International Internships (2001–04). He is an award-winning educator, with an appointment as "University Teaching Scholar" at UNB (2005–08). He received the Association of Atlantic Universities Instructional Leadership Award (1995) and the Allan P. Stuart Memorial Award for Excellence in Teaching (1984). His special areas of teaching embraced qualitative and phenomenological research approaches, interpersonal relations, human development and consciousness, cross-cultural studies, the sociology of culture, of music, and of Eastern religions. David lives in Vancouver, Canada, where he studies jazz piano, with particular emphasis on the creative art of composition. Contact: rehorick@unb.ca

Valerie Malhotra Bentz, MSSW, PhD (Editor) is Professor of Human and Organization Development, Fielding Graduate University, where she served as Associate Dean for Research. Her current interests include somatics, phenomenology, social theory, consciousness development, and Vedantic theories of knowledge. Her books include: *Contemplative* *social research: Caring for self, being, and lifeworld*, with Vincenzo M. B. Giogino; *Transformative phenomenology: Changing ourselves, lifeworlds and professional practice*, with David Rehorick; *Mindful inquiry in social research*, with Jeremy Shapiro, and *Becoming mature: Childhood ghosts and spirits in adult life.* She also authored a philosophical novel, *Flesh and mind: The time travels of Dr. Victoria Von Dietz.* She is a Fellow in Contemplative Practice of the American Association of Learned Societies. Valerie was editor of *Phenomenology and the Human Sciences* (1994–98). She has served as president and board member of the Clinical Sociology Association, the Sociological Practice Association, and the Society for Phenomenology and the Human Sciences. She founded and co-directed an action research team and center in Mizoram, India. Valerie was co-founder of the Creative Longevity and Wisdom program at Fielding. She is the Director of the Doctoral Concentration in Somatics, Phenomenology, and Communicative Leadership (SPL). She has twenty years experience as a psychotherapist, and is a certified yoga teacher and certified massage therapist. She is a member of the board of the Carpinteria Valley Association, an environmental activist group. She also plays bassoon and piano. Contact: vbentz@fielding.edu

About Fielding Graduate University

Fielding Graduate University, headquartered in Santa Barbara, CA, was founded in 1974, and celebrated its 40th anniversary in 2014. Fielding is an accredited, nonprofit leader in blended graduate education, combining face-to-face and online learning. Its curriculum offers quality master's and doctoral degrees for professionals and academics around the world. Fielding's faculty members represent a wide spectrum of scholarship and practice in the fields of educational leadership, human and organizational development, and clinical and media psychology. Fielding's faculty serves as mentors and guides to self-directed students who use their skills and professional experience to become powerful, socially responsible leaders in their communities, workplaces, and society. For more information, please visit Fielding online at www.fielding.edu.

Made in United States
North Haven, CT
30 April 2022